40-00

ST ANTONY'S/MACMILLAN SERIES

General Editors: Archie Brown (1975-85) and Rosemary Thorp (1985-), both Fellows of St Antony's College, Oxford

Recent titles include

Gail Lee Bernstein and Haruhiro Fukui (*editors*)
JAPAN AND THE WORLD

Archie Brown (*editor*)
POLITICAL LEADERSHIP IN THE SOVIET UNION

Deborah Fahy Bryceson
FOOD INSECURITY AND THE SOCIAL DIVISION OF LABOUR IN TANZANIA, 1919–85

Victor Bulmer-Thomas
STUDIES IN THE ECONOMICS OF CENTRAL AMERICA

Helen Callaway
GENDER, CULTURE AND EMPIRE

David Cleary
ANATOMY OF THE AMAZON GOLD RUSH

Roger Cooter (*editor*)
STUDIES IN THE HISTORY OF ALTERNATIVE MEDICINE

Robert Desjardins
THE SOVIET UNION THROUGH FRENCH EYES, 1945–85

Guido di Tella and Carlos Rodríguez Braun (*editors*)
ARGENTINA, 1946–83: THE ECONOMIC MINISTERS SPEAK

Guido di Tella and D. Cameron Watt (*editors*)
ARGENTINA BETWEEN THE GREAT POWERS, 1939–46

Guido di Tella and Rudiger Dornbusch (*editors*)
THE POLITICAL ECONOMY OF ARGENTINA, 1946–83

Saul Dubow
RACIAL SEGREGATION AND THE ORIGINS OF APARTHEID IN SOUTH AFRICA, 1919-36

Anne Lincoln Fitzpatrick
THE GREAT RUSSIAN FAIR

Heather D. Gibson
THE EUROCURRENCY MARKETS, DOMESTIC FINANCIAL POLICY AND INTERNATIONAL INSTABILITY

David Hall-Cathala
THE PEACE MOVEMENT IN ISRAEL, 1967-87

John B. Hattendorf and Robert S. Jordan (*editors*)
MARITIME STRATEGY AND THE BALANCE OF POWER

Linda Hitchcox
VIETNAMESE REFUGEES IN SOUTHEAST ASIAN CAMPS

Derek Hopwood (*editor*)
STUDIES IN ARAB HISTORY

Amitzur Ilan
BERNADOTTE IN PALESTINE, 1948

J. R. Jennings
SYNDICALISM IN FRANCE

Maria D'Alva G. Kinzo
LEGAL OPPOSITION POLITICS UNDER AUTHORITARIAN RULE IN BRAZIL

Bohdan Krawchenko
SOCIAL CHANGE AND NATIONAL CONSCIOUSNESS IN TWENTIETH-CENTURY UKRAINE

Robert H. McNeal
STALIN: MAN AND RULER

Amii Omara-Otunnu
POLITICS AND THE MILITARY IN UGANDA, 1890-1985

Ilan Pappe
BRITAIN AND THE ARAB–ISRAELI CONFLICT, 1948-51

J. L. Porket
WORK, EMPLOYMENT AND UNEMPLOYMENT IN THE SOVIET UNION

Brian Powell
KABUKI IN MODERN JAPAN

Alex Pravda (*editor*)
HOW RULING COMMUNIST PARTIES ARE GOVERNED

H. Gordon Skilling
CZECHOSLOVAKIA, 1918–88
SAMIZDAT AND AN INDEPENDENT SOCIETY IN CENTRAL AND EASTERN EUROPE

J. A. A. Stockwin, Alan Rix, Aurelia George, James Horne, Daichi Itô, Martin Collick
DYNAMIC AND IMMOBILIST POLITICS IN JAPAN

Verena Stolcke
COFFEE PLANTERS, WORKERS AND WIVES

Jane E. Stromseth
THE ORIGINS OF FLEXIBLE RESPONSE

Joseph S. Szyliowicz
POLITICS, TECHNOLOGY AND DEVELOPMENT

Jane Watts
BLACK WRITERS FROM SOUTH AFRICA

Philip J. Williams
THE CATHOLIC CHURCH AND POLITICS IN NICARAGUA AND COSTA RICA

Series Standing Order

If you would like to receive future titles in this series as they are published, you can make use of our standing order facility. To place a standing order please contact your bookseller or, in case of difficulty, write to us at the address below with your name and address and the name of the series. Please state with which title you wish to begin your standing order. (If you live outside the United Kingdom we may not have the rights for your area, in which case we will forward your order to the publisher concerned.)

Standing Order Service, Macmillan Distribution Ltd,
Houndmills, Basingstoke, Hampshire, RG21 2XS, England.

Studies in Arab History

The Antonius Lectures, 1978–87

Edited by

DEREK HOPWOOD
*Director of the Middle East Centre
St Antony's College, University of Oxford*

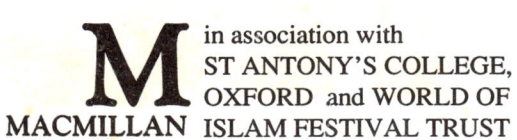 

MACMILLAN in association with ST ANTONY'S COLLEGE, OXFORD and WORLD OF ISLAM FESTIVAL TRUST

© St Antony's College 1990

All rights reserved. No reproduction, copy or transmission
of this publication may be made without written permission.

No paragraph of this publication may be reproduced, copied
or transmitted save with written permission or in accordance
with the provisions of the Copyright, Designs and Patents Act 1988,
or under the terms of any licence permitting limited copying
issued by the Copyright Licensing Agency, 33 – 4 Alfred Place,
London WC1E 7DP.

Any person who does any unauthorised act in relation to
this publication may be liable to criminal prosecution and
civil claims for damages.

First published 1990

Published by
THE MACMILLAN PRESS LTD
Houndmills, Basingstoke, Hampshire RG21 2XS
and London
Companies and representatives
throughout the world

Typeset on a Lasercomp at Oxford University Computing Service

Printed in Great Britain by WBC Print Ltd, Bristol

British Library Cataloguing in Publication Data
Studies in Arab history: the Antonius lectures, 1978–87.
1. Arabia, history
I. Hopwood, Derek, *1933–*
953
ISBN 0-333-52348-2

Contents

Editor's Preface   vii
An Introduction by E.C. Hodgkin   ix

Antonius Lectures

1976   George Makdisi
On the Origin and Development of the College
in Islam and the West   1

1977   Albert Hourani
The Arab Awakening Forty Years After   21

1978   André Raymond
The Ottoman Conquest and the Development of
the Great Arab Towns   41

1979   Afaf Marsot
Muhammad Ali and Palmerston   61

1981   Thomas Hodgkin
George Antonius, Palestine and the 1930s   77

1982   Magdi Wahba
Cairo Memories   103

1983   Harold Beeley
Ernest Bevin and Palestine   117

1984   Mahmud Manzalaoui
Mouths of the Sevenfold Nile: English Fiction
and Modern Egypt   131

1985   Oleg Grabar
The Meaning of the Dome of the Rock in Jerusalem   151

1986   Tarif Khalidi
Space, Holiness and Time: Palestine in the
Classical Arab Centuries   165

1987   Norman Daniels
Orientalism Again   175

To the memory of Katy and George Antonius

Editor's Preface

The editing of this volume has been made very easy by the willing cooperation of the contributors, to whom warm thanks. Only one lecturer failed to respond and unfortunately his paper has had to be omitted. I would like to thank also Jennifer Baines for typesetting the manuscript and Diane Ring for her help with the proofreading.

I am happy to acknowledge the agreement of *Encounter*, Macmillan Press and the *International Journal of Turkish Studies* to print the lectures of Magdi Wahba, Albert Hourani and Andre Raymond.

Finally I am most grateful to Alistair Duncan and the World of Islam Festival Trust for its generous support

Derek Hopwood

Antonius Lectures
An Introduction by E.C. Hodgkin

For many people the Antonius Lecture has become one of the most enjoyable events of the year, more eagerly awaited than Epsom, Wimbledon, Eights Week, or any other of the summer season's fixed points. It is an occasion at which the attender can be certain of enlarging his or her knowledge in a most agreeable fashion, of meeting old friends and making new ones. And now comes this sort of posthumous *Festschrift* in which eleven of the first twelve lectures find a permanent home in print.

Contributions to some of the *Festschrifts* I have seen appeared often to have little relevance to the person they were supposed to be honouring. That is far from being the case here. Each lecture is directly relevant to some part of George Antonius's interests – historical, political, literary, topographical, all to do with some aspect of the Middle East, and more particularly with the relations between that area and the West. George, who admired scholarship and enjoyed chat, would have greatly appreciated the chattiness as well as the scholarship here displayed. There can be no higher praise than that.

In his 1983 lecture Harold Beeley said that he was 'one of the few people in the room who met George Antonius and talked, or more accurately listened, to him,' having met him during the 1939 St James's conference. I can upstage Harold, having first met George in London in 1934 and got to know him well in Jerusalem and Cairo in the winter and spring of 1935/36. This was when, having left Oxford, I was travelling in the Middle East, often staying with my brother Thomas, whose chequered career as a colonial servant he described in his 1981 lecture and which is reflected also in his *Letters from Palestine 1932–36*, which I edited and which apppeared in 1986.

In a letter to his mother, written in May 1933, Thomas described George as a man with rather the manner of a young fellow of All Souls and a mysterious profession – travelling expensively round, interviewing Amirs, Sultans, Grand Rabbis and Secretaries of State, and opening all their eyes.' In a letter to me a year later he recalled a meeting we had had with George at the Maison Basque (a very good restaurant in Dover Street, alas no more), during which George had 'talked passionate politics.' Thomas went on: 'He is even more charming here [Jerusalem] than in England, because in England there are more people rather like him, whereas here there are very few – no one that I have ever met that so admirably combines the passion of

Introduction

the Syrian patriot with the lucidity of the Cambridge don in stating his patriotic beliefs.' There is a subtle Oxford/Cambridge nuance in these two passages which I leave to higher criticism. What I can confirm is that George was splendid company – seldom in my memory passionate, but always lucid.

To be a guest at Karm al-Mufti in those days was a rare privilege, as it was later after George had died, an oasis of civilization in the last unhappy years of the mandate. On all occasions it was Katy who showed the guest to what heights hospitality could rise. To speak of that remarkable person in a single pendant sentence seems a crime, but there are, fortunately, so many who have attended these lectures, as she herself also did as long as she was able, who will have their private memories of her that any tribute to her or to Soraya in this context would be otiose.

The institution of these lectures was made possible by the generosity of an admirer of George Antonius who has from the outset desired to be anonymous and still wishes to remain so. He will, however, I think be not unaware of the enormous pleasure he has provided for so many over the past thirteen years – a pleasure which can be keenly looked forward to in the years to come.

E.C. Hodgkin

On the Origin and Development of the College in Islam and the West

FEW chapters in the history of Western culture are as fascinating as that of the rise and development of universities. These institutions of learning are justly the pride and joy of those who cherish the traditions of Western culture. Such names as Salerno and Bologna, Paris and Montpellier, Oxford and Cambridge, carry a resonance richly deserved, which has not ceased to vibrate in the annals of Western civilization, since their early foundations in the Middle Ages. Small wonder, then, that claims on their origins as possibly owing to influence from the Muslim East should be opposed, at times politely, more often by simply ignoring the claim.

There is no doubt in my mind as to the legitimacy of such opposition. The claims which have been made for the *madrasa* as the prototype of the university should be regarded as devoid of a sound basis in fact. The idea of the university as it first arose in the West is one which is totally alien to classical Islam.

The university in its early history is strictly a product of Western Europe in the Middle Ages. Islam borrowed it in modern times, in the second half of the nineteenth century. In his excellent book on *The Rise of Universities*, Charles Homer Haskins made it clear that the institution was a medieval one, the likes of which had not been seen by Athens or Rome in ancient times.[1] He did not insist on its European character; he merely took the matter for granted; and this is spite of claims by Islamists placing its origin in Baghdad or Cairo. Haskins was right, irrespective of his awareness of such claims. This fact of the medieval European origin of the university should be kept in mind when speaking of 'the rise of universities'.

On the other hand, when we speak of the rise of colleges, we are speaking of an institution that is peculiarly Islamic in origin. And there is ample reason to believe that the medieval West borrowed it from Islam. This is what I hope to show in what follows.

In a study that seeks to understand institutions of learning from their genesis, it behooves the student first to seek a clarification of the key terms involved. In a comparative study of such institutions in Islam and the West, clarification is nowhere more necessary than in the signification of the basic insitutional terms, 'college' and 'university'.

If we were to consider the college and the university as we first find them in Paris in the latter part of the twelfth and early thirteenth centuries, we would find that there was no ambiguity whatsoever as to the functions of each of these two institutions. The faculties, the curricula, the examinations and the granting of degrees were all confined to the university. The college was merely a boarding house for certain students, mostly those who needed financial aid.

If we were then to skip over the centuries and come to the United States today, we would see a distinctly different situation. Faculties, curricula, examinations and degrees are not the private preserve of the university; the college has them all as well. Indeed, the terms 'college' and 'university' are used almost synonymously.[2]

Between late twelfth-century Paris and Colonial America the college had undergone an important transformation. Grafted on to its original essential nature was another nature which belonged to the university. Whence the resulting ambiguity. In Colonial America, Yale is referred to as the *University* of Yale *College*; and to this day, Harvard *University* is headed by the President and Fellows of Harvard *College*.

The origin of the ambiguity can be traced back to Colonial times, and beyond that to the antecedents of the Colonial College in Ireland and Scotland, and these, in their turn, to Oxford.

But in order to grasp the significance of the whole development across the centuries, one must reach further back in time, not only to the original home of the university itself on the European continent, not only to Paris, home of the college in the West, but further back still, to the original home of the college in Islam, some four centuries earlier than Paris, back to its first humble beginnings in the lands of the Eastern Caliphate.

In going back to the origins, I hope to show that, as it first appeared in Paris, Oxford, and elsewhere, the college was a previous product of Islam; and that, in Merton College in Oxford, we have a watershed in the history of the college. Merton stands as a dividing point between the college of Islam on the one hand, and that of the United States on the other.

Let us first look at the 'college' and the 'university' as we know them today in the United States. In Webster's Collegiate Dictionary, the term 'university' is explained as 'an Institution of higher learning providing facilities for teaching and research and authorized to grant academic degrees . . .'[3] 'College' is explained as 'an independent institution of higher learning offering a course of general studies leading to a bachelor's degree . . .'[4] An Oxford college, such as Balliol or Magdalen, is explained as 'a self-governing constituent body of a university offering living quarters and instruction but *not* granting degrees' (emphasis added).[5] In an earlier edition, this Dictionary explains the term college as 'a *university* or one of its schools.'[6] It explains 'university' as 'typically a *college* and one or more graduate or professional schools' (emphasis added).[7]

The legal encyclopedia, *American Jurisprudence*, after giving its own definitions for college and university, draws the following conclusion:

'... the terms 'college' and 'university' *convey the same idea, differing only in grade*...' (emphasis added).[8]

This ambiguity in the use of the two terms has existed for a long time in the United States. The matter has simply been taken for granted. Americans familiar with education in Europe are aware of the fact that our colleges have little or nothing in common with European colleges. Our historians have to point out to us that the colleges of Oxford and Cambridge served as models for our early collegiate history. But the Oxonian type of college remains unique: it is a constituent part of the university and does not grant degrees. The Parisian *collège* is not a college at all in our sense of the word. A *collège* and a *lycée*, both of which offer the same level of instruction, are below the college level in the U.S.[9] A graduate of a *collège* or *lycée* will normally be admitted to the second year of an American college, with three years to go for his bachelor's degree.

'College' in the Oxford English Dictionary is explained as follows:

> an independent self-governing corporation or society (usually founded for the maintenance of poor students) in a University, as the College of the Sorbonne in the ancient university of Paris, and the ancient colleges of Oxford and Cambridge...
>
> From the fact that in some Universities only a single college was founded or survived, *in which case the University and College become co-extensive*, the same has come, as in Scotland and the United States, to be interchangeable with 'university'; 'a college with university functions.'
>
> In the U.S. 'college' has been the general term, and is still usually applied to a *small* university (or degree-giving educational institution) having a single curriculum of study, the name 'university' being chiefly to a few of the larger institutions, which in their organization, and division into various faculties, more resemble the universities of Europe (emphasis added).[10]

In the case of Yale University *v.* New Haven, we have the following statement regarding the foundation of that institution:

> 'In 1698...ten of the principle ministers agreed to stand as trustees to found, erect and govern a college. They formed themselves into a society at New Haven in 1700, and the same year, at a meeting at Branford, they founded *the University of Yale College* (emphasis added).'[11]

Previous to the foundation of Yale, Ireland and Scotland had the same ambiguity in the use of the two terms. In Dublin, Trinity was indiscriminately called 'Trinity College, Dublin', 'Dublin University', and 'The University of Trinity College, Dublin'.[12] In Aberdeen, Scotland, in 1593, Marischal College was founded as both 'a college and university'.[13]

The development of higher institutions of learning in the American colonies followed a trend which was the reverse of that of England and the European Continent. Rather than having first a university, and then colleges, they began with a college and made *it* into a university. This trend is described as follows in the case of Yale University *v.* New Haven:

> In establishing the universities in the new world, the limitations of the people compelled the founders to follow the example of Trinity College, Dublin, and Marischal College, Aberdeen, and not that of Oxford and Cambridge. Upon the same corporation was conferred the power of the university in granting degrees and of the college in government; and such community and the buildings required for its use were known as 'The College'.[14]

In Harvard's case, the General Court at Boston appropriated £400 to establish an institution of higher learning. This was in 1630. In 1642 the Court established overseers of 'a college founded in Cambridge'. This was later to mean 'a university', in the usage of Mather, who, in 1692, said the General Assembly granted 'a charter to this University'. The Massachusetts Constitution of 1779 recognized 'The University at Cambridge'.[15]

In the American Colonies, in Dublin, and in Aberdeen, the development of higher institutions of learning went a stage beyond what had earlier taken place in Oxford and Cambridge.

What happened in Oxford with regard to the foundation of colleges is very important for the understanding of the collegiate system. It not only illuminates what later took place in Dublin, Aberdeen, and the American Colonies, but by contrast, it also throws light on what had taken place previously.

To get a clear view of the rise and development of the college let us first go back to its very beginnings in Islam. This means going back to the origins of the *madrasa*. For the *madrasa*-college and the college of the West are essentially one and the same type of institution. That institution remains the same until the advent of Merton College in the second half of the thirteenth century.

When digging into the Islamic past in search of the origins of colleges one has to be satisfied with rather inadequate sources. Histories of colleges were written only by late authors, and are of only local interest. For instance, the sixteenth century *Daris fī tarikh al-madaris* of an-Nuʿaimi (*d.* 927/1521) is a study of the various types of colleges in Damascus.[16] He begins with twelfth-century colleges, except for a few isolated cases from the previous century. Such works, though excellent as far as they go, do not treat of the early collegiate period. Our information must therefore be derived from other sources, especially the biographical works.

Since the college was a charitable foundation owing its existence to the generosity of benefactors, it would be well for us to look into the history of charity as practised by Muslim men and women of means. Some of these benefactors were possessors of great wealth, and practised their philanthropy on a wide scale; others, not so wealthy, practised it on a more modest one.

Isolated charitable gifts of men of modest means may have created an institution of learning earlier than the dates here considered. This should be granted, if only to avoid the pitfall of arguing from silence in an area where the sources are anything but adequate. But there is a better reason for granting this: the foundation of certain institutions on a large scale is usually preceded by their prior foundation in isolated instances. Considerable sums of money are usually invested in institutions only after they have proven to be successful and socially desirable.

Throughout the centuries we meet with philanthropists expending great sums of money on objects socially and religiously desirable. Such sums were provided for distribution among the poor, the widows and orphans; they were provided for the shrouding of the dead; for the pilgrims to Mecca and their various needs; for camps and relay stations, and wells and supplies of fodder, all along the pilgrims' road; for the upkeep of the sanctuaries; for individual scholars, or different groups of scholars and such like. However, this category was of a transitory, fleeting character; good for as long as it pleased the donor, or for as long as he lived, but cut off with his displeasure, his dismissal from office or his death.

It was not this category of philanthropy that brought institutions of learning into existence. On the contrary, these institutions came into existence after the institutionalization of charity by the law of *waqf*. With the *waqf*, or charitable trust, institutions of learning were made perpetual, and independent, in some cases, of the donor himself, and in all cases, of the donor's life-span. This type of philanthropy we meet on a very wide scale when we come to the tenth century.

It is true that mosques were founded in great number by Muslim benefactors long before the tenth century. The question arises, however, as to when they were first used as colleges. For the first type of college in Islam was not the *madrasa*-college, but rather the *masjid*-college. By *masjid*, or mosque, I mean the smaller of the two types of mosques in Islam, that which served a small community within one quarter of the city; not the *jamiʿ*, the larger mosque, variously referred to in English as the Friday Mosque, or the Cathedral Mosque, or the Congregational Mosque. The medieval city of Baghdad, for instance, had thousands of the smaller type, but only six of the larger.

The smaller mosque served as a college before the tenth century, as early as the eighth, and perhaps earlier. In the biographical dictionary of Ibn Khallikan we have a mosque referred to as that of the Prophet, in which Koranic science was taught by a scholar who died in 132/750.[17] In the biographical dictionary of Yaqut we have several mosque-colleges where grammar was taught, one of them belonging to al-Kisai who died in 189/805.[18] The eleventh century Shirazi taught law in the mosque-college of Shafiʿi who died in 204/820.[19]

These and other mosque-colleges belonged to the eighth and ninth centuries, and perhaps earlier. How much earlier is not known, and may never be known exactly. What is certain is that this is the first type of college in Islam; and that it is a charitable foundation, governed by the law of *waqf*.

As a charitable foundation the mosque was endowed, and the income of the endowment paid the salary of the professor who was usually its *imam*, or leader of the prayer. The student benefitted in that he had no tuition to pay; but he had to provide for his own lodging and subsistence. The mosque could not be used for lodging, except in the case of travellers and pious learned men who led an ascetic life.[20]

Among the wealthy philanthropists of the tenth century the name of Badr b. Hasanawiah al-Kurdi should stand out as one of the most significant for the history of Islamic institutions of learning. His father, Hasanawiah, who died in 369/979,[21] a man of power and influence, is said to have expended great amounts of alms-giving. But neither he nor any of the other philanthropists of that century are cited for having endowed institutions of learning on a wide scale. Among these were the mother of the Caliph, al-Muqtadi, known as *as-Saiyida*, the Grand Dame (*d.* 321/933), whose annual income from her estates amounted to one million *dinars*;[22] Bajkam the Turk (*d.* 329/941) who held the title of *amir al-umara'*, a title which was the precursor of that of *sultan*, and who began the construction of the great hospital in Baghdad;[23] the Buwaihid ʿAdud ad-Daula (*d.* 372/983) who completed the construction of that hospital;[24] as-Sahib b. ʿAbbad (*d.* 385/995) vizier and patron of learning;[25] and other philanthropists of lesser renown, who instituted mosque-colleges, such as Diʿlij as-Sijistani (*d.* 351/962) who established such colleges in Baghdad, Mecca and Sijistan.[26] His mosque-college in Baghdad, which bore his name,[27] was located in the Fief of Rabiʿ, on Abu Khalaf Road, of Baghdad's West Side.[28]

But with Badr (*d.* 405/1015)[29] we have a new development. When his father died in 369/979, he was appointed in his place as governor over several provinces[30] by ʿAdud ad-Daula. The length of his tenure was thirty-two years. As in the case of his predecessors he established pensions, gave alms to scholars, to the poor descendants of the Prophet, to orphans and to poor masses. He spent considerable sums in connection with the pilgrimage to Mecca.[31] In all of this there was nothing that was essentially different from previous philanthropy. When Badr died, this side of his philanthropy died with him: the beneficiaries suffered, and the pilgrimage was cut off, because the roads were no longer safe now that annual payments had ceased for the safe-passage guarantee of the pilgrims.

But Badr established one type of institution which was of a more permanent character. Because of its permanence and widespread diffusion, it constituted an advance of great significance in the history of Islamic institutions of learning. He established, throughout the realm of his administration, three thousand *masjid-khan* complexes: these were mosque-colleges (*masjid*), with adjacent inns (*khan*) for out-of-town students.

To my knowledge, this is the first extant text to mention a development of such magnitude. The text runs as follows: 'he built anew, in the provinces of his administration, three thousand *masjids* and *khans*, (the latter) for those away from home.'[32]

Fortunately, we are in a position to explain the significance of the inn built next to the mosque. We can identify the complex as such thanks to a description given by one of its student residents in Baghdad, in the second half of the eleventh century.

The student, Abu ʿAli al-Fariqi, was from out-of-town, and had come to study law under the direction of the great Shirazi who was soon to occupy the chair of Shafiʿi law in the new *madrasa*-college of Baghdad, the Nizamiya. Meantime, Shirazi was teaching law in a mosque-college with its adjacent inn. The year was 456/1064, one year before ground was broken for the new Nizamiya. The following text is an autobiographical note of the student describing the situation as it existed in that year. Here is what he says:

> I took up residence in an inn facing the mosque-college of Abu Ishaq (ash-Shirazi) in the quarter of Bab al-Maratib wherein resided the fellows of the Shaikh and the scholars studying under his direction. When we were many, there were about twenty of us; when we were few, there were about ten. The Shaikh Abu Ishaq was teaching us the law course (taʿliqa) in a period of four years; so that when the scholar had learned his course during this period of time, it was no longer necessary for him to study anywhere else. He used to give us a lesson following the morning-prayer (ghadaʿ), and another following the prayer of nightfall (ʿisha'). In the year 460/1068, I crossed over to the west side (of Baghdad) to the Shaikh Abu Nasr b. as-Sabbagh and studied ash-Shamil under his direction; then I returned to Abu Ishaq and became his fellow until he died.[33]

The term *khan* is variously translated as an inn; a caravanserai; a place in which travellers lodge; a building for the reception of merchants and travellers and their goods; a shop; a house; etc. There was obviously more than one type of *khan*.[34] The type which interests us here was a place of residence, an inn or residence hall for law students.

Other texts make this quite clear. One historian of Baghdad describes an uprising by the inhabitants of the Karkh Quarter in the following terms: '... When (they) had learned what had happened, they went to the *Khan* of the Hanafi fellows and scholars in the Fief of Rabiʿ and seized what they found, setting fire to the *khan* and taking houses of the lawyers by surprise.'[35]

The Fief of Rabiʿ was a popular quarter of the city.[36] It had mosque-colleges for the Hanafi and Shafiʿi students of law. These were nearby inns for the law students and professors. As mentioned previously, the mosque-college itself could not be used for purposes of residence.[37] That is why the inn was built near the mosque-college as a residence hall for students. Such was the case with the mosque-college of Shirazi, with its inn facing it and the ten-to-twenty students residing there. The number is typical of the number of students attending any one of the colleges of law that were later to be founded; and the fluctuation in their number was due to the fluctuation in the income of the endowment.

The mosque-inn complex undoubtedly existed before Badr b. Hasanawaih built them on such a grand scale. This we know to be the case later with the *madrasa*-college which preceded Nizam al-Mulk's vast network of *madrasas*. Badr's foundations constituted a great step forward in the development of institutions of learning, especially as regards the provision of lodging for students. There might be some question as to whether students shared in the income of the endowments. But the fact that they later had still to provide for their own subsistence would lead us rather to believe that, generally speaking, endowments, at this stage of development, did not yet include stipends for subsistence. Well into the eleventh century students were still providing for their own subsistence by taking part-time work, such as the copying of manuscripts,[38] the guarding of silos, and the job of night watchman in the quarters of the city.[39]

Further proof of this is supplied by the fact that some professors of the eleventh century are known to have given financial aid to their students from their own pockets, for the purchase of school supplies. Such was the case of the great tradition-expert and biographer of Baghdad, al-Khatib al-Baghdadi. And when he died he bequeathed his possessions to the scholars of tradition.[40] Others are known to have contributed to the subsistence of their students; as in the case of the Professor of law, Imam al-Haramain al-Juwaini, of Nishapur, who helped his students financially in this way from his pay and from what he had inherited until he had used up his whole inheritance.[41]

The most significant aspect of this stage of development is that it foreshadowed the development of the college of law: the *madrasa*. The transition from Badr's vast network of mosque-inn complexes to Nizam al-Mulk's vast network of *madrasas* is seen most clearly in the example of Baghdad with the introduction of the Madrasa Nizamiya in 459/1067.

One of the values of the autobiographical note, quoted previously, lies in the dates cited: 456/1064 and 460/1068. These dates cover the transition made in Baghdad from the mosque-college and its inn to the *madrasa*-college combining both. For Fariqi and his classmates it meant complete financial support for their scholarly pursuits.

I might recall at this point that Shirazi had at first refused to accept the chair of law in the new *madrasa* for reasons which I have discussed elsewhere at length, and which had to do with the misappropriation of materials used in the construction of the *madrasa*. For twenty days his rival, Ibn as-Sabbagh, had occupied the chair, to the delight of the latter's students, but to the distress of Shirazi's students who threatened to leave him and follow Ibn as-Sabbagh unless he accepted the chair which was rightfully his. Shirazi finally accepted. His refusal would have meant a real financial loss for his students.[42]

The status of the *madrasa* differed legally from that of the mosque, though they were both charitable trusts governed by the law of *waqf*. The founder of a mosque had no control over his foundation once he established it. The lawyers assimilate its status to the manumission of a slave. Once manumitted, a slave is absolutely free; so also the mosque once founded.[43] By contrast, the founder of a *madrasa* had virtually unlimited freedom in deciding the course of its existence. It is true, however, that once the instrument of *waqf* was drawn up and signed, and the foundation was thus brought into existence, the founder was forever bound by its contents.[44] But up to that point his freedom of choice was limited only by the restriction that nothing in the foundation could be done which would contravene the tenets of Islam.[45]

The innovation of the *madrasa* was one that involved the legal status of the institution, not one involving the curriculum. As far as the studies were concerned they remained the same. So that the fact that *madrasa* were first instituted outside of Baghdad had nothing to do with the level of culture of the regions in which they were founded. Baghdad was, and remained for long the cultural center of the Islamic world. What it did mean was that Nizam al-Mulk and the Saljuqids were strong enough to set up such institutions in Baghdad, which encroached upon the patronage of the Caliph in his own backyard. Before them, *madrasa* founded by powerful patrons were confined to areas outside of Iraq.

Nor were the *madrasa*, or the mosque-colleges, state institutions. As charitable trusts (*waqf*) they were founded by individual Muslims committing private property to public purposes, as in all cases of *waqf*. This is also the case even when statesmen were the founders.[46]

It should be borne in mind that the motive is not considered a determining factor in judging whether a trust is charitable or not. What matters is the public purpose to which the private property is devoted immediately or in the future. Generally speaking, charitable purposes include the promotion of education, the relief of poverty, the advancement of religion, the improvement of health, and such other items as the building of bridges and the ransoming of captives.

But if motives are of no interest to the law of *waqf* or charitable trust, they can be of more than passing interest to the historian. Besides the obvious motive of charity for establishing charitable trusts, there were still other motives not as obvious. The establishment of charitable trusts, in a form other than mosques, was one way of protecting property against confiscations and securing the financial future of one's family in perpetuity. For in the case of *waqfs*, the public purpose could be served after the extinction of the founder's descendants. This explains the family dynasties of learned men succeeding one another to the endowed professorships of colleges. The founder was free to appoint himself as professor-administrator and to keep that position for his descendants after him down to the last of his line. The Maliki law is the only law that did not allow the setting up of *waqfs* for one's own benefit. I have discussed this matter elsewhere to explain the relative absence of *madrasa* in regions where Maliki law was predominant, especially in Spain where *madrasa* were almost nonexistent.[47]

With statesmen of great wealth and power there was the additional motive of attracting the ʿulama to their fold in order to secure the support of their followers among the masses. This motive appears quite clearly in a statement made by Bajkam the Turk in the tenth century, a major part of whose philanthropy went to the support of ʿulama. The reason for his eagerness to support them is revealed in the following statement: 'Although I am not capable of scholarship and literary excellence', he says, 'yet it is my desire that there should not be on this earth a man of letters, or a man of religious learning, or the head of any field of knowledge, but that I have him under my protection, indebted to my largesse!' (*In kuntu la uhsinu l-ʿilma wa'l-adab, fa-uhibbu an la yakuna fi 'l-ardi adib, wa-la ʿalim wa-la ra'su sinaʿa, illa fi janbati wa-tahta 'stinaʿi.*)[48]

Neither Badr nor Nizam were innovators when they established their networks of institutions of learning.[49] They made use of a successful institution already in existence, taking their lead from the ʿulama themselves, whose wishes they were eager to grant in return for their influence with the masses of their followers. Rather than innovators, Badr and Nizam were great statesmen[50] and consummate politicians. Any man who could maintain himself in high office for three decades, in those turbulent days when highly competitive top positions were coveted by ambitious rivals who would stop at nothing to unseat the incumbents—such a one shows true political genius. Badr was governor over several provinces for thirty-two years; and Nizam, for thirty years, a prime minister under two of the great Saljuqids. These two master politicians knew how to harness the steeds of power and keep a firm grip on their reins. The ʿulama, indebted to their largesse, were a guarantee of their continued success. In return, the ʿulama were provided for, and the schools of law to which they belonged found the colleges to be excellent recruiting centers for their respective schools of legal thought. Between an institution which provided for the student and another that could not, the student in need had little difficulty in choosing between the two. And, in doing so, he had to adopt, as his own, the school of law represented by the institution.

The development of the college in Islam went, therefore, from the mosque, to the mosque-inn complex, to the *madrasa* and other like institutions. At some point in the eighth century or earlier, the *masjid*-mosque had become a college providing salaries for its staff, and gratuitous learning for the student; the mosque-inn went a step further and provided the student with lodging; and finally the *madrasa* provided him with all his essential needs for learning.[51]

Let us now look into the rise of colleges in the West. The earliest known college was founded in Paris. The founder was a certain John of London who had just returned in 1180 from Jerusalem where he had gone on pilgrimage. Founded in that year, the college eventually took its name from the eighteen poor students who were its resident members; hence the name 'Collège des Dix-Huit'. Many other colleges followed this one in Paris. Rashdall lists some seventy colleges for Paris by the year 1500.[52]

The earliest colleges in Oxford are Balliol, University, and Merton. Rashdall and, later, Emden, have sought to trace their origins to a simple benefaction dating as early as 1243,[53] or to a graduate society consisting of four masters and one bachelor of arts who lived in a house of a pre-collegiate type. Rough accounts relating to this house were found in a manuscript of Latin translations of works of Avicenna. Emden concludes that 'it may be claimed . . . for this "domus scholarium" house of scholars that it is the first known example of the type of graduate society which the founders of the earliest colleges were to establish later in a permanent form by means of endowment and incorporation. Hitherto an example of this prototype had been lacking. After the foundation of colleges it would seem', continues Emden, 'that non-collegiate graduate halls with Masters of Arts as fellows disappeared, and that only among the lawyers similar societies of fellows, under the name of Inn of Hall, continued in Oxford.'[54]

Unaware of the Islamic experience, Rashdall and Emden sought the origins of Oxford colleges in Oxford, while admitting that Paris was the home of the collegiate system.

There are two strong arguments for the borrowing of the college from Islam by the West. One is the law of *waqf*, or charitable trust. The other is the internal organization of the college itself.

Legal historians have long been puzzling over the origin of trusts. Pollock and Maitland make the following statement: 'We should be nearer the truth if we said that, to all intents and purposes, the first persons who in England employed the 'use' on a large scale were, not the clergy, nor the monks, but the Friars of St. Francis.'[55] According to Bracton, the earliest date of the trust in England is 1224.[56] Henry Cattan, after tracing the history of the use and comparing it with the Islamic *waqf*, comes to the conclusion that the early English use may have been derived from the Islamic system of *waqf*. He bases his conclusion on the essential similarities between the two, and on the priority of the *waqf* in time, developing as it did in the eighth and ninth centuries.

The colleges of Islam and those of the West are strikingly similar in their internal organization. Not only are they similar in their essential elements, relating to their government and management,[57] but also in their two classes of student foundationers. Both systems had fellows and scholars. The fellows were the graduate students; the scholars, undergraduates. In the *madrasa*-college of Islam the equivalent of fellow was *sahib*, and that of scholar, *mutafaqqih*. It is significant that the term fellow, the Latin equivalent of which was *socius*, is the exact translation of the Arabic Islamic term *sahib*, a term which goes back to the origins of Islam itself. What is much more significant, however, is that the *content* of the two terms is also exactly the same.

The first three known colleges in Oxford shed further light on the evolution of this institution in the West. There is a long-standing dispute as to which of the three is the oldest. This very dispute adds its own light to the nature and development of the collegiate system. Rashdall offered a solution in the following terms: 'On the whole, perhaps Merton has the best claim to be the earliest Oxford College: Balliol existed before it, we may say, *de facto* but not *de iure*, and University *de iure* but not *de facto*. Merton alone existed both *de iure* and *de facto* in 1264.'[58]

In the light of the Islamic experience, however, it is Mallet's judgement which makes more sense, and Emden is right in drawing attention to it.[59] 'To dismiss Balliol as an almshouse because it represents an older and simpler type of foundation than the Merton model, is surely to ignore the way in which the earliest colleges came into existence, not only at Balliol, but at Paris and elsewhere ... Walter de Merton's plans began as early as 1262 ... : John Balliol's plans began still earlier. William of Durham's bequest dates from 1249, but it was not used immediately to found a college ... Balliol represents the oldest House of Scholars in Oxford whose existence can be proved and not merely conjectured. Merton represents the oldest corporation organized on what became the regular English collegiate system. University represents the oldest benefaction out of which a college subsequently grew.'[60]

This statement of Sir Charles Mallet, relegated by him to a footnote, settles the question quite nicely. We can be certain that he did not know that the essence of his statement had the solid backing of the Islamic collegiate system, which, centuries before, had preceded that of the West. The essence of Mallet's statement, if I may paraphrase it, is that if we are talking about colleges, then we must see that Balliol is, of the three mentioned, the *first college* of Oxford; University college is the *first benefaction* which later resulted in a college; and Merton, the *first incorporated college*. We thus have not one, but *three firsts*.

The place of the professor in Islam was the mosque-college: in the West, his place was the university. The place of the student in Islam and the West was the inn, or hospice. Eventually, professor and student were brought together into one institution. In Islam, the institution which brought them together was the *madrasa*. In the West there was a tug of war between the two institutions, college and university. The struggle ended in Europe by the absorption of the college into the university, except at Oxford and Cambridge. Here, the college, rather than being absorbed by the university, took on the essential attribute of the university, incorporation. Later colleges, such as Dublin, Marischal, and the American Colonial colleges went a step further and became themselves, college-universities.

Oxford in the middle ages, as also today, had many colleges, but only one university. The university was a guild of masters, that is to say, *all* the masters of a given city. To this day, the old universities of Europe are still one university to a city. This was the case until recently[61] in a great city such as Paris, it is still the case in a small one such as Oxford. But, on the other hand, colleges could be multiple in a given city; there was nothing all-inclusive about them. That is why American college-universities which, at their inception, shared with the university the legal status of incorporation, are numerous in many of our cities. This characteristic they derive from their collegiate origins. The United States never had a university which was only a corporation and inclusive of all professors in a given city; its college-university was always a combination of a corporation and a charitable trust. Hence the ambiguity.

When we place Merton college against the background of the Islamic collegiate experience we have a key to the understanding of the long history of the collegiate system. For Merton ranks as a watershed in this history from the beginnings in Islam down to modern times. Its significance lies in the fact that it was incorporated. *That* is its rightful claim to primacy. Indeed, that is a primacy far more significant than that Merton should be merely the first college of Oxford. For, after all, Oxford was preceded by Paris in the matter of colleges by close to a full century; and by those of Islam, by several centuries more.

To sum up: the college and the university, as they have developed through the centuries, are each based on a legal concept: one Islamic in origin; the other, Western European.

Until modern times, Islam knew only the charitable trust and therefore developed only the college, not the university. And the college it developed was one which was later known in Europe up to the second half of the thirteenth century.

This century of corporations in the West was also one of charitable trusts. We find the two kept separate until after the middle of the century, at which time the charitable trust was further strengthened by the corporations. The marriage of the two concepts produced the collegiate system which is still to this day peculiar to Oxford and Cambridge, and through them to the college-universities of the United States. Henceforth the college was no longer simply an eleemosynary institution, it was also incorporated.

The University, at first, was strictly European; and the college, strictly Islamic. But as the university absorbed the functions of the college, it took on characteristics which had their origins in Islam. Similarly, when the college took on a university status, it preserved those characteristics which were Islamic in origin. The fusion of the elements of the two institutions brought about confusion in the terminology; it also caused Islamists to have the partly mistaken, partly correct, notion of the *madrasa* being at the origins of the university. In this fusion of the elements, the medieval West benefitted greatly by marrying the corporation to the charitable trust. For it is doubtful whether the university could have survived down to the present day as a corporation pure and simple. It was merely a guild, a union of masters, and nothing else. It possessed no wealth, no real estate, no property of substantial value. On the other hand, the college, as purely and simply a charitable trust, although endowed in perpetuity, suffered in many cases from a lack of stability and flexibility. It was the combination of both concepts that gave the composite institution the stability and flexibility it needed. Its remarkable longevity is due in great measure to a marriage of the two concepts. Although Islam had developed the college over the centuries to the limit of its potentialities, it suffered from the absence of the corporation, which it finally borrowed from the West in recent times. Until then, Islam was limited to the charitable trust as its only form of perpetuity. The corporation was foreign to it, based as it was on juristic personality, a concept alien to Islamic law. And while the West enjoyed the element of stability in the charitable trust, and the element of flexibility in the corporation, Islam was limited with its *waqf* to a stability which eventually turned to stern rigidity. For the *waqf* is mortmain (*main morte*, dead hand), incapable of unshackled development, soporific in its effects, qualities that weighed heavily on its object and kept it back from keeping up with the times. Nevertheless, the great institutions of learning that have lasted for eight centuries, and will soon be entering their ninth, whether universities, colleges, or the later college-universities, bear the unmistakeable stamp of Islamic institutions to which they owe many of their most enduring elements.

The College in Islam and the West

Notes

[1] C. H. Haskins, *The Rise of Universities* (Ithaca, NY: Cornell University Press, 1957, reprint of the Colver Lectures in 1923 in Brown University), p. 1.
[2] See below, pp. 3–4.
[3] *Webster's Collegiate Dictionary* (7th edition), s.v. 'university'.
[4] *Op. cit.*, s.v. 'college'.
[5] *Ibid.*
[6] *Webster's Collegiate Dictionary* (5th edition), s.v. 'college'.
[7] *Op. cit.*, s.v. 'university'.
[8] *American Jurisprudence* (2nd edition), paragraph 1, s.v. 'Definitions'.
[9] The *collège* is funded by the municipality; the *lycée*, by the state.
[10] *The Compact Edition of the Oxford English Dictionary* (Oxford: University Press, 1971), s.v. 'college'.
[11] *U.S. Reports*, Case of Yale University v. New Haven, 71 Conn. 316, January 1899, pp. 325–326.
[12] *Op. cit.*, p. 324.
[13] *Ibid.*
[14] *Ibid.*
[15] *Ibid.*
[16] ʿAbd al-Qadir b. Muhammad an-Nuʿaimi, *ad-Daris fi tarikh al-madaris*, 2 vols. (Damascus: at-Taraqqi Press, 1367–1370/1948–1951).
[17] Ibn Khallikan, *Wafayat al-aʿyan wa-anbaʾ abnaʾ az-zaman*, ed. Muhammad Muhyiʿd-Din ʿAbd al-Hamid, 6 vols. (Cairo: as-Saʿada Press, 1948–9), vol. 5, p. 318 (no. 785).
[18] Yaqut, *Irshad al-arib ila maʿrifat al-adib*, ed. Ahmad Farid ar-Rifaʿi, 20 vols. (Cairo: Dar al-Maʾmun Press, 1936–38), vol. 18, p. 61.
[19] Abu Ishaq ash-Shirazi, *Tabaqat al-fuqahaʾ*, printed with the *Tabaqat ash-shafiʿiya* of Hidayat Allah al-Husaini (Baghdad: Baghdad Press, 1956/1937), p. 82 (lines 12–13).
[20] See D. Santillana, *Istituzioni di diritto musulmano malikita con riguardo anche al sistema sciafiita*, 2 vols. (Rome: Istituto per l'Oriente, 1925), vol. 1, p. 324: '... non possono essere nè venduti, nè locati, nè adibiti ad uso privato' (here, a note to the effect that the foundation of a mosque causes the right of the founder to cease, except in certain cases, as for example, for the teaching of the religious sciences): 'le moschee appartengono a Dio'.' (Koran, LXXII, 18). There are certain exceptions to this rule. For instance, a traveller could spend the night there, or several nights; also the poor and destitute. There are cases of ascetic men of religious learning who lived and taught in a mosque for long periods of time; as in the following cases: Abu ʿUmar al-Baqillani (d. 402/1012), see Ibn al-Jauzi, *al-Muntazam fi tarikh al-muluk waʾl-umam*, ed. Krenkow, 6 vols., 5–10 (Haidarabad: Daʿirat al-Maʿarif Press, 1357–59/1938–40), vol. 7, pp. 258–259; Abu ʿAbd Allah ash-Shirazi (d. 439/1048), who reconstructed a mosque in the quarter of ash-Shuniziya and lived in it with his poor followers, see *ibid.*, vol. 8, p. 134; Abu ʿAli ash-Sharmaqani (d. 451/1059), who lived in a mosque on Darb az-Zaʿfarani, see *ibid.*, vol. 7, pp. 212–213; Abu ʾl-Maʿali as-Salih (d. 496/1102), an ascetic who lived in a mosque in the left bank quarter of Bab at-Taq, and whose mosque was still known by his name nearly a century later when Ibn al-Jauzi was writing his *Muntazam*, see *ibid.*, vol. 9, p. 136; and Muhammad, known as Akhu Jumada (d. 503/1109), an ascetic who lived in seclusion in his mosque for about forty years, leaving it only on Fridays to perform the Friday prayers at the Cathedral Mosque, see *ibid.*, vol. 9, p. 164. The rule was not always followed, apparently, since others, who could not qualify as exceptions to the general rule, were found now and then to be residing in the *masjid*-mosques. This was the case in the year 483, when the Caliph's vizier asked for a *fatwa* regarding the professors who were occupying these mosques as

places of residence. The legal opinion went against them and they were evicted, except for one poor juriconsult who acted as leader of the prayer (*imam*) and as caretaker. An exception was made in his case on the basis of his piety and indigence. See *Muntazam*, vol. 9, p. 53.

²¹ Ibn al-Jauzi, *Muntazam*, vol. 7, p. 101.

²² *Muntazam*, vol. 6, pp. 253–254; Ibn Kathir, *al-Bidaya wa 'n-nihaya fi ʿt-tarikh*, 14 vols. (Cairo: as-Saʿada Press, 1348/1929 ff.), vol. 11, pp. 175–176. Her name was Shaghab ('The nightingale's plaintive cry'). Her gifts, for the most part, consisted of alms. She also contributed annually to the needs of travellers who went on pilgrimage to Mecca, sending physicians and medicines along with the caravans and providing for the maintenance of wells on the road to the Holy City. Of course, alms-giving could have conceivably included indigent men of learning; they are simply not as yet *specifically* mentioned in the sources as the object of generosity *as a class*.

²³ *Muntazam*, vol. 6, p. 320.

²⁴ *Ibid.*, vol. 7, p. 115. As a patron of learning, ʿAdud ad-Daula was known to have assigned from his treasury regular stipends paid directly to juriconsults, to men of letters and to scholars of the *Koran*. No mention is made, however, of his having endowed institutions of learning in perpetuity, unless we take into consideration the hospital which he completed and where instruction in the medical arts and cognate fields of knowledge took place.

²⁵ He was himself a learned man, with a library of his own the size of which is said to have required four hundred camels to transport. His philanthropy took the form of emoluments in the amount of five thousand *dinars* sent annually to Baghdad for distribution among juriconsults and men of letters. He endeared himself to the traditionalists by his animosity toward those who pursued the study of Greek philosophy. See *Muntazam*, vol. 77, pp. 179–181.

²⁶ *Ibid.*, vol. 7, p. 10, and p. 13 (1.23). Diʿlij was a tradition-expert who travelled widely in pursuit of the science of traditions (to Khurasan, Raiy, Hulwan, Baghdad, Basra, and Mecca).

²⁷ *Ibid.*, p. 12 (1.15). The chair of law in his mosque-college in Baghdad was occupied by the professor of law, the Shafiʿi juriconsult ad-Dariki (*d.* 375/986).

²⁸ *Ibid.*, p. 29.

²⁹ For his full name, see Ibn Kathir, *al-Bidaya*, vol. 11, p. 353; Nasir Ad-Daula Abu 'n-Najm Badr b. Hasanawaih b. al-Husain al-Kurdi; his honorific title and patronymic (*laqab, kunya*) was given him by the Caliph al-Qadir (reign: 381–422/991–1031).

³⁰ Including al-Jibal, Hamadhan, Dinawar, Burujird, Nuhawand, and Asadabad, among others.

³¹ He gave one thousand *dinars* annually to outfit twenty men to perform the pilgrimage to Mecca in lieu of his mother and of the Buwaihid ʿAdud ad-Daula who had given him his position of power. To Mecca and Medina, the two Holy Cities of Islam, he sent one hundred thousand *dinars* for the upkeep of the sanctuaries and to pay for the safe-passage guarantee (*khafr at-tariq*) of the pilgrims. Three thousand *dinars* went annually to shoemakers located between Hamadhan and Baghdad to make shoes for the needy among the pilgrims. Twenty thousand *dirhams* monthly went for the shrouding of the dead; and ten thousand weekly to widows and the poor. He built many bridges and is said never to have passed a place with running water without building there a settlement. *Muntazam*, vol. 7, pp. 271–272.

³² *Ibid.*, '*wa-'stahdatha fi aʿmalihi thalathata alafi masjidin wa-khanin li 'l-ghuraba*'', see also Ibn al-ʿImad, *Shadharat adh-dhahab fi akhbar man dhahab*, 8 vols., (Cairo: al-Oudsi Press, 1350/1931), vol. 3, pp. 173–174 (based on Ibn al-Jauzi's *Shudur al-ʿuqud*); see also Ibn Kathir, *al-Bidaya*, vol. 11, p. 354 (lines 10–11) where the text reads as follows:

'wa-ʿammara fi aiyamihi mina 'l-masajidi wa 'l-khanati ma yunifu ʿala alfai masjidin wa-khan' ('he built during his administration by way of masjids and khans a number of them well above two thousand.').

[33] For the Arabic text, see *Muntazam*, vol. 10, p. 37; for the translation, with some modifications, and for details, see G. Makdisi, 'Muslim Institutions of Learning in Eleventh-Century Baghdad', in *Bulletin of the School of Oriental and African Studies*, vol. 24 (1969), p. 54.

[34] There is a text in at-Tanukhi (329-384/940-994), *Nishwar al-Muhadara wa-akhbar al-mudhakara*, 8 vols. (Beirut: Dar Said, 1971-1973), vol. 2, p. 99 which refers to a *khan* on the Tigris where a guard watches over merchandise belonging to merchants conducting business between Baghdad and Mosul. In another text of the same work, the author quotes Abu Nasr al-Bins who lived during the caliphates of al-Muqtadir. al-Qahir and ar-Radi (i.e. AH 295-329/AD 908-940): 'I was once in a city where I was a stranger, so I took up residence in a *khan* where youth and men visited me frequently and I taught them law in my room'; (see *ibid.*, vol. 1, p. 46). There was a *Khan* al-Khalifa in the Caliphal Quarter on Baghdad's Left Bank (see G. Makdisi, 'The Topography of Eleventh-Century Baghdad; Materials and Notes', in *Arabica*, vol. 6 (1959), p. 291 and note 10), and a Khan ar-Raqiq, 'the Slaves' House', and Dar ad-Daqiq, 'the Flour House'; (see Le Strange, *Baghdad during the Abbasid Caliphate* (Oxford: Clarendon Press, 1900), p. 123 and note 1). Le Strange cites Khan al-Khail, 'the Riding House', where envoys to Baghdad were taken first, and which he describes as a palace in the following terms: ' . . .built with porticos of marble columns. On the right part of this house stood five hundred mares with saddles of gold and silver, while on the left stood five hundred mares with brocade saddle-cloths and long head-covers; and each mare was held by a groom wearing a magnificent uniform'; (see *ibid.*, p. 296 and note 8). Of Dar ar-Raqiq (=Khan ar-Raqiq) Le Strange writes in the following terms: 'The Slaves' House had been originally used in the days of Mansur as barracks for his domestic slaves, who were brought and imported from the Turk borderlands, to be placed on their arrival in Baghdad under the superintendance of his chamberlain Rabiʿ; and also near the Slaves' House Yaʿkubi mentions the fief where the pages (*Ghulams*) of the chamberlain had their lodgings'. (See *ibid.*, pp. 123-124.) From the foregoing texts and descriptions it is clear that the *khan* was a building that served many purposes, among which teaching or tutoring on a private basis, and that the term *khan* itself was interchangeable with that of *dar*, 'a house', 'a mansion' of palatial proportions, reminiscent of the colleges which were later to evolve from it.

[35] *Muntazam*, vol. 8, p. 150 (ll. 18-20): 'fa-lamma ʿarafa ahlu 'l-Karkh ma jara, saru ila khani 'l-fuqaha'i 'l-hanafiyina bi-Qatiʿat ar-Rabiʿ, fa-akhadhu ma wajadu, wa-ahraqu 'l-khan, wa-kabasu dura 'l-fuqaha'.

[36] See Le Strange, *Baghdad during the Abbasid Caliphate* (Oxford: Clarendon Press, 1900), index, *s.v.*

[37] See note 19 below.

[38] Such was the case of Ibn al-Khadiba (d. 489/1096) who tells of a dream he had after copying seven times the monumental *Sahih* of Muslim, an authoritative collection of traditions (one of the canonical six) in four volumes. He dreamt that he had died and gone to heaven: 'When I went through the gate', he says, 'and was safely within, I lay down on my back, crossed one leg over the other, and said: "At last! I am done, by God, with copying!"' See *Yaqut Irshad*, vol. 13, p. 228.

[39] Such was the case, for instance, of the Chief Qadi of Baghdad, and Professor of Hanafi Law, Abu ʿAbd Allah ad-Damaghani (d. 478/1085), who hired as a night watchman in his student days in order to earn enough for his subsistence; see al-Bundari, *Tarikh Baghdad*, MS Paris, fonds arabe 6152, fol. 46a (in the margin; based on Samʿani's lost history of Baghdad); for this and further details on Damaghani see G. Makdisi, *Ibn*

ʿAqil et la résurgence de l'Islam traditionaliste au XIᵉ siècle (Damascus: Publications de l'Institut Français de Damas, 1963), pp. 171 ff., esp. p. 172 and n. 4.

⁴⁰ Ibid., vol. 4, p. 33.

⁴¹ See Subki, Tabaqat ash-shafiʿiya al-kubra, 6 vols. (Cairo: al-Husainiya Press, 1323–24/1905–06), vol. 3, p. 252 (ll. 7): '... wa-yanfuqu ma warithahu wa-ma kana yadkhulu lahu ʿala 'l-mutafaqqiha'. Students who worked for their subsistence were proud of the fact that they were 'working their way through college' as a student of modern days would say. The Andalusian Abu 'l-Walid al-Baji was not only proud of it but used it as an excuse for not being up to par in a disputation he had with Ibn Hazm. After the disputation was over, he said to Ibn Hazm: 'You will excuse me, for most of my studying was done by the light of the night-watchman's lantern'. To which Ibn Hazm retorted: 'And you will excuse me also, for most of my studying was done on desks inlaid with silver and gold'; pointing out to al-Baji that the luxuries of wealth are more of a deterrent to learning than are the straits of poverty, a condition which rather tends to spur one on to achieving success. See Yaqut, Irshad, vol. 12, p. 239.

⁴² For the details, see G. Makdisi, 'Muslim Institutions of Learning', pp. 32 ff.

⁴³ See G. Makdisi, 'The Madrasa as a Charitable Trust and the University as a Corporation in the Middle Ages, in Actes du Vᵉ Congrès International d'Arabisants et d'Islamisants (Bruxelles, 31 août–6 septembre 1970), Correspondance d'Orient Nº 11 (Bruxelles: Publications du Centre poᵘʳ l'Étude des Problèmes du Monde Musulman Contemporain, 1971), pp. 329–337 esp. pp. 334 and note 10, 335 and note 11.

⁴⁴ Ibid., p. 331.

⁴⁵ Ibid., p. 330.

⁴⁶ Thus Nur ad-Din Zanki (511–569/1118–1174) insisted that he did not use a single dirham from the treasury (bait al-mal) in order to build his endowed institutions. The inscription on the Dar al-Hadith an-Nuriya in Damascus, in its final part, cites the founder as hoping to find reward and recompense awaiting him on the Day of Judgement. Such facts point to Nur ad-Din's personal involvement in his endowed institutions. To endow them, he insisted by solemn oath that he used the income he earned from the ransoming of the prisoners he had taken, and that none of his endowed institutions benefitted from a single dirham drawn from the treasury: 'wa-kana Nur ad-Din yahlifu bi'llahi taʿala anna jamiʿa ma banahu mina 'l-madarisi wa 'l-auqafi wa'r-rubuti wa-ghairiha min hadhihi 'l-mufadat (ransom from captured kings and nobles), wa-jamiʿa waqfihi minha, wa-laisa fiha min baiti 'l-mali 'd-dirhamu 'l-fard.' See Nuʿaimi, ad-Daris, vol. I, p. 614 (lines 8–10). On Nur ad-Din, see the excellent work of Nikita Elisséeff, Nur ad-Din: Un grand prince musulman de Syrie au temps des croisades, 3 vols. (Damas: Institut Français de Damas, 1967).

⁴⁷ See G. Makdisi, 'The Madrasa in Spain: Some Remarks', Mélanges Roger Le Tourneau, in Revue de l'Occident Musulman et de la Méditerranée (Aix-en-Provence, 1973), pp. 153–158.

⁴⁸ Muntazam, VI, 320.

⁴⁹ Badr's network would seem to preclude the prior existence of the masjid-khan complex. The verb used in the above quoted passage, 'istahdatha' (see n. 28), 'he built anew', could mean that the complex itself was an innovation. It was an innovation not in the sense that the khan had not been used before as a place of lodging for students, but rather as an establishment legally linked with the masjid-college as a place of residence exclusively for the latter's students, the legal link being that of the charitable trust, or waqf. This ambiguity in the term istabdatha has already been productive of a long-standing puzzlement in connection with Nizam al-Mulk's foundation of madrasas (see G. Makdisi, 'Muslim Institutions', pp. 50 ff.). Care must be practised regarding the interpretation of 'primacy' in the establishment of institutions of learning. The innovation

of Badr is not in the institution of the *khan* itself, but rather in adapting it to the exclusive use of students of a *masjid*-college on a wide scale and providing the students with free lodging.

⁵⁰ Their deeds lived on long after them making it difficult for their successors to measure up to them. (Cf. al-Mutanabbi, in *Poems of al-Mutanabbi*, ed. A. H. Arberry (Cambridge: University Press, 1967), p. 26 (lines 23–24), p. 27 (lines 23–24). Nizam was highly praised by Ibn ʿAqil; see G. Makdisi, *Ibn ʿAqil*, pp. 485–486. Badr's name was invoked in order to shame others into emulating his generosity; as, for instance, in the petition made to the Ghazanwid Mahmud b. Sabuktakin (388–421/998–1030) which subtly recalled the generosity of Badr in the following terms: '...Badr b. Hasanawaih —and there is not a man among your officials who is not a greater man than he was—used to provide for the organization and expenditures of the annual pilgrimage to Mecca for twenty years from his own pocket. Consider the matter, for the sake of God, and give it a measure of your concern...' (*Muntazam*, vol. 8, p. 2). This passage implies that until Mahmud b. Sabuktakin came along, the last of the great philanthropists was Badr. Mahmud could not easily ignore the petition's subtle implication that to ignore it would mean not merely that he is second to Badr who, after all, was his peer, but to his own officials, who were his subordinates.

⁵¹ So also the other institutions of learning such as the dar *al-hadith*, dar *al-Qurʾan* and the various monasteries (*ribat, khanqah, zawiya*).

⁵² H. Rashdall, *The Universities of Europe in the Middle Ages*, new edition by F. M. Powicke and A. B. Emden, 3 vols. (Oxford: University Press, 1936, first edition 1895), pp. 536–539.

⁵³ *Ibid.*, vol. 3, p. 175; the benefaction was that of Alan Basset, according to Rashdall, but later said to be that of Bishop Grosseteste, see *ibid., loc. cit.*, n. 3.

⁵⁴ A. B. Emden, 'Accounts relating to an Early Oxford House of Scholars', in *Oxoniensia* (Oxford: The Oxford Architectural and Historical Society, 1968), vol. 31 (1966), pp. 77–81, esp. pp. 79–80.

⁵⁵ F. Pollock and F. W. Maitland, *History of English Law* (Cambridge, 1952), vol. 2, p. 229; quoted by H. Cattan, 'The Law of Waqf', in *Law in the Middle East*, vol. I, *Origin and Development of Islamic Law*, ed. M. Khadduri and H. J. Liebesny (Washington, D.C.: The Middle East Institute, 1955), pp. 203–222, see p. 213 and n. 4.

⁵⁶ See H. Cattan, *op. cit.*, p. 213.

⁵⁷ One has only to compare the law of *waqf* with that of the charitable trust; see *American Jurisprudence*, 2nd edition, on the charitable trust, *s.v.*, and for the *waqf*, see H. Cattan, *op. cit.*.

⁵⁸ Rashdall, *op. cit.*, vol. 3, pp. 192–193.

⁵⁹ See Emden's note in Rashdall, *op. cit.*, vol. 3, p. 181 note 1.

⁶⁰ C. E. Mallet, *A History of the University of Oxford*, 3 vols. (London: Methuen, 1924–1927), vol. 1, p. 83 note 1.

⁶¹ Recently the University of Paris was divided into thirteen universities: Paris I, Paris II, etc., each with its own president. Note that each is still designated as Université de Paris, the only distinguishing mark being the Roman numeral. Paris IV is designated 'Université de Paris-Sorbonne'.

The Arab Awakening Forty Years After

GEORGE Antonius was born in 1891 of Lebanese Christian parents who had settled in Alexandria. He studied at Victoria College, the English school in Alexandria, and then at King's College, Cambridge, where he obtained first-class honours in the Mechanical Sciences Tripos. After working during World War I in the censorship department of the Egyptian Expeditionary Force, he served in the British Mandatory Administration in Palestine, in the Education Department, 1921–7 and the Secretariat, 1927–30. He then left official service and began a new career as Middle Eastern associate of the Institute of Current World Affairs, an American organisation of which the aim was to spread understanding of what was happening in the outside world by the circulation to subscribers of confidential newsletters; it had been founded by Charles Crane, a Chicago business man who had himself played some part in the Middle East as a member of the King–Crane Commission, sent to the region by President Wilson in 1919. In 1938 he published his only book, *The Arab Awakening: the Story of the Arab Nationalist Movement*, and dedicated it to Mr Crane. He died in 1942.[1]

Why, it may be asked, should a book published forty years ago, and dealing with an early phase in the history of a national movement which has taken more than one new direction since then be taken seriously enough for a study to be devoted to it? There must be some intrinsic merit or significance in it to make it still deserving of serious study and consideration. In answer to such a question, at least three claims may be made for the book without much fear of contradiction.

First of all, most readers would agree that *The Arab Awakening* has literary merit of a high order. It is written in an excellent narrative style, precise, vivid, highly coloured, at times moving, carrying the reader easily and swiftly from one episode to another, and compelling belief as he reads it, even if some doubts may come later; its explanations are clear even if not always profound or sufficient. There is no extended analysis of ideas, but there are sharply expressed depictions of human personalities. Here is what he says of Mark Sykes:

> His mind was both perceptive and quick, and at the same time strangely inattentive and undiscerning; and, in his nature, he had something of the improvidence as well as all the warmth of the enthusiast. He knew a good deal about the Arabs at first hand, but his knowledge was as remarkable for its gaps as for its range, and his judgments alternated between perspicacity and incomprehension, as though his mental vision were patterned like a chessboard ... This placed him at a disadvantage in the game of diplomatic bargaining ...[2]

Here again is his memory of King Husayn in old age:

> ... ill at ease, in an armchair far too large for his small frame, shrunken with paralysis, his beautiful face blanched by the pallor of death, his eyes suddenly glowing from the vacancy of resignation to flashes of controlled passion ... his mind seemed less flexible and the mannerisms of expression which were a feature of his conversation obtruded themselves with greater frequency, as though habit had begun to steal upon reasoning. His old craving for justification had become an obsession.[3]

His judgement of T. E. Lawrence, once more, is perceptive:

> ... that very inconsistency which pervades his revelations and causes him to appear unreal, now as a man of vision and then as a victim of self-delusion, alternating between candour and affectation ... There are errors and misfits in [his book], which cannot be disposed of as mere lapses or defects of knowledge or memory and point rather to some constant psychological peculiarities. It seems as though Lawrence, with his aptitude to see life as a succession of images, had felt the need to connect and rationalise his experiences into a pattern; and in doing so had allowed sensations to impinge upon facts.[4]

This was indeed almost the first attempt to break away from the picture of Lawrence propagated by his friends on the basis of what he had himself told them, and at that time generally accepted almost as an article of faith. Antonius was taken to task by at least one of Lawrence's friends; since then, others have tried to answer the questions he posed—Richard Aldington, Sulayman Musa, John Mack[5]—but we still lack what Antonius suggested that we needed, a study of *Seven Pillars of Wisdom* as a work of the imagination in which events are transmuted into myths.

It cannot, secondly, be doubted that the book had a great impact at the time when it appeared. It came out near the end of 'Britain's moment in the Middle East',[6] that strange interlude in Middle Eastern history, when the region was not, as it had for so long been and was to become again, the point where the interests of all the Great Powers met in concert or in rivalry, but was under the effective domination of one of them. Russia, Germany and Austria-Hungary had collapsed or withdrawn at the end of World War I, the United States was not yet involved in more than a marginal way. France was, indeed, present in the Middle East, but as a nation weakened both politically and economically by the War and its aftermath. Final power over most of the area lay with Great Britain, but that power was now being challenged, by the growth of German and Italian influence, by the emergence of nationalist movements, in Egypt, Iran and the Arab countries of Asia, and by the posing of questions, inside England itself, about the legitimacy of rule over other nations. To these questions a certain answer was being given, that it was possible to respond to the challenge of nationalism and give a moral basis to the retention of final power, by establishing a new relationship with the peoples ruled by Great Britain, and one which offered them the ultimate prospect of independence: Ireland had been given independence, within certain limits, in 1921; the Government of India Act of 1935 had provided for a certain transfer of responsibility from British to Indians; the Anglo-Iraqi Treaty of 1930, and the Anglo-Egyptian Treaty of 1936, had also led to such a transfer, although within limits imposed by a continuing British presence. On the other hand, there had now appeared another problem which could not easily be resolved in this way. Jewish immigration into Palestine, under the pressure of events in Europe, had aroused among Palestinian Arabs a mass reaction, of an order different from the political opposition to foreign rule in Syria or Iraq; Jews all over the world and Arabs in the countries surrounding Palestine were being drawn into the conflict, which threatened to have repercussions upon British interests and policies all over the world. The report of the Royal Commission, proposing the partition of Palestine, had been published, accepted in principle by the British government, and then virtually abandoned because of the difficulties of carrying it out, and Great Britain seemed to be moving towards another kind of solution.

It was in this context that Antonius's book appeared. It was written quickly and urgently, and was indeed a shortened and altered version of another book he had intended to write, a detailed historical study of the origins and early development of the Arab movement; and it was written for a particular audience at a particular moment in time. The readers to whom it was addressed were primarily British, politicians, diplomats, officials, journalists and scholars, members of the élite of a few thousand people who were seriously concerned about imperial policy and in a position to exercise some influence upon decisions. It provided them with historical information, and with an explanation of political attitudes; it gave the clearest exposition which had ever been given of the Arab fears in regard to Palestine (Antonius had given evidence to the Royal Commission when it was in Palestine in 1937, and had deeply impressed members of it). It strengthened the sense, which by now was widespread among British officials, that some serious errors of policy had been made, but at the same time appeased it by suggesting a way out.

There is no doubt that it had a great and immediate influence. Documents studied recently by Elie Kedourie bear witness to its influence among civil servants, although by no means all of them accepted its version of events. When the 'Round Table Conference' was held at St James's Palace in 1939, Antonius was chosen as Secretary-General of the Arab delegations, apparently at the suggestion of the British Government.[7] He played an important part in drafting documents submitted by the Arab delegations to the conference, and a dominant one in the committee set up to consider the meaning of the various letters exchanged and agreements made during World War I; it was largely because of his advocacy that the British members of the committee admitted that there was more force to the Arab contentions than had appeared hitherto, an expression which came as near as any great government does to agreeing that it had been mistaken.[8] During World War II, before his early death, he continued to have some influence on British officials in the Middle East, and here again his persuasive tongue and pen seem to have helped incline them to the belief that some kind of Arab unity, and some concessions to the Arabs in regard to Palestine, would be in harmony with British interests.

Thirdly, there is no doubt that *The Arab Awakening* has had a great influence (although not everyone, as we shall see, would think it a good one) on academic studies of the modern Middle East, in both England and the United States. It stands in fact near the beginning of the development of these studies. Before Antonius and a few others of his generation wrote, those who wished to know about the modern history of the Middle East did not have much to rely on. There were books by travellers and memoirs of former officials, studies of the 'eastern question' and of colonial policy. The former tended to be superficial or partial, the latter might be more solid but had a certain limitation which by then was becoming apparent. Writers on the 'eastern question' studied the relations of the European Powers with each other, within a framework of generally accepted conventions about the ways in which those relations should be carried on, and in regard to the problems posed by the weakness of the great Islamic states of early modern times, Morocco, Iran and the Ottoman Empire. They tended to look on those states as passive bodies over which the Powers argued, quarrelled and agreed, not as active parties, however weak, in the process; it is only in recent years that such work as that of Thomas Naff and Allan Cunningham has begun to change this view.[9] Books on colonial policy tended to base themselves on the writings of officials or the archives of colonial governments, and to accept that what happened was what governments or officials thought was happening or wanted to happen. Once again, it is only in recent years that a view of British rule derived from Lord Cromer's apologia in his *Modern Egypt* has been modified by such work as that of Afaf Lutfi al-Sayyid, Alexander Schölch and Jacques Berque; the Egypt of the time can now be seen not as the matter on which Lord Cromer imposed form, but as one party in a relationship (even if it was one of unequal power) in which each party had its own motives and direction of change.[10]

Seen in retrospect, *The Arab Awakening* was one of two books published in the period between the two wars which played an important part in preparing the way for such changes of view. The other was Arnold Toynbee's *The Western Question in Greece and Turkey*,[11] a book less well-known than his later *Study of History*, but which contains in embryonic form some of the ideas later expounded there, about contacts between civilisations, and in particular about the relationship of unequal strength between Great Powers and small states or nationalist movements, and the nature of conflicts between powers which are fought out not directly but by means of client states and movements:

> ... the illusions of local nationalities have been utilised by the Western diplomats in order to save something from the wreck of their schemes ... Greeks and Turks can be swayed and stampeded by visions of 'The City', 'Ionia', 'The Abode of Felicity' or the Holy Sepulchres of Edirné ... a kind of 'Juggernaut' national personality can be conjured into existence and induced, by offerings attractive to its divinity, to drive over its worshippers' bodies. On the international chess-board such pieces make excellent pawns ... [But] the trap in which the victims have been caught in order to be exploited was not cunningly hidden. They rushed into it because they could not resist the bait ... They did not suspect how quickly pawns in distress become an embarrassment, or how little the players care if they disappear from the board.[1,2]

Implicit in statements like this is an understanding of the tragic nature of such relationships. Great powers are primarily concerned with their relations with other great powers; their clients must fit into this framework, but often forget this, and in doing so may draw their patrons into conflicts they do not desire, or find too late that their patrons abandon them at the moment of crisis, in order to avoid a conflict. In an age when the 'shadow of the West' falls across the whole world, and takes the shape of nationalist movements, this process may end by the disruption of ancient communities and the dissolution of ancient ties of neighbourliness. The episode which Toynbee studied in this book ended with the destruction of the Greek communities of Asia Minor: Greeks and Turks, who had lived together in city and countryside for centuries, faced each other as strangers and enemies.

Although Toynbee and Antonius knew each other, there is no evidence that Antonius had read *The Western Question* or been influenced by it, but his book points much the same moral. At the heart of it there lies a detailed account of the dealings of one Great Power with one nationalist movement, and it ends with a fear that, under the shadow of British policy, what had happened between Greeks and Turks in Asia Minor might happen between Arabs and Jews in Palestine.

Since *The Arab Awakening* was published, interest in the Middle East has grown, and has moved in a direction to which it is relevant. It has had a major impact on later scholars, and one might say that it is the point from which many of them have started. It is still used by students, and liked by many of them, and still present in the minds of later writers on the same range of subjects, most of whom find it necessary to define their areas of agreement and disagreement with it. Even if this were not true, it would still have played an important part in the growth of a certain field of study, and that is as much as can be said for most works of scholarship of a past generation. Since it *is* true, however, we must ask how far the book can be regarded as a permanent and valuable contribution to our knowledge of its subject. Some later writers have expressed serious doubts about this, and to some extent Antonius himself must be held responsible for this. His book is a slightly uneasy combination of two different kinds of writing. It is a work of historical narrative, but also of political advocacy. This is clear from the style, which moves from one register to another, and from the intrusion of moral judgements, sometimes strongly expressed. We are forced therefore at least to pose the question, to what extent his own political feelings and convictions determined his principles of selection and emphasis. Moreover, it is difficult to judge the depth and range of the documentation on which the book is based, because there is almost none of the apparatus of scholarship; there are few footnotes and no bibliography. This may be explained partly by the haste with which it was written, but also perhaps in another way: the book was not primarily addressed to scholars, but to the kind of reader who might have been put off by too great a display of learning. Antonius may have judged his readership well, for he was addressing himself to the kind of Englishman who, in that generation, might have had a certain cult of the amateur and a suspicion of anything which might appear to be 'showing off'.

Antonius's own correspondence makes it clear that the book was in fact based on wide reading. He had worked in the Public Record Office in London, at a time when the fifty years' rule was in force and documents were not available beyond the 1880s; he had been allowed to see some papers of the Foreign Office and the Committee of Imperial Defence; he had been given access to the private papers of D. G. Hogarth, Sir Gilbert Clayton and Sir Mark Sykes. In the United States he had seen documents in the State Department and some private papers, those of Colonel House and Professor Westermann.[13] The extent of his Arabic documentation is more difficult to judge. He certainly made use of newspapers, and of printed works containing documents, like Amin Saʿid's *al-Thawra al-ʿarabiyya al-kubra*,[14] and he appears to have had access to documents in the possession of the Hashimite family, some of which seem to have disappeared since then.[15] Above all, the book is based on many conversations and interviews with those who had taken an active part in the Arab movement.

Since he wrote, many more documents have become available. In particular, those in the Public Record Office are now open for the whole period with which the book deals, and have been studied by a number of later writers. In the course of time, too, concerns and convictions have changed, and no writer today perhaps would place the emphasis exactly where Antonius did. We must therefore ask at least two questions: how far have the documents now available shown that Antonius's narrative or interpretation is erroneous, and how far did his personal convictions lead him to distort the story, even within the limits of the materials which were available to him? These questions have clearly been present in the minds of such later writers as Elie Kedourie and Sylvia Haim, A. L. Tibawi, Z. N. Zeine and C. E. Dawn.[16] On the whole, they express considerable disagreement and disquiet. Some at least of these are justified, but it may be that certain parts of the book have greater and more lasting value than others.

The book falls into three parts, all rather different from each other in both matter and style. The first of them narrates the early development of the Arab nationalist movement down to the outbreak of war in 1914; the second studies in detail the relations between various Arab groups and the British government during the War and the subsequent period when questions raised during the War were being settled; and the third describes the development of the Arabian Peninsula, and of the successor states of the Ottoman Empire placed under British and French mandate, in the 1920s and 1930s.

Of these three parts, the first may have seemed to most readers to be the most valuable and original when it was first published. It provided information about some aspects of the modern history of the Middle East which, although not completely new, must have been unfamiliar to most English and American readers: for example, it was one of the first accounts in English of the Lebanese literary movement. In one respect at least it was almost wholly new: its description of the origins and nature of the Arab societies of the Young Turk period was based to a great extent on information given by former members of them, and it still appears to be substantially accurate so far as it goes, although Majid Khadduri and others have corrected it in detail.[17] When we pass from facts to explanations, however, a sharp criticism has been made, and with some reason, by Zeine, Dawn, Tibawi and others.

Such criticism is directed towards Antonius's view of the nature of Arab nationalism in that early period. It can best be approached by asking three kinds of question. First, who were the nationalists and why did they become nationalists? Antonius gives the impression that they were men of differing origins, Lebanese, Syrians and Iraqis, Muslims and Christians, who had one thing in common: they had been moved by the rediscovery of the Arabic language and its literature, and 'the contemplation of its beauty'[18] revived in them the consciousness of being Arabs, and gave birth to a resolve to recreate a society in which Arabs could live together and rule themselves. Once this seed had been planted, it had to grow in a certain way: a reform of the Ottoman Empire, of such a kind as to enable the Arabs to continue living in it, was impossible, for it was based on the idea of an 'unnatural alliance of Turks and Arabs'.[19]

Because the alliance of Turks and Arabs was in fact dissolved, we may easily assume that it had to be; but it was not so obvious at the time as Antonius implies. In fact, those who joined the societies before 1914, and who later emerged as members of the ruling élite of the Arab successor states of the Ottoman Empire, were men who on the whole came from a certain milieu, and who became nationalists gradually, reluctantly, and to some extent unconsciously. There were among them a few members of the new educated Christian class of Syria, Lebanon and Palestine, and a few members of the traditional Muslim learned class, in particular those who had been brought within the range of the ideas of 'Islamic modernism' put forward by Rashid Rida in his periodical *al-Manar*. For the most part, however, they were members in some sense of the Ottoman ruling élite; or, to be more precise, members of those great families in the cities of the Arab provinces who had a tradition of learning and social leadership, had always played a part in the Ottoman system of local government, and from the late nineteenth century were being drawn more fully into the Ottoman service as officers or civil servants.

C. E. Dawn has the credit of being the first scholar to draw attention to this fact. His thesis is that the rise of Arab nationalism in the years before 1914 can be explained in terms of an 'inter-élite conflict defined in terms of ideologies': the real conflict was not one of ideas, it was one of personal, family and factional rivalries, the purpose of which was to obtain or keep office or influence within the Ottoman system of government.[20] This is a good starting point, but it may be that Dawn's view needs to be further refined.

It is true, to begin with, that such families had always been linked with the Ottoman system of government. The failure to make this clear is indeed one of the most serious defects in Antonius's book. He missed the framework of institutions within which the Arab movement arose. At the time when he wrote, little work had been done in the Ottoman archives, and the dissolution of the Empire was still a recent memory, so that it was possible for Arabs, as for the peoples of the Balkans, to think of the Ottoman government as an alien despotism which had held its subject-peoples back until they broke away from it. It is common for nationalist movements to think of the immediate past with revulsion, and to appeal against it in the name of some more distant past, real or imagined. In the last generation, however, views have changed. Study of the Ottoman archives, both by western scholars and by the new school of Turkish historians, has thrown new light on the institutions of government; this has recently been described, so far as the classical period is concerned, in Halil Inalcik's book, *The Ottoman Empire: the Classical Age 1300–1600*.[21] More recently there have been some studies of the Arab provinces which take Ottoman documents into account, such as those of Raymond and Shaw for Egypt, and Rafeq, Cohen and Barbir for the Syrian provinces.[22] Such work makes it possible to look at Ottoman rule in Syria in a light different from the familiar one. The eighteenth century, which is usually regarded as a period when Ottoman power was seized by local despots, was one in which that power was in fact reasserted in a new way, by 'Ottoman governors with local roots'.[23] It was at this time that certain notable families in cities like Aleppo and Damascus consolidated their social power by means of their links with the Ottoman government: they held local offices or in other ways had access to the rulers, and were sensible of the prestige of Ottoman culture, whether expressed in the literature of the ruling élite or in the Hanafi legal code which was the code officially recognised by the government. In the nineteenth century, during the earlier period of Ottoman reform, the balance of local power between Ottoman governors and local notables moved for a time in favour of the second, but towards the end of the century it moved back in the other direction: the Ottoman policy of administrative centralisation began to succeed, and some of the local families began to send their sons to the professional schools in Istanbul and from there into the Ottoman army or civil service.

After the Young Turk revolution of 1908, new conflicts began to appear within such families, and in particular among those members of them who had taken service in army or administration, but it would be best not to take Dawn's view to extremes and think of these conflicts as being simply struggles for position or power, nor to accept Antonius's distinction between those who became Arab nationalists by passion and conviction (the 'suffering idealists',[24] as he calls them) and those who clung to the 'unnatural alliance between Turks and Arabs'. Intermingled with the struggles for position, there were genuine differences of opinion and conviction, but for the most part these were local forms of certain differences which existed throughout the Empire, and concerned the problem of what should be done if the Empire was to survive: there was a difference between those who wished it to remain an Islamic autocracy within the bounds of the shariʿa, and those who wanted it to be a constitutional state on the western European model, and also between those who supported the Young Turk policy of centralisation and those who wanted a greater measure of decentralisation. A few individuals apart, the idea that the Arabs should break away from the Empire scarcely arose until two events brought it to the surface: the entry of the Empire into the War in 1914, at a moment when Arab-Turkish relations were strained; and the collapse of the Empire in 1918, which faced everyone, and in particular the members of the ruling élite, with an inescapable choice.

The second kind of question we need to ask concerns the ideas in terms of which these differences of opinion were expressed. In so far as they were expressed in 'Arab' terms, what exactly were they and where did they come from? Here again there is no doubt that Antonius gave too simple an answer. The Lebanese Christian literary movement was not a major factor. No strong line of descent can be traced from Nasif al-Yaziji and Butrus al-Bustani to the nationalists of the next generation; curiously enough, Antonius does not mention the one writer of this kind who can in some ways be considered a precursor, Ahmad Faris al-Shidyaq. Two other lines of thought were more important. One was a certain development of the 'Islamic modernism' of the Salafi school. Re-interpreting Islamic law in the light of what the 'pious elders' were believed to have done and said, it naturally laid more emphasis on the period of Arab domination in Islamic history. At some point the Islamic community had taken a wrong turning; this was connected with the ascendancy first of Persians and then of Turks in the Muslim world, and the conclusion was drawn that the centre of gravity must move back to the Arabs—the advocacy of an Arab caliphate was one aspect of this. Secondly, and perhaps more important, there were ideas picked up by Arab students in the professional schools of Istanbul or by officers and officials in Ottoman service: ideas which were the commonplaces of the Ottoman ruling élite, drawn from French books or German military instructors, and which were restated in an 'Arab' idiom by some students, officers and officials, perhaps under the stress of a sense of exclusion from the inner circle of the élite, which remained largely Turkish. (In the same way, at much the same time, Jews, Armenians and Turks in the Russian Empire, who had gone far enough on the road of assimilation to have absorbed the ideas of the Russian intelligentsia, had restated these ideas in their own idiom as Zionism, Armenian nationalism and Pan-Turanism.)

Why was it, thirdly, that such ideas in their Arab form began to attract members of the ruling élite, and what difference did they make to their actions? Here once more it would be best to take a middle path between the explanation suggested by Antonius and a contrary opinion. Antonius seems to be saying that certain Arabs experienced a kind of sudden conversion, moved as they were by the beauty of their language and the memory of their ancestors. On the other hand, it is sometimes suggested that Arab nationalism was little more than a form of words, which indicated at most some changing fashion of the imagination, but did not serve as a guide to action: the reality behind it was either the desire of individuals to secure power and office, or the desire for political domination which, according to such formulations, is intrinsic to Islam, at least in its Sunni form.

A change of words and images must, however, be significant of something beyond itself. In all communities, there is a kind of rhetoric which is used at moments of high tension, as a spur to action. In stable communities it tends to express ancestral pieties; an example of this has been given by the sociologist Robert Bellah in his essay on 'The civil religion of America', in which he analyses the language used by Presidents in their inaugural addresses.[25] If this language changes, if it expresses the past in some different way or turns away from the past towards an imagined future, this may be a sign of some other kind of change: some fundamental, rapid and unexpected change in the social order, of such a kind that old beliefs, symbols and rituals can no longer serve as guides to social action. The point has been well expressed by Clifford Geertz:

> In politics firmly embedded in Edmund Burke's golden assemblage of 'ancient opinions and rules of life', the role of ideology is marginal. In such truly traditional political systems the participants act as . . . men of untaught feelings . . . which do not leave them 'hesitating in the moment of decision, sceptical, puzzled and unresolved' . . . But when . . .those hallowed opinions and rules of life come into question, the search for systematic ideological formulations flourishes. The function of ideology is to make an autonomous politics possible by providing the authoritative concepts that render it meaningful.[26]

Such changes were indeed taking place in Ottoman society in the late nineteenth century, and by the end of the century were having a deep effect on the life of the provinces and the minds of the educated class. Ottomans, whether Turkish or Arabic-speaking, found themselves living under a different system of administration and law; their wealth and social position were affected by changes in patterns of production and trade; faster communications gave them a different relationship with other parts of the Empire and with the outside world; new media of expression made it possible for ideas and news to be spread and discussed widely; and the shadow of European power lay over all of them. It is in this context that we should try to understand the significance of the new ideology of 'Arabism'. It had by no means driven out other ideologies, those of Ottomanism and Pan-Islamism, nor had it replaced, throughout society, something far older, the acceptance of the rule of a just Muslim sultan. That it was emerging and spreading at this time, however, indicates that for some at least of the Arabic-speaking Ottomans neither the traditional idea of authority nor the other ideologies could provide a guide to social action. The analysis of 'Arabism' as an ideology, with all that this implies, is missing from *The Arab Awakening*, but it is also missing from the work of most of its critics.

We come now to the second part of the book, which deals with World War I and the peace settlement after it. There is evidence here of wide reading of documents not generally available at the time it was written, and of information drawn from personal contacts. Antonius gives us a clear description of Arab participation in the Arabian and Syrian campaigns, and one of special interest to Middle Eastern historians because they can see in it almost the last example of a recurrent process in the history of the region, before modern technology changed the world. He shows us how a new dynasty emerged, springing as usual from an urban initiative. An urban family, that of the Hashimite Sharifs of Mecca, created around itself a combination of forces, partly by the formation of a small regular army but even more so by making alliances with rural leaders, and it was able to do this by providing both a leadership which could be regarded as standing above the different groups in the alliance, and an aim which could persuade them to rise above their divisions. The combined forces moved along a line of communications linking a chain of oasis-settlements and market towns, towards a great city; but—and here is the difference from the traditional process—it fails at the moment of victory to establish its control over the city by allying its interests with those of the urban population, because circumstances have changed, the strength it has been using is not its own but borrowed from a more powerful patron which in the end has abandoned it.

There is, however, a point of weakness in the narrative. Antonius tends to ascribe to this fragile combination of forces around the leadership of the Hashimites a unity and solidity which it did not possess. The rural leaders, in particular those of pastoral groups, could not be subjected to discipline beyond a certain point, and, what was more important, there were differences of conception and purpose between the two forces which composed the 'Arab movement' at that time: the nationalist societies, formed mainly of Syrians, with their centres of activity in Damascus and Cairo, and the Hashimite family whose power was rooted in the Hejaz. The relationship between them, and between each of them and the British authorities in Cairo and Khartoum, was shifting and unstable. It passed through at least three different stages. In the first year or so of the War, there was a concentration of Arab elements in the Ottoman army in Syria, and the British were thinking of a possible landing on the Syrian coast at Alexandretta; this explains the rather mysterious negotiations with the Arab Ottoman officer al-Faruqi, who claimed to speak on behalf of the nationalist societies but had also some contact with the Sharif Husayn, and the sense of urgency with which they were conducted by the British. Then, after the end of the Dardanelles campaign, there seemed to be a possibility of a Turco-German advance from Syria, westwards against the Suez Canal and southwards in western Arabia; in these circumstances, an agreement with the ruler of Mecca became more important for the British, and he for his part was afraid that such an advance would mean an extension of direct Ottoman control in the Hejaz. Finally, in 1917 and 1918, there came the successful British advance from Egypt into Palestine and Syria. The British needed to make decisions about the future of the conquered territory, and to achieve some kind of balance in their relations with all parties concerned, Hashimites, Syrians, Zionists and French; and tensions between Syrians and Hashimites, and even within the Hashimite family itself, began to come to the surface. Antonius must have been aware of all this, given his unusual contacts with all parties, but he tended to obscure it, partly because his main information came from the Hashimites, and partly perhaps because, throughout the book, his main emphasis was on the underlying unity of the Arab movement. A reader may be conscious here of some confusion between historical explanation and political advocacy. It should be said, however, that apart from C. E. Dawn,[27] other writers too have tended to underrate the importance and independence of the Syrian nationalists.

Together with the description of the campaign there went an analysis of the network of discussions and agreements which surrounded it. This shows a political sense which is rare among historians. Much modern history is written on the level of the higher civil service; Antonius himself had been a civil servant, but by temperament he was more of a politician, and understood how politicians think and make decisions. Although, for example, in the last part of the book he drew a contrast between what he regarded as the failure of French policy in Syria and the success of British policy in Iraq, he had a complete understanding of the reasons why French policy was as it was: the overriding concern to do nothing in the Middle East which might affect the French position in North Africa, and the sense of weakness which Frenchmen in the Middle East felt vis à vis the British, so that French policy was really a sequence of tactical replies to what appeared to be British threats to French interests.[28]

To take an even more striking example, Antonius gave perhaps the first cogent explanation of the reasons for which the British Government issued the Balfour Declaration of support for the establishment of a Jewish National Home in Palestine. It was issued, he suggests, primarily because the British Government and the Zionists found they had a common interest: the British wished to prevent any potential rival acquiring a position of power in Palestine, so close to the Suez Canal, while the Zionists wanted a powerful patron. They were thus able to reach an agreement, by which Great Britain would support the Zionist idea and the Zionists would ask for British protection.[29] Antonius's suggestion must have been more than a guess, it was surely based on documents to which he had access, interpreted by his fine sense of the way in which political negotiations take place. It has been in general confirmed by the most careful and judicious study made since the opening of the relevant British archives, that of Mayir Vereté in his article on 'The Balfour Declaration and its makers'.[30]

In other ways, however, his treatment of the war-time agreements has been exposed to much criticism. It is inevitable that much of what he says should be out-dated. He first provided some of the essential documents in an easily accessible form, but in the last decade or so many more have become available and been studied: by Sulayman Musa and A. L. Tibawi, by I. Friedman, J. Nevakivi and R. Adelson, and most recently by Elie Kedourie in his *In the Anglo-Arab Labyrinth*.[31] A vast construction of scholarship and argument now exists, and no attempt will be made to add to it. It is necessary, however, to ask where Antonius stands on the main points at issue, and whether his stand is a tenable one.

Antonius was concerned to make three essential points: in the Husayn–McMahon correspondence of 1914–15, the British Government gave certain undertakings to the Arab nationalists in order to induce them to revolt against the Ottoman government; in the Sykes–Picot Agreement of 1916, the British made concessions to the French which were incompatible with the undertakings given to the Arabs; in the Balfour Declaration of 1917, the British gave an undertaking to the Zionists which was no less incompatible with those given to the Arab nationalists.

Some later writers have denied all these claims. Elie Kedourie maintains that no undertakings were given to the Arabs, and that such hopes as they might have conceived on the basis of badly drafted letters were not incompatible with the precise undertakings given to France, undertakings which were in any case explained to the Sharif Husayn.[32] I. Friedman for his part claims that Palestine was never included in whatever pledges were given to the Arabs, and the Balfour Declaration was therefore compatible with those pledges.[33]

The evidence which they and others have produced, however, can be regarded as pointing in the direction of conclusions different from theirs. There seems no doubt that in the letters sent by McMahon, expressions were used which Husayn could legitimately regard as constituting pledges, and they were so used not because of bad draftsmanship, since in fact they were drafted by an official of high intelligence, Gilbert Clayton, and approved at every stage by the Foreign Office, but because they expressed British policy and intentions at that time. Once they were used, they were regarded by the British government as constituting binding engagements. Very few of those who studied the documents at that time had any doubt of this: that is true not only of comparatively junior officials like Arnold Toynbee and Harold Nicolson, but of the Foreign Secretary, Sir Edward Grey. It was stated forcefully by a later Foreign Secretary, Arthur Balfour, in his famous memorandum of August 1919, and by the Prime Minister, Lloyd George, in a conversation with Husayn's son Faysal in September of that year.[34]

If George Antonius is right on this, however, he appears to be on less safe ground when he maintains that the pledges given to the Arabs were incompatible with those given to the French. It seems clear now that the intention of the British government, when it made the Sykes–Picot agreement, was to reconcile the interests of France with the pledges given to the Sharif Husayn, and the agreement can be regarded as having reconciled them, if it is interpreted in a certain way, but not if it is interpreted in another. Once more, there is no question of inept draftsmanship; if the agreement was ambiguous, it was not because it was badly expressed, but because it was a war-time agreement. Such agreements were made in a hurry and under stress, and for an immediate purpose: not to decide what should happen once the War was ended, but to achieve the minimum of agreement without which campaigns could not be fought in common. In a difficult negotiation, when there is an urgent need to reach agreement, it is natural and legitimate to try to devise a formula which can be interpreted in more than one way, and to leave the question of which interpretation should prevail to be decided by the balance of strength when the war was over.

Ambiguous agreements secretly arrived at can cause difficulties for historians fifty years on, but still more at the time, for they do not end the discussion, they provide a new basis for it to be carried on. Each party sets himself to ensure that his interpretation should prevail, either by argument or by trying to obtain a position of power. It was not only British, French and Arabs who could interpret pledges and agreements in different ways. British officials seem to have given different interpretations when talking to the other parties, and such differences of interpretation may have reflected different views of policy. When talking to Husayn or the Syrian nationalists, there seems no doubt that British officials did all they could to persuade them that their government accepted the Arab interpretation. When Sir Mark Sykes met Husayn in May 1917, Professor Kedourie maintains that he gave Husayn full information about the Sykes–Picot Agreement; but the evidence he produces appears to show that Husayn may only have been told of 'the principle of the agreement as regards an Arab confederation or state', and that he may have been encouraged to believe that even on the Syrian coast, where France was to be free, according to the Agreement, to set up any administration she wanted, she would in fact act as favourably to Arab aspirations as the British had recently proclaimed they would act in that part of Iraq where they too would be free to do as they wanted.[35] Similarly, in June 1918, the British High Commissioner in Egypt, Sir Reginald Wingate, told Husayn's agent in Cairo that the Sykes–Picot Agreement was 'merely a record of old conversations and of a provisional understanding'.[36] A little later, in November 1918, an Anglo-French declaration gave the most unequivocal support for Arab independence, and Antonius is surely right to lay stress upon it.[37] It is difficult, therefore, to blame the Arab nationalists for having been encouraged to believe that the Sykes–Picot Agreement meant one thing, only to discover after the War that the French meant by it something else. (In the same way, Sykes tried to reassure the Zionist leaders when he met them in February 1917; they seem to have had some kind of information about the recent Anglo-French Agreement and asked him whether the British Government had given any pledge to its allies in regard to Palestine. The Agreement in fact provided for an international administration of Palestine, but Sykes assured them that 'with great difficulty the British Government had managed to keep the question of Palestine open'.[38])

As for the third question, that of whether Palestine was excluded from the area in which the Arabs were given hopes of independence, the balance of the evidence seems to be that, at the time of the Husayn–McMahon letters, the British probably did intend to exclude Palestine, not for the absurd reason later advanced that it could be regarded as part of the area lying to the west of Damascus, Homs, Hama and Aleppo which could not be regarded as being wholly Arab, but on the ground that it was part of the area within which Britain was not 'free to act without detriment to the interests of her ally France'. That phrase was intended to apply specifically to the region west of the four Syrian cities, but it might have been intended to apply generally to Palestine as well.[39] It was a vague phrase of uncertain extension, and Husayn was willing to leave it as such, because he was aware of the complexity of international interests in Palestine, and because he needed British support against the French in Syria, and was willing as the price of such support to leave aside the question of Palestine, or to recognise Britain's special position there. The question of Zionism had not yet arisen, and his acquiescence in possible British claims did not imply acceptance of Zionist claims. When the Balfour Declaration was made, the Syrian nationalists soon reacted against it, but Professor Kedourie may well be right in saying that the Hashimites did not oppose it strongly until after Britain withdrew its support for Faysal in Syria.[40]

The argument about the interpretation of these agreements is one which is impossible to end, because they were intended to bear more than one interpretation. If later historians have tried to end it by supporting one or other of the possible interpretations, it is partly because those interpretations have a significance beyond themselves, as symbols of certain attitudes or policies, and historians, whether or not they know it, are carrying on the political discussion which began the agreements. This is true of Antonius himself, writing as he did at a time when the question of French policy in Syria and the implications of the Jewish National Home were burning political issues about which he had strong convictions; it is equally true of more recent writers, since the end of 'Britain's moment in the Middle East' is recent enough to generate controversy about the success or failure of British policy, and the question of Palestine is still with us.

About the last part of the book there is less to say. It gives a clear account of events from the peace settlement to the time when it was written, and makes certain suggestions about British policy in Palestine and French in Syria. It is important for another reason than its explicit content, however. A text can be read for what it tells us about the author and his times, and from these pages there emerges an image of the colonial relationship in the penultimate phase of British and French domination of the world. It was a relationship of unequal strength, and in such situations the weaker party, being unable to compel the stronger to change its policy, must try to use arguments, and persuade it of an identity of real interests between the two. In pages such as those of Antonius there is no idea of revolutionary change, of a victorious liberation which creates another kind of human being, but rather of a peaceful resolution of conflict by agreement between men of reason and goodwill, searching for points of common interest and smoothing the transition to independent rule. In such a process of persuasion, the production of documents and the attempt to interpret them precisely has a special place.

The relationship is also one of cultural dependence. The weaker party tries to assure the stronger that its essential interests will be safe even if its power is surrendered, and does so by demonstrating its own mastery of the culture and values of the stronger, and showing therefore that the transition to independence can take place without shock, and will not appear as a radical change. The experience of the last thirty years, indeed, has shown that the first phase of independent rule, in many countries, has been almost like a continuation of the last phase of colonial rule; the real shock of change has come later.

In such situations, there is a need for intermediaries who can explain each party to the others, and find and express their points of common interest. George Antonius was exceptionally good at such work, and his career in fact contained a series of successful mediations. Thus in 1925 he helped Sir Gilbert Clayton on his official mission to negotiate with ʿAbd al-ʿAziz Ibn Saʿud about recognition and frontiers. His role was to talk persuasively to the king's officials and advisers, and he was very successful in this: 'I am quite convinced I could not have succeeded without him', Clayton declared.[41] In 1926 he went with Clayton on a similar mission to Yemen, and in 1928 on a second one to Ibn Saʿud. In 1927, while on vacation in Egypt, he helped the Egyptian Government and the British High Commissioner, Lord Lloyd, to resolve a crisis which had arisen in regard to the Egyptian army, by finding a formula which both could accept. In 1929, during the crisis over the Wailing Wall in Jerusalem, he was the member of the Secretariat who maintained liaison with the Arab political leaders. After 1930, when he left the government's service, he was free to undertake a wider range of activities. In 1932 his correspondence shows him to have been engaged almost at the same time in at least half a dozen negotiations. He was involved in the controversy within the Orthodox Christian community over the Patriarchal election, and discussing it with the different candidates, the Greek consul-general, the Fraternity of the Holy Sepulchre and leaders of the laity. He was talking to leaders of the Islamic conference recently held in Jerusalem about the future of Islam, and to Nallino and other orientalists about a project for a new Arab lexicon. He was discussing with the Prime Minister of Egypt, Sidqi Pasha, the vexed question of tariffs on Palestinian oranges, and with Chauvel, the *chef de cabinet* of the French High Commissioner for Syria and Lebanon, the more difficult question of Syrian nationalism; and all the time he was talking to the British High Commissioner in Palestine about British policy there.[42]

Anyone who reads *The Arab Awakening* now may end it with a certain feeling of sadness. This is partly a reflection of the anxiety which the author himself felt and expressed. Already by 1938 a shadow of what was to come had fallen across his pages: a new age of mass-politics, when issues would be determined otherwise than by delicate negotiations between men who understood and trusted one another. In his final section on the problem of Palestine, he makes clear that what is at issue is not simply the question of who should have sovereignty, but that of physical possession of the land. He records the beginning of mass action: the Palestine revolt continuing as he wrote was not, he insisted, inspired or manipulated by urban politicians but a genuine rural upheaval. Once more, recent research by T. Bowden has confirmed his view.[43]

There is another cause of sadness, however. Contemplation of the life of George Antonius will reveal how difficult is the path of the intermediary; he may so easily fall into the chasm he is trying to bridge. His official career showed that he was too large and complex for the kind of intermediate position which was all that was available to an Arab in the mandatory administration; he was squeezed out of the Education Department in a way which reflected little credit on his colleagues. There was, at that time, no other government or institution to which he could give all his talents and devotion. His personal tragedy was that of someone who could not fit easily into any of the moulds available to him at a time when, with the disintegration of ancient societies and systems of government, and the rise of nationalism, men were being forced to define their identities in new and narrower terms. In the last analysis, he belonged to an earlier world: he was a citizen of Alexandria in the last phase of Franco-Ottoman civilisation, the city where all men could be at home, all could be more than one thing, and all matters could be resolved by delicate compromise. He belonged to a world lost and irrecoverable, but embalmed for ever in the poems of Cavafy—in such a poem as that which portrays a Syrian eager to serve his country:

> I am young and in excellent health.
> I have a wonderful mastery of Greek
>
> (Aristotle, Plato, I know them forwards and backwards:
>   And orators, and poets, and anything you mention).
>   Of military matters I have a notion,
> And I have friendships with leaders of the mercenaries,
> I have plenty of entries to administrative things too . . .

Wherefore I believe that I fill the bill,
Marked out to be of service to this country,
My own dear land of Syria.

Whatever work they put me to I will endeavour
To be of use to the country. That is my purpose.
If on the other hand they hinder me . . .
    it isn't my fault . . .

The almighty gods ought to have seen about
Creating a fourth man and an honest one.
I should have been delighted to work with him.[44]

Notes

[1] Some biographical details in Bernard Wasserstein, *The British in Palestine: the Mandatory Government and the Arab-Jewish Conflict 1917–1929* (London, 1978) p. 182 f.
[2] George Antonius, *The Arab Awakening* (London, 1938) p. 250.
[3] *Ibid.*, pp. 182–183.
[4] *Ibid.*, pp. 321–2.
[5] Richard Aldington, *Lawrence of Arabia, a Biographical Inquiry* (London, 1955); John E. Mack, *A Prince of our Disorder: the Life of T. E. Lawrence* (Boston, 1976).
[6] Elizabeth Monroe, *Britain's Moment in the Middle East 1914–1956* (London, 1963).
[7] Antonius Papers (Middle East Centre, St. Antony's College, Oxford): Antonius to W. S. Rogers, 15 February 1939.
[8] Great Britain, Cmnd. 5974, *Report of a Committee set up to consider certain Correspondence between Sir Henry McMahon . . . and the Sharif of Mecca in 1915 and 1916* (London, 1939) p. 10.
[9] Thomas Naff, 'Reform and the conduct of Ottoman diplomacy in the reign of Selim III, 1789–1807' in *Journal of the American Oriental Society*, 83 (1963) p. 295; Allan Cunningham, 'Stratford Canning and the Tanzimat' in W. R. Polk and R. L. Chambers (eds.), *Beginnings of Modernization in the Middle East: the Nineteenth Century* (Chicago, 1968) p. 245.
[10] Lord Cromer, *Modern Egypt* (London, 1908); Afaf Lutfi al-Sayyid, *Egypt and Cromer* (London, 1968); Alexander Schölch, *Ägypten den Ägyptern! Die politische und gesellschaftliche Krise der Jahre 1878–1882 in Ägypten* (Zurich, 1972); Jacques Berque, *L'Egypte, impérialisme et révolution* (Paris, 1967).
[11] Arnold J. Toynbee, *The Western Question in Greece and Turkey: a Study in the Contact of Civilizations* (London, 1922).
[12] *Ibid.*, pp. 61, 100.
[13] Antonius Papers: Annual Report to the Institute of Current World Affairs, 1933–4 and 1934–5.
[14] Amīn Saʿīd, *al-Thawra al-ʿarabiyya al-kubrā*, 3 vols (Cairo, 1934).
[15] Antonius Papers: Antonius to W. S. Rogers 18 April 1933 and 16 May 1933.
[16] Elie Kedourie, *England and the Middle East: the Destruction of the Ottoman Empire 1914–1921* (Cambridge, 1956) and *In the Anglo-Arab Labyrinth: the McMahon-Husayn Correspondence and its Interpretations 1914–1939* (Cambridge, 1976); Sylvia G. Haim, 'The Arab Awakening—a source for the historian?' in *Welt des Islams*, new series 2 (1953) p. 236; A. L. Tibawi, *A Modern History of Syria* (London, 1969) and *Anglo-Arab Relations and*

the *Question of Palestine 1914–1922* (London, 1977); Z. N. Zeine, *The Emergence of Arab Nationalism* (Beirut, 1966); C. E. Dawn, *From Ottomanism to Arabism: Essays on the Origins of Arab Nationalism* (Urbana, 1973); R. I. Khalidi, *British Policy towards Syria and Palestine 1906–1914* (London, 1980).

[17] Majid Khadduri, ''Aziz 'Ali al-Maṣrī and the Arab nationalist movement' in A. Hourani (ed), *Saint Antony's Papers 17, Middle Eastern Affairs 4* (London, 1965) p. 140.

[18] Antonius, *The Arab Awakening*, p. 60.

[19] *Ibid.*, p. 103.

[20] C. E. Dawn, 'The Rise of Arabism in Syria' in *From Ottomanism to Arabism*, p. 148.

[21] London, 1973.

[22] André Raymond, *Artisans et commerçants au Caire au XVIIIe siècle*, 2 vols (Damascus, 1973–4); S. J. Shaw, *The Financial and Administrative Organization and Development of Ottoman Egypt 1517–1798* (Princeton, N.J., 1962); Abdel-Karim Rafeq, *The Province of Damascus 1723–1783* (Beirut, 1966); Karl Barbir, *Ottoman Rule in Damascus 1708–1758* (Princeton, N.J., 1962).

[23] Barbir, ch. 1.

[24] Antonius, *The Arab Awakening*, p. 13

[25] Robert N. Bellah, 'Civil religion in America' in *Beyond Belief: Essays on Religion in a Post-Traditional World* (New York, 1970).

[26] Clifford Geertz, 'Ideology as a cultural system' in *The Interpretation of Cultures* (London, 1975) p. 218.

[27] C. E. Dawn, 'The Amir of Mecca al-Ḥusayn ibn-'Ali and the origin of the Arab Revolt' in *From Ottomanism to Arabism*, p. 1.

[28] Antonius, *The Arab Awakening*, pp. 355–6.

[29] *Ibid.*, pp. 260–2.

[30] Mayir Verité, 'The Balfour Declaration and its makers' in *Middle Eastern Studies*, 6 (1970) p. 48.

[31] Sulaymān Mūsā, *al-Ḥaraka al-'arabiyya* (Beirut, 1970); Isaiah Friedman, *The Question of Palestine 1914–1918: British–Jewish–Arab Relations* (London, 1973); Jukka Nevakivi, *Britain, France and the Arab Middle East 1914–1920* (London, 1969); Roger Adelson, *Mark Sykes: Portrait of an Amateur* (London, 1975); for Tibawi and Kedourie, see note 16.

[32] Kedourie, *In the Anglo-Arab Labyrinth, passim*.

[33] Friedman, *The Question of Palestine, passim*.

[34] References to Nicolson, Toynbee and Grey in Kedourie, *In the Anglo-Arab Labyrinth*, pp. 207 f, 209 f, and 230 f; references to Balfour and Lloyd George in review of Friedman's book in *Times Literary Supplement*, 2 November 1973.

[35] Kedourie, *In the Anglo-Arab Labyrinth*, p. 163 f.

[36] *Ibid.*, p. 197.

[37] Antonius, *The Arab Awakening*, pp. 274–5, 435–6.

[38] 'Memorandum of a conference held on the 7 February 1917', p. 11, in Samuel Papers (Middle East Centre, St Antony's College, Oxford).

[39] Kedourie, *In the Anglo-Arab Labyrinth*, p. 84.

[40] *Ibid.*, p. 233 f.

[41] Gilbert Falkingham Clayton, *An Arabian Diary* (Berkeley, 1969) p. 120.

[42] Antonius Papers: Antonius to W. S. Rogers, 12 February 1932, 9 April 1932, 23 April 1932, 13 May 1932, Annual Report to the Institute of Current World Affairs 1931–32.

[43] Tom Bowden, 'The Politics of the Arab rebellion in Palestine 1936–39' in *Middle Eastern Studies*, 11 (1975) p. 147.

[44] 'They ought to have thought' in *The Poems of C. P. Cavafy*, English trans. John Mavrogordato (London, 1952), p. 190.

The Ottoman Conquest and the Development of the Great Arab Towns

THE period of the Ottoman domination over the Arab provinces is still looked upon as characterized by a decline uninterrupted up to the nineteenth century. Therefore, historians feel entitled to condemn it wholly, or to ignore it. Such an attitude is in itself worth study: if one were to try to explain it briefly, one would have to take into account the perhaps natural tendency to paint the entire Ottoman period with the dark colours of the recent decline and collapse and the violence of the closing period of the Empire, that is to say, the end of the nineteenth century and the beginning of the twentieth century. One would also need to allow for the fact that Arab historians feel reluctant to study a phase of their past which they tend, by analogy with a more recent period of their history, to consider as colonial. The general obscurity which still overshadows the Ottoman era must account for the rest of its lack of credit in the eyes of modern historians. It is, however, a somewhat incomprehensible obscurity, as sources exist for that period, more numerous, more abundant, and more varied than for any other period of Moslem history, especially in the field of archival documentation. This biased view of the Ottoman era has facilitated the falsifying of the modern history of Arab countries for the purpose of justifying European colonization. This is particularly the case for the Maghreb countries, where the intrusion of the colonists was represented as the unavoidable (and happy) conclusion to an era of poverty and barbarity.

This prejudice against the Ottomans becomes particularly conspicuous in the histories of the towns. Urban history has been, for a long time, the province of art historians, who describe the towns through their monuments and who, consciously or not, tend to equate artistic splendour with urban prosperity and growth, and vice versa. The tendency to write the history of the towns as a chapter of a general history of the fine arts proved particularly damaging to the reputation of the Ottoman era, whose architectural achievements in the Arab provinces did not match the size and originality of those of the preceding period. These art historians are guilty of an exaggerated worship of antiquity, finding it difficult to conceive of the existence of an urban organization which would not follow the ancient patterns (or, at the other extreme, those of Western modern urbanism).

Any study of Arab towns from the sixteenth century to the eighteenth century ought to consider towns as coherent ensembles, organized according to their particular rules, in which monuments are urban tokens of that organization, 'des signes urbains,' and are to be studied as such. When researchers have gathered enough objective facts concerning, on one hand, global economic movements and the evolution of demography and, on the other, the concrete history of the towns, then the history of the Arab towns in the Ottoman period can progress. For the time being we can only present tentative conclusions and venture to generalize, sometimes broadly, from the facts we have.

The economic development in the Arab provinces in the sixteenth and seventeenth centuries.

The Arab countries are generally described as having undergone a severe decline from the beginning of the Ottoman occupation; being deprived of their political role by the Turkish conquest and affected by intellectual and cultural sclerosis, they are also supposed to have suffered economic decline mainly due to the European advance which took place at the beginning of the sixteenth century—an advance which was marked by the appearance of Western sailors in the Eastern seas and by the conclusion of the Capitulations. None of those assumptions can be accepted without discussion.

Let us, first of all, emphasize a fact which is well known, but not sufficiently taken into account: the decline of the Arab countries began well before the arrival of the Ottomans. In the fifteenth century, the Maghreb was already going through a dark period. The territories which today constitute Algeria were breaking up into various political divisions, with anarchy threatening in the background, while Hafsid Ifriqiyya (which is modern Tunisia) was surviving with great difficulties. In the East the decline of the Mameluk state, which included Hejaz, Palestine, and Syria under Egyptian rule, had begun long ago. In about 1420 the Egyptian historian Maqrīzī was sadly reckoning the losses which Cairo had suffered since the middle of the fourteenth century. Ransacked by Tamerlane in 1400, Damascus 'had never quite recovered and the town was half in ruin when Sultan Selīm took possession of it in 1516'.[1] Iraq was still suffering the effects of the blow received during the Mongol invasion of 1258 when its capital was plundered by Tamerlane. It was described as follows by Maqrīzī in 1437: 'Baghdad is but a heap of ruins; there is neither mosque, nor congregation, nor market place. Most of its waterways are dry, and we can hardly call it a town.'[2] So, it was an impoverished Arab world with fallen capitals that the Ottomans conquered between 1516 (occupation of Syria) and 1574 (definitive conquest of Tunisia).

It is true that the Ottomans turned the Arab States into mere provinces of an empire whose centre was Istanbul and whose predominant component was the Turkish element. Admittedly this could have been an additional cause of decline. But the Ottoman Empire, stretching from the frontiers of

Morocco to those of Persia, and from the steppes of Southern Russia and the Austrian border to Yemen, was a unified whole; indeed, it was the most extensive political entity to arise in the West since the Roman Empire, embracing (in 1606) about 2.5 million square kilometres, including the vassal states. In spite of the difficulties it met with in the seventeenth century, the Empire as constituted by Selīm I (1512–1520) and Sulaimān I (1520–1566) remained on the whole unimpaired to the end of the seventeenth century and even made territorial gains in the north and east. It was only after the aborted attempt on Vienna in 1683 that the tide of Empire started to ebb.

During all of the period from 1516 to 1683 and even long after, 'every subject of the Emperor could henceforth go from the Danube to the Indian Ocean and from Persia to the Maghreb without ceasing to be submitted to the same laws and to the same administrative organization, to speak the same language, to use the same currency, a fact favourable to a large inner stream of exchanges'.[3] This easy circulation of men and goods was hindered only by natural obstacles (mountains and deserts), or by insecurity due to political difficulties (such as local upheavals or the actions of wandering tribes). It was a considerable advantage which must be seen to have made up for the diminution in political stature suffered by some large cities such as Cairo.

When the Empire was constituted, a huge market was opened to towns favourably situated along the main routes of international trade. This was particularly the case for the great cities of Egypt and Syria. Located at the hinge of Europe, Asia, and Africa, these cities traditionally played the part of redistribution centres for the products of both western countries (manufactured goods and, especially, materials) and eastern countries (spices, woven fabrics). Cairo was the standard transshipment centre for the ocean trade from the Red Sea and the Indian Ocean, while Aleppo controlled an important segment of the land routes. Even an event as important for the future as the arrival of the Europeans in the Indian Ocean at the end of the fifteenth century did not for a long time threaten the commercial power of Cairo. If the distant trade (to and from South East Asia and the Far East) began to be directed towards the great European places of market, the commerical relations with nearer areas (the Red Sea, the Persian Gulf, Persia and India) remained mainly under the trading control of Cairo and Aleppo. On the whole, the great Arab cities of the Middle East benefitted from the favourable circumstances created by the Ottoman conquest and did not suffer unduly from European trading encroachment. It is no wonder, therefore, that signs of an increase in commercial activities can be noticed at that time.

The discovery of the Indian route did not divert at once the stream of Eastern goods which had enriched the *Kārimī* merchants. In the accounting of the big merchants of Cairo, shipments of spices, particularly pepper (*filfil*), continued to be reckoned up in great number; more than thirty sorts of products were still coming from the East in the seventeenth century. It was only in the eighteenth century that the Cairo merchants saw any noticeable diminution in the number of products imported from the East and spices began to appear in increasingly large quantities in the sales made by the Europeans in the Levant 'Echelles'. But, by this time, a new product, coffee (*bunn qahwa*), had appeared to replace profitably the Eastern spices in the great international trade of Cairo.

Appearing in Egypt at the beginning of the sixteenth century, sometimes accepted (with reluctance) by the pious men and sometimes forbidden (in 1534, for example), coffee soon became the object of an active trade, first within the Empire (as early as 1554 a coffee house opened in Istanbul) and then with the European countries (which discovered it in the middle of the seventeenth century). During this period the volume of the trade in coffee became greater than the volume of the spice trade which had preceded it. Of the 200,000 quintals of coffee, exported by Yemen, about half (100,000 ql.) transitted through Cairo; out of this amount, 50,000 quintals were redistributed inside the Empire (Istanbul's share alone being estimated at 15,00 ql.) while much of the rest went to the various countries of Europe. At the beginning of the eighteenth century, a little more than 20,000 quintals of coffee accounted for half of the value of French purchases in Egypt. Towards the end of the eighteenth century imports of coffee were evaluated at 300 millions of paras, that is to say, more than a third of Egypt's total import, and the trade of this single product accounted for the business activities of about 60 out of the 360 *wakāla* in Cairo.[4] Those figures show clearly the leading part played by the great Eastern trade in the economic activity of Cairo and of Egypt, and suggest as well the extent of the wealth and power of the major coffee merchants (the *tujjār*).

Cairo therefore remained one of the main centres of the great international trade up to the beginning of the eighteenth century. It kept on redistributing Eastern products—some to Europe of course, but most to the interior of the Ottoman Empire. It was only in the eighteenth century that the direction of trading exchanges began to reverse. Soon after 1700, pepper appeared in the lists of goods entering Egypt from Marseilles. In 1737, coffee from the West Indies began to arrive from Europe. Finally then, the traditional Egyptian markets for products within the Empire became endangered. But this was an event following long after the Ottoman conquest brought Egypt into the Empire as one of its provinces, and Cairo had benefitted greatly up until that time.

As for Aleppo and the northern part of Syria, these drew even larger economic benefits from the Ottoman conquest as the territories submitting to the rule of the Sultans of Constantinople were extended to the Caucasus and the frontiers of Iran. A frontier town during the Mameluk period, Aleppo became, in the sixteenth century, the centre of a vast area and the place where the great international trade routes met. It had become an unavoidable transit city fo rluxury goods from the Persian Gulf, Persia and India—goods which were in great demand at the imperial court of Istanbul. The early establishment of European trading posts ('comptoirs') is a pertinent indication of the international role played by Aleppo. In 1548 the Venetian consulate was transferred there, to be followed shortly by the French 'Nation' (settled in Aleppo in 1562) and the English (in 1583). Sauvaget quotes (quite rightly), as a proof of the fame of Aleppo at this time, the line from *Macbeth*: 'Her husband's to Aleppo gone, master o' the Tiger.'[5]

Until the middle of the eighteenth century, Aleppo remained the main market of the whole East, astride two commercial streams: the stream of manufactured goods going from the West to the East and the stream of Eastern products and raw materials moving from the hinterland to Europe. All of the commerical goods flowing in these streams were received and distributed from Aleppo. Even at the end of the nineteenth century, in spite of the rise of Smyrna and in spite of the blows against its Eastern trade as a result of the wars against Persia and the competition of European merchants, Aleppo remained a very active trade centre. The bulk of its trade with Marseilles was more important than the trade between Marseilles and Egypt: in 1786–1789 the sales and purchases between Marseilles and Egypt were worth 4.2. million French pounds, while for the same period the trade between Marseilles and Aleppo and Alexandretta was worth 5.6 million pounds.[6]

The establishment of an immense Empire throughout which people could travel quite easily resulted in the development of the pilgrimage (*hajj*), with beneficial effect for Egypt and Syria, the two countries where the caravans gathered before departing for Hejaz. The Ottoman sultans, who were the supreme authorities of Sunni Islam, made it a point of honour to facilitate the pilgrimage. They organized the caravans that came from all part of Africa towards Cairo and from the Balkans and Asia towards Damascus; they provided the route of the *hajj* with caravansaries, bridges, places where water could be found, and small forts. In this way, 30,000 to 40,000 pilgrims used to gather every year in Cairo, and 20,000 to 60,000 in Damascus. The gigantic pilgrimage caravans were the vehicles of a trade whose bulk it is difficult to estimate with accuracy: products from the remotest corners of the Empire and neighbouring Islamic lands—from the Maghreb, Black Africa, the Balkans, Anatolia, and the Near East—all were brought by these caravans to Egypt and Syria to be sold there or to continue on the route towards the Holy Places; on the way back, the caravans carried products from the East (fabrics, spices) to be distributed all over the Empire.

Moreover, the thousands of pilgrims who passed through Aleppo, Damascus or Cairo had to buy the necessary equipment for a journey which was to last three months. In the *sūq* of these cities, they purchased mounts, tents, food, and, during their rather long stays in the pilgrimage towns, they enhanced greatly the commercial activity which contributed to prosperity. Such was especially the case in Mecca: 'During the pilgrimage the town is perhaps the richest fair in the world since, in this short lapse of time, several million (pounds' worth) of goods coming from India are sold, in addition to coffee, myrrh, incense and other products of the country' consul De Maillet wrote, towards 1700.[7]

The pilgrimage was thus a powerful stimulus for the intra-Empire trade, whose importance we have already stressed; it also gave incentive to craftsmen in the remotest provinces of the Empire and, even more, to those in Damascus and Cairo where the pilgrims gathered.

Statistical data concerning this period are late and unreliable. They do not allow us to appreciate the economic rise which resulted from the foundation of the Ottoman Empire. But the evidence of the impressive commercial facilities with which the great Arab cities were equipped may be relied on as surely as figures. As for Cairo, a bare comparison between the number of trading centres (caravansaries and markets) counted by Maqrīzī at the beginning of the fifteenth century and the number we find mentioned in Arab sources (and in the *Description de l'Egypte*) seems quite significant: the number of markets (*sūq*) increased from 87 at the time of Maqrīzī to 145 in the Ottoman period.[8] What is more significant, the number of caravansaries (*khān, qaisāriyya, wakāla, funduq*), where the wholesale trade and the international trade was concentrated, increased sixfold. Maqrīzī lists 57 caravansaries; the *Description* mentions 220 of them, and we have numbered a total of 360 for the Ottoman period. On a map of Cairo the area of great activity at the beginning of the fifteenth century is seen to be limited to the *Qasaba* (the central thoroughfare of Cairo) and to the nearby districts (about 32 hectares). During the Ottoman period, the commercial area spread to cover about 58 hectares, even growing beyond the limits of the Fatimid town into new areas where varied trading activities were conducted (around bāb al-Shariyya, the Citadel, Ibn Tūlūn, bāb al-Lūq). The amount of Egypt's foreign trading activity inferable from the archives makes a truly impressive total: at the end of the eighteenth century, in spite of an incipient economic slump, the value of Cairo's foreign trade was still shown to be 94.6 million pounds, that is to say, about 24 pounds per inhabitant.[9] That figure is, in fact, probably on the low side. In France at the same time, the figure was shown to be an average of 44 pounds per inhabitant (1,153 million pounds for 26 million inhabitants). If we take into account the relatively high level of economic development of France as compared with Egypt at that time, we must conclude that Egyptian foreign trade was remarkably active. Also significant is the evidence of the economic activity of Būlāq, the outer port of Cairo, where the French in 1798 numbered as many as 53 *wakāla*, and of the extraordinary rise of Rashīd (Rosetta), whose wealth in the Ottoman period was made conspicuous through architectural adornments, which have remained partly undamaged through the passing centuries.

In Aleppo, it was during the sixteenth century that the building of the great trading premises took place in the economic centre of the town, which the inhabitants called 'the City' (*madīnah*). The 'City' was extended towards the south during the course of about 40 years by successive stages that the history of the great *waqf* allow us to trace: *waqf* of Khusrū pasha (about 1544), *waqf* of Muhammad pasha Dūqakīn Zāda (about 1555), of another Muhammad pasha (1574), of Bahrām pasha (1583). In this very period we can deduce, by comparing Sauvaget's maps, that the 'City' reached almost its final stage of development, expanding in area from 4 hectares at the beginning of the sixteenth century to more than 9 hectares at the beginning of the nineteenth century—an increase of about 140 per cent. Impressive vestiges still remain of the great trading centres built during the period of expansion: Khān of Qurt Bey (1540), Khān al-Gumruk (1574), Khān al-Wazīr (1682). In about 1680, the Chevalier d'Arvieux numbered 68 *khān* and 187 *qaisāriyya* in Aleppo, and he wrote: 'Aleppo is undoubtedly the largest, the richest and the most beautiful town of the whole Ottoman Empire after Constantinople and Cairo. The splendour of Aleppo is not confined to mosques only, but it is just as striking in the khans and Bazars, where goods from all the parts of the world can be found.'[10] Aleppo's power lay not only in commerce. Commercial statistics from Marseilles reveal impressive activity of local 'industries': in 1750–54, out of a total of 2,074,000 pounds' worth of trade, the purchases of Marseilles included 1,326,000 pounds' worth of goods from local linen manufactories, that is to say, more than 60 per cent. At that time Marseilles bought from Aleppo linen fabrics worth more than its sales to that city (1,326,000 pounds as against 1,130,000).[11]

Thus the Ottoman conquest gave rise to a brisk commercial activity which, we have just seen, resulted in a spectacular growth of the economic substructures of some of the biggest Arab towns of the Empire. However, one must remember that this growth was attributable primarily to growth in intra-Empire trade, which the very size of the Empire had made so profitable. In Egypt, at about the end of the eighteenth century, the wholesale trade with the East represented 36 per cent of the exchanges, the Mediterranean trade with the various provinces of the Empire 50 per cent, and the trade with Europe only 15 per cent of the total. The real 'foreign' trade was therefore marginal even at the end of the eighteenth century, when the penetration of the West was becoming more noticeable. It was the establishment of an immense and relatively unified empire that provided the elements and catalyst for the commercial boom (which can be traced to as early as the sixteenth century)—not the development of commercial links with the West. The breaking of this internal cohesion, an effect of Western economic penetration beginning as early as 1750 but increasing drastically in the nineteenth century, was one of the main causes of the decay of the Ottoman world in the nineteenth century. It also paved the way for colonial penetration.

The development of the great Arab towns

The development of the great Arab towns in the sixteenth and seventeenth centuries was the result of two main factors. First there was the economic growth resulting from the creation of a huge intra-Empire market, the reality of which we have tried to demonstrate. Towns like Aleppo, Damascus, and Cairo which were most favourably situated on the borders of three continents could play fully the role of redistribution centres for the Empire and around the Mediterranena world.

The second factor was the presence in the capitals of the provinces of a large class of persons with a high level of consumption of luxury goods (the 'ruling institution' of Gibb and Bowen). This was the caste established to ensure the protection and proper administration of the provinces: these army officers, 'civil servants,' took the places of the sultanian and provincial courts of the Mameluk period, and they contributed greatly to the economic prosperity of the towns (even if their exploitation of the countryside and of the working people also had pernicious effects). In Algiers, for example, the Turkish Janissaries, mainly recruited in Anatolia, numbered about 20,000 in the sixteenth century and still numbered 10,000 in the eighteenth century, while the total population amounted to less than 50,000 inhabitants. The influx of this large number of representatives of the conqueror was doubtless one of the causes of the extraordinary growth of Algiers during the Ottoman period. Less numerous, but richer, were the privateers (*ra'īs*), whose standard of living depended on the profitable expeditions launched against the merchant navy of the maritime powers: in the seventeenth century the ten or so bagnios set up in Algiers were reported to be peopled by 30,000 prisoners who furnished cheap labour or were sold at high profit. In Cairo in the sixteenth and seventeenth centuries, the militias (the most important of which were those of the Janissaries and 'Azab) must have numbered about 15,000 men, not including the households of the Mameluk emirs. Towards the end of the eighteenth century, the ruling caste numbered about 10,000 men, not reckoning the families and servants, and was still therefore an important part of the Cairo population. As for Aleppo, the English consul Devezin thought that the number of Janissaries amounted to 12,000.

The Development of the Great Arab Towns

This ruling population drew its income from the exploitation of country people (through the *iltizām* in Egypt) and of urban population through the urban farms (*muqāta'a*) as well as from the protection of artisans and merchants. The most powerful emirs were also extremely rich. We shall mention only in Egypt Ibrāhīm Çūrbajī al-Sābūnjī, the emir of the 'Azab, and 'Uthmān Katkhudā al-Qāzdughlī, chief of the Janissaries. When Ibrāhīm Çūrbajī al-Sābūnjī died in 1719, he was worth 6.5 million paras. In 1736, 'Uthmān Katkhudā al-Qāzdughlī left a total of 21.5 million paras, not including the landed estate. Their fortunes were larger than those of the wealthiest coffee merchants of the time. The enormous levies made on 'industrial' and agricultural production, and on trading benefits, were for the most part kept in the capitals of the provinces where the emirs and army officers lived with their retinues. The portion of these levies sent to Constantinople as tribute varied according to the degree of subordination of the provinces to the Sublime Porte. In Egypt the *khazīna* never went beyond 30 million paras—not a very large sum in comparison with the total fiscal and parafiscal levies. The bulk of the levies was spent on the spot for commodities and luxury goods, contributing to the vigorous economic activity to which the number of trade guilds bears witness: the 250 trade guilds of Cairo are obviously indicative of that city's economic vitality in the Ottoman period.

The case of Algiers must be set aside in this study of the urban growth of the great Arab cities in the Ottoman period. The extraordinary rise of that town, a modest republic of 20,000 inhabitants towards the end of the fifteenth century, was mainly due to political factors. By making Algiers the capital of a state unified for the first time; by endowing it with a port from which, for three centuries, privateers left to scour the Western Mediterranean; by setting up an effective war machine in Algiers (the *odjaq* of the Janissaries, which was to rule over the Maghreb for two centuries), the Ottomans actually created a new town. With its *shaikh al-balad*, who controlled the trade guilds and the national communities, its *qā'id al-zabal*, presiding over the scavenging, and its *qā'id al-'uyūn*, in charge of the water mains, aqueducts and fountains, Algiers had an urban organization which was relatively advanced and sophisticated, a fact which should lead us not to accept without further examination what is generally written about Ottoman urban administration. The organization in Algiers was of an entirely new pattern (though it may be a Maghrebi phenomenon to be linked with what we know of Fez and Tunis). But the growth of Algiers is so special as to deserve a more complete study; therefore, we shall just consider here the cases of three ancient capitals: Cairo, Damascus and Aleppo.

In the last century of the Mameluk period, Cairo expanded only slightly beyond the limits of the Fatimid town of Qāhira. The location of the *hāra* (districts) mentioned by Maqrīzī (26 in Qāhira, 6 in the southern region, 1 in the western part) corresponds exactly to that of the public baths (*hammām*) in use in 1420: 25 in Qāhira, 4 in the southern districts, none in the western part.[12] The same can be said of the location of the mosques. The comparison of these figures leads us to suggest, on the one hand, that the population of Cairo was at the time concentrated in Qāhira, the southern district being only partly urbanized and the western part urbanized practically not at all, and, on the other hand, that the population of Cairo was less than 200,000 at the beginning of the Ottoman period. Entirely different is the situation of the town we may describe from the detailed *Description de l'Egypte*. In 1798, the whole area covered by the map of Cairo given in the *Description* was rather evenly populated. We infer this fact from the location of two sorts of public structures, the building of which evidently depended on the density of population in an area. Public baths (*hammām*) and public fountains (*sabīl*) were evenly distributed within the different districts of Cairo: one third in Qāhira; two fifths in the northern districts; between one fifth and a quarter in the western districts.[13] Those figures probably are a good indicator of the distribution of the population between the different districts of Cairo in 1798. The overall area of the town was then 730 hectares, 660 of which were actually built up—certainly much more than in 1517 and probably more than in the fourteenth century (450 hectares?). We can figure out the actual increase of the population by comparing the number of public baths at different periods (51 in the fourteenth century, 29 only in the beginning of the fifteenth century, 72 in 1798) if we have correctly postulated the correlation between the number of *hammām* and the number of the population, i.e., one *hammām* for about three to five thousand people. In the *Description*, this population was reckoned to have been 263,000 in 1798, that is to say, an average of 400 inhabitants per hectare; but we suppose that it exceeded 300,000 inhabitants towards the end of the seventeenth century, before the crisis undergone by Egypt, particularly in the last decades of the eighteenth century. As we estimated the population of Cairo as well under 200,000 in 1517, our conclusion is that the Ottoman period was a period of important urban development (see map 1).

The urban growth of Cairo under the Ottoman government was particularly swift at the beginning of the period, in the sixteenth and seventeenth centuries. This is evidenced by several urban factors. One of the more typical is the moving of the tanneries (*madābigh*) which, until the sixteenth century, covered an area of more than four hectares some 300 metres to the southwest of bāb Zuwaila. The Egyptian historian of the nineteenth century, ʿAlī Pasha Mubārak, who mentions the transfer of the tanneries, links it explicitly with the growth of the population in this part of Cairo, right to the south of the Fatimid wall. The more densely settled populace found the tanneries, particularly their smells, unbearable. So the tan-yards of Cairo were transferred to a more remote location, near the gate

The Development of the Great Arab Towns

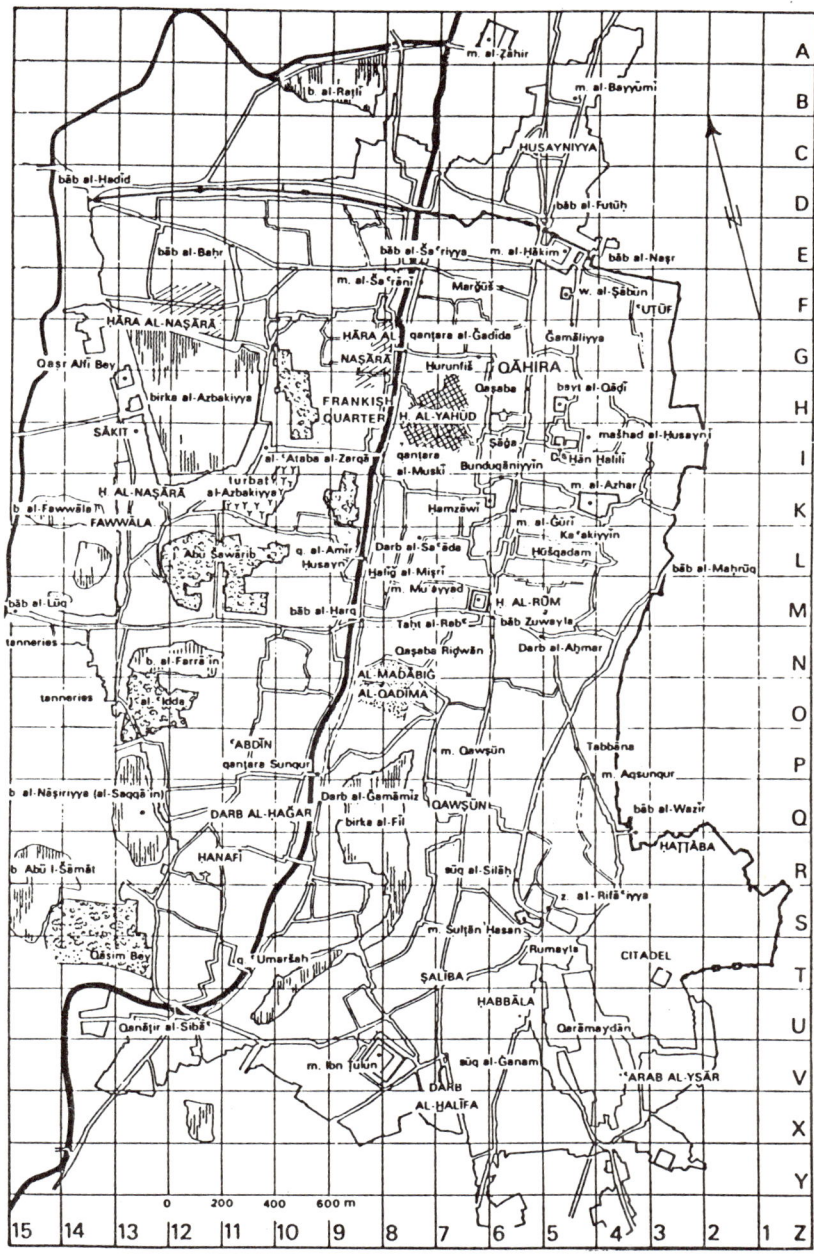

1. Plan of Cairo
(from *Description de l'Egypte*)

of bāb al-Lūq. ʿAlī Pasha gives only an indication for the date of this operation—the eleventh century *hijra*, which means some time between 1591 and 1689; but various archive documents allow us to ascertain that it took place after 1580 and before 1630, most probably about 1600. The transfer permitted the building of some of the great mosques of Ottoman Cairo, that of Malika Safiya (1610), for example, and that of Burdainī (1616), in the area stretching between bāb Zuwaila and birkat al-Fīl. This change of location also permitted the development of the districts situated in the south of Qāhira, where the overflow of the population could settle (Ridwān Bey's buildings in the south of bāb Zuwaila are dated 1630 to 1650).[14] The progressive growth of Cairo is also testified to by the successive shifts of the rich residential districts. The overcrowding of the economic centre of the town inside Qāhira and in the area nearing the Citadel, as well as the development of commercial activities which resulted in the multiplication of caravansaries (*khān* and *wakāla*), led the emirs to settle first in the southern section of the town, round birkat al-Fīl and the Khalīj away from the bustle of the markets. Later on, the same motives may have accounted for a new shift of the 'fashionable' districts towards the western part of the town, beyond the canal which had, for a long time, marked the limit of Cairo: there 'industrial' and commercial activities were comparatively few and there were numerous unoccupied areas such as gardens and ponds so that there was room for the erection of large palaces. Whereas at the beginning of the sixteenth century, more than half of the emirs' houses were built in Qāhira and near the Citadel, in the period 1650–1700, they clustered around birkat al-Fīl (40 per cent) and the Khalīj. Finally, in the second half of the eighteenth century, 45 per cent of those dwelling places were built in the western part of the town, around the pond of the Ezbekiyya.[15]

This progressive build-up, first of the southern districts, then of the western districts of the town, resulting from the increase in population, accounts clearly for the construction of public fountains (*sabīl*), with of course some time-lag, the building of new *sabīl* being normally subsequent to the growth of the population in a given area. If we consider the *sabīl* whose construction we can date accurately, we notice that in the sixteenth century 5 were built in Qāhira, and 4 in the southern area; none, as far as we know, was built in the western part of the town. In the seventeenth century, 17 *sabīl* were built inside Qāhira, 24 in the southern area (then in full expansion), and only 2 in the West area. The number of public fountains built during the eighteenth century was 24 in Qāhira, 27 in the southern area, and 11 in the western area which was then becoming newly urbanized.[16] The conclusion which may be drawn from these figures seems obvious. The increase of the Cairo population resulted in a strong outpouring of residents from Qāhira as the saturation point in that district was reach, i.e., as the area became more and more dedicated to trading activities and the density of population became greater. (There were in 1798 well over 600 inhabitants per hectare.) The excess population first poured into the southern districts; then the town began to expand towards the west, into areas which had undergone little urbanization up to that time. That expansion, which began as early as the sixteenth century, culminated in about 1700.

While Cairo was outgrowing the limits of Qāhira, the two great Syrian cities were expanding beyond their walls, as a result of their high population growth. The development of the Empire, and the setting up of new political and military frontiers far enough from the heart of Syria to protect it from foreign invasion, made the ancient fortifications useless for the security of the town. In both Aleppo and Damascus the moats round the walls were filled up and occupied by dwelling houses, and the population settled in the large, unprotected suburbs which were the most conspicuous features of the two towns during the Ottoman period.

Damascus was in a less favourable position than Aleppo or Cairo. Situated at a distance from the great land and sea trade routes, the city had no easy access to the Mediterranean and had no extensive 'hinterland'; but it nevertheless turned to its advantage the Ottoman occupation, which led, as we have already seen, to a considerable development of the pilgrimage, with Damascus as one of its rallying centres. This is the main cause of the important expansion of the town during the Ottoman period. From Sauvaget's maps (see map 2) we see that the built-up area grew from 212 hectares at the beginning of the sixteenth century, to 313 hectares in the middle of the nineteenth century; that is, an increase of about 50 per cent.[17] The urban development in Damascus took the shape of an impressive development of the commercial centre, spreading from the Mosque of the Omayyads to the 'rue Droite'. Many caravansaries were built there in the period from the beginning of the sixteenth century to the middle of the eighteenth century. But the town centre was already too thickly populated to be able to absorb such urban growth. Thus the city expanded outside its walls, towards the west, with the growth of the Sūq Sārūjā and of the districts of Qanawāt and Suwaiqa, whose areas doubled during the period. The expansion to the west of the town was marked, as early as the sixteenth century, by the building of monuments which were among the most stately constructions of the Ottoman period: the mosque of Sinān Pasha (1586), the mosque and sepulchral monument of Darwīsh Pasha (1571 and 1579) and, even further west, the *takiyya* and *madrasa*-mosque of Sultan Sulaimān (1554–1566). However, it was especially towards the south, along the pilgrimage road, that the expansion moved: the built-up area of the two Mīdān increased from 8 hectares in about 1516 to 64 hectares in about 1850; this was located between the Murād Pasha mosque (built in 1572) and the Qadam mosque (also sixteenth century). Right outside the southern wall of the city was a cluster of *sūq* where the people who travelled with the

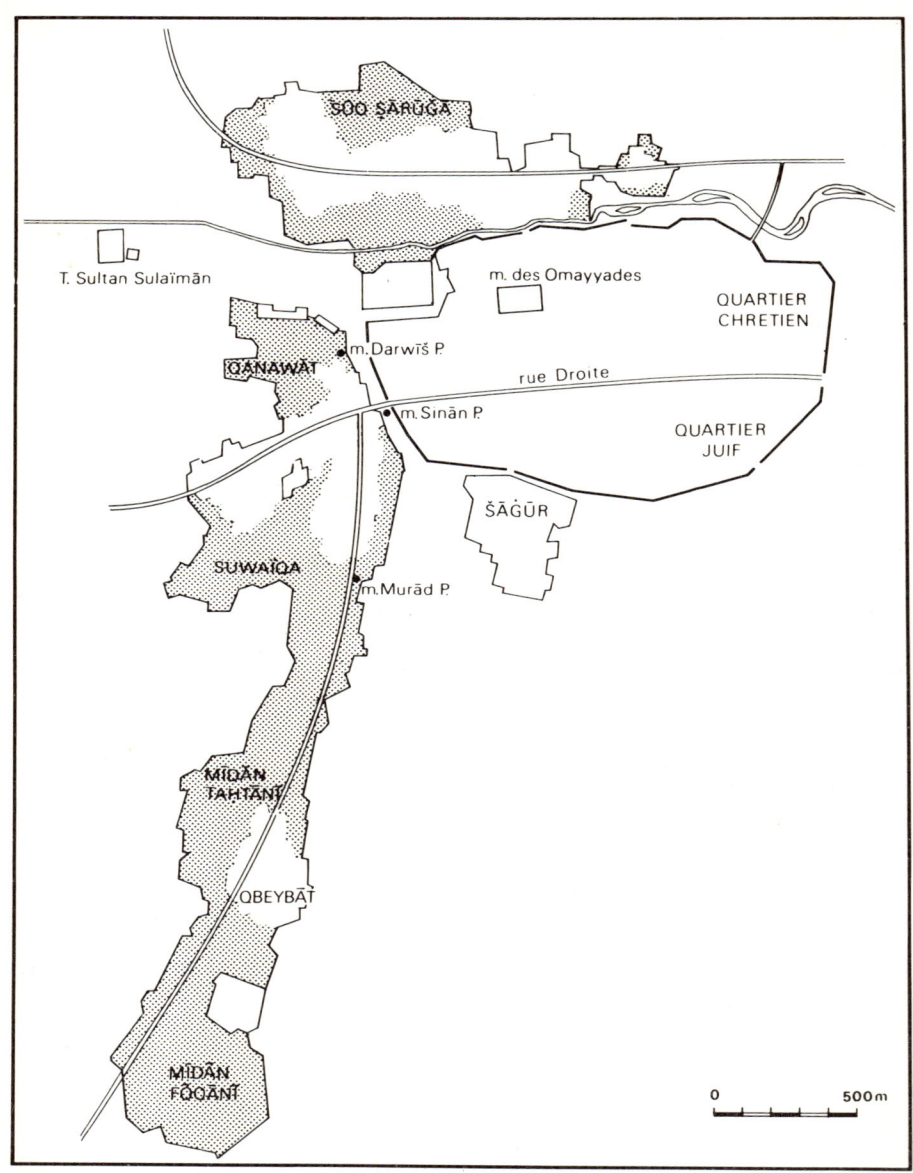

2. Growth of Damascus during the Ottoman period
(beginning of the XVIth century–beginning of the XIXth century):
from J. Sauvaget's maps (*Esquisse*, VIII and X).
The dotted areas indicate the zones of urban growth.

caravans, the country people who brought their corn to town and the nomads who hired their camels, bought all they needed: clothes, travelling and camping equipment. Further along the way leading to the Hejaz and the rich wheat-growing lands of the Hawrān, the wheat warehouses constituted a suburb stretching over three kilometres which had engulfed the village of Qubaibāt ('the small domes') as well as the ancient hippodrome (*mīdān*) after which the suburb was called.

As for Aleppo, again the comparison of the maps (see map 3) drawn by Sauvaget for the beginning of the sixteenth century and for the nineteenth century enables us to see the magnitude of the town's development as well as the direction of the thrust during the Ottoman period. If we follow Sauvaget, Aleppo, at the time of the occupation of Syria, must have covered an area of 238.5 hectares: at the beginning of the nineteenth century, when the map of Rousseau, which Sauvaget used as a model, was drawn, the area covered 349 hectares; it had, therefore, increased by about 50 per cent. Comparing Sauvaget's maps with Russell's (for the middle of the eighteenth century) and comparing the lists of the districts (*mahalla*) given by Ghazzī (for the nineteenth century) with those of Russell (for the eighteenth century), d'Arvieux (1683) and the archives from the sixteenth century, we deduce that the expansion was, for the most part, achieved as early as the end of the sixteenth century.[18] The seventeenth century was for Aleppo and its province, as well as for the whole of the Empire, a period of disorder and decline. The eighteenth century witnessed a revival of urban growth. This general pattern is evidenced by the progression of the building of monuments during the Ottoman period: there was clearly a slackening in the seventeenth century, between two periods of urban growth.

The sixteenth century was a period of strong urban development in Aleppo, with the vigorous expansion of the 'City' towards the south, beyond the west–east line connecting Antioch gate *bāb Antākya*) to the Citadel (*Qalʿa*). Along this street were disposed the main *sūq* of the town; and this line was also the limit of the 'City' during the Mameluk period. The free areas stretching to the south were gradually occupied in about forty years' time through a series of urban construction projects. We know some of these through the *waqf*.[19] The building of one of the first Ottoman monuments in Aleppo, the great mosque built by Khusrū Pasha in the southwest of the Citadel, was closely related to that kind of project. Governor of Aleppo between 1531 and 1534, and later governor of Cairo, this high official ordered the mosque which bears his name to be built in Aleppo. (The construction ended in 1544.) He endowed this monument with important *waqf* including, for example, the great *khān* of Qurt Bey and, above all, the buildings erected in the 'empty space' (*fadā*) surrounding the four sides of the mosque. The information given by the *waqfiyya* enables us to delimit a large region, encompassing an area of 4 to 5 hectares in the southwest of the

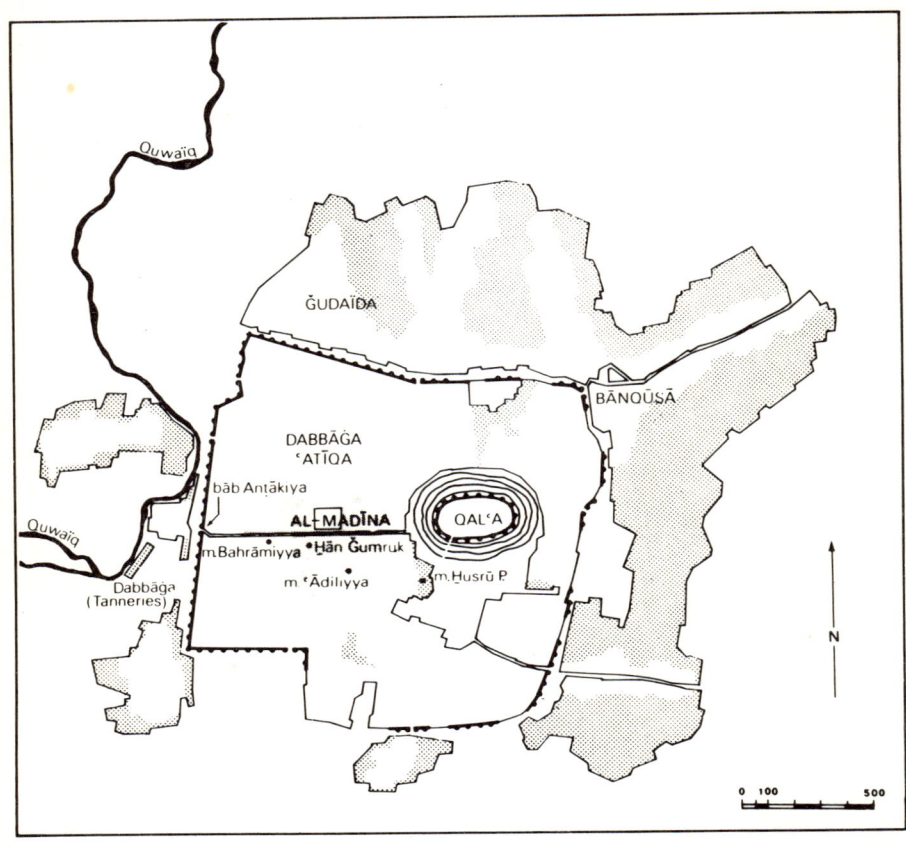

3. Growth of Aleppo during the Ottoman period
(beginning of the XVIth century–beginning of the XIXth century):
from J. Sauvaget's maps (*Alep*, LXII and LXX).
The dotted areas indicate the zones of urban growth.

Citadel, in which the *waqf* developed. In this area were built particularly several *khān*, *qaisāriyya*, and shops of which we know nearly nothing because of the deep changes this district underwent in the nineteenth and twentieth centuries.

We know much more about the building operation undertaken, towards 1555, by Muhammad Pasha Dūqakīn Zāda, a very important person related to the sultan himself, pasha of Aleppo (1551–1553) and, later on, of Cairo (1553–1555). His own constructions spread round the great mosque al-Ādiliyya (finished in 1556) just west of the constructions of Khusrū Pasha. It was a thinly populated area during the period of the Mameluks(who had there a *mīdān* where they practised the javelin). Around the beautiful Turkish-style mosque which was erected on a slight eminence to enhance its beauty, three great *khān* were built: the khān al-'Ulabiyya (5550 square metres, 47 shops on the ground floor), the largest in Aleppo after the khān al-Gumruk: the khān al-Nahhāsīn and the khān al-Farrā'īn. To these were added three *qaisāriyya* and four *sūq* (including 157 shops). The whole compound covered more than three hectares.

Twenty years later, another Muhammad Pasha constituted one of the most important *waqf* of the time; it included a total of 125 articles, 34 of which concerned Aleppo and involved 937 commercial or industrial premises. In the *Madinah* the constructions of Muhammad Pasha were erected on a plot just to the west of the area which had been occupied in 1555. The most remarkable element of the ensemble was the Khān al-Gumruk (*khān* of the Customs) built in 1574, one of the masterpieces of Ottoman architecture in Aleppo. This monument is as impressive in the quality of its construction and decoration as in its size, which was quite exceptional for a building of that type (0.6 hectares, 52 rooms on the ground floor, 77 upstairs, a mosque in the courtyard and a *qaisāriyya*). To this splendid monument were connected, through a device of cupolas which marked the axis of the construction and extended the monumental entrance, several business buildings including two beautiful covered *sūq* made of hewn stones, plus another *sūq*—a total of 344 shops and a built-up area of about one hectare.

This great urban construction inside the City ended about 1583 with a project in the west part of the area where the previous construction had taken place. The heart of this final project was, again, a mosque, the Bahrāmiyya, built, like the two former ones, in pure Ottoman style. Here, too, the builder linked the mosque with two markets whose profits were to ensure the up-keep of the religious building. The architectural unity of the construction rested on a system of domes connecting the gate of the mosque to the *sūq*.

Two things should be especially noticed about this spectacular expansion of the City towards the south: first, the westward thrust was a steady one, every new *waqf* developing just beyond the former one; and second, the scale of the undertakings was gradually reduced (4 to 5 hectares in 1544; 3 hectares in 1555; between one and two hectares in 1574; and, finally, half an hectare in 1583). Rather than suppose the existence of a pre-established plan, we must think that the need to find unbuilt areas near the main east–west line of the *sūq* compelled the builders to shift progressively the sites of their urban projects towards the west, where thinly populated districts could still be found. On the other hand, the diminishing size of the undertakings does not seem to come from a slackening of the creative impulse, but rather from a diminution of the space available in the City, a result of its increasing urbanization. Both the thrust towards the west and the decrease in size of the architectural works must have been caused by the gradual overcrowding of the centre of Aleppo which resulted from its fast urban growth. This situation made it necessary to contemplate building projects *out of the town*; and as early as 1574 the building plans of Muhammad Pasha included an important extension *extra muros*, i.e., outside bāb Antākya.

In Aleppo, as well as in Cairo, the shifting of the tanneries was a consequence of the growth of the old urban centre.[20] The population increase and the development of the commercial districts of the centre made it necessary to transfer beyond the town limits the premises of artisans whose activity involved noticeable drawbacks for the population. During the Ayyoubid period a district dedicated to the leather work had developed in the northwest angle of the *intra-muros* town; it was called Dabbāgha, the Tanyard. When Muhammad Pasha's *waqf* was laid out in 1574, the tanneries had already been transferred out of the town, outside bāb Antākiya, to the banks of the Quwaiq river. The *waqf* had erected there a building of impressive size (170 m. by 40 m., with 111 rooms) for the *dabbāgha*, plus 4 *khān*, two public baths and two mosques, partly meant for the tanners. At that time, the district where the tanneries were previously located was already known as the 'Ancient tan' (Mahalla al-Dabbāgha al-ʿatīqa) and this name remained that of the very old mosque which is still standing there (Jāmiʿ al-Dabbāgha al-ʿatīqa). Thus the shifting of these industrial activities, due to the economic and demographic growth of the old town, gave birth to a new suburb on the west outskirts of Aleppo.

But especially towards the north and east did the expansion of Aleppo result in a vigorous growth of suburbs.[21] Towards the north there was a merger of the separate developments which had risen along the street leading from the town, and a new district was formed. On the east, an entirely new town developed between the Sūq Bānqūsā on the north and the district of the nomads in the south. Sauvaget's maps enable us to have a precise idea of the magnitude of the urban growth. The whole area of the suburbs increased from 91 hectares in about 1516 to 198 hectares in the nineteenth century, that is to say, an increase of over 100 per cent. Just like Muhammad Pasha, who had realized his architectural programme partly outside the ancient town centre in the west part of the town, Bahrām Pasha in 1583 built a *hammām* and a *qaisāriyya* in Judaida to the north of the *intra-muros* town in a place where urban growth was particularly rapid at that time. The urban thrust Aleppo underwent in the sixteenth century pushed the town out of its medieval boundaries and gave it the features it kept till the end of the nineteenth century.

Conclusion

The reality of a vigorous urban growth in the great Arab towns from the very beginning of the Ottoman conquest can hardly be questioned. This growth is evidenced by features of the urban physical structure as well as by various recorded events in the history of Cairo and Aleppo. This urban thrust was linked with the commercial expansion which followed the constitution of the Empire. That commercial expansion still needs careful study, but it probably reflected a demographic expansion. The existence of such demographic expansion has been proved, at least for the Balkans and Anatolian provinces of the Empire, by the researches of European and Turkish scholars, following the pioneer work of Omar Lutfi Barkan. The development of urban life in Rumelia and in Anatolia in the sixteenth century seems well established; it would be logical to think that the Arab towns developed in the same way. The case of the great Arab towns would therefore be a regional aspect of a general evolution, and their prosperity would not cause any surprise if the decay of Ottoman Turkey in the nineteenth century had not cast a dark shadow on the whole of Ottoman history.

Our knowledge of the economic history of the Arab provinces of the Ottoman Empire is not precise enough to allow us to state either that a global economic development took place there during the decades which followed the constitution of the Empire, or, on the contrary, that the towns experienced their expansion within an area of general stagnation. As to the towns themselves, we do not see any inconsistency between material development of the cities and the cultural apathy which, no doubt, characterized the Arab world at that time. It is important to mitigate the harshness of the judgments which have been passed against the Ottoman legacy in the field of the architectural and urban development. Careful studies like those of John Williams and Michael Rogers[22] have recently shown that the heritage was not as negative as it had long been thought to be and that it ought not to be totally ignored. After all, the numerous *sabīl* erected all over Cairo from the sixteenth to the eighteenth century; the carefully built *mahalla* and streets of Aleppo; the aqueducts and water distribution system of Algiers, all bear testimony to a genuine governmental interest in the inhabitants of these towns. The matter is worthy of further study.

Notes

This is a revised version of the George Antonius Lecture, given and St Antony's (Oxford) in June, 1978. It was translated into English by Mrs O. Rudigoz.

[1] J. Sauvaget, *Esquisse d'une histoire de la ville de Damas*, REI, 1934, p. 467.

[2] *Sulūk*, III, 100, quoted by A. A. Duri, s.v., 'Baghdād,' *Encyclopédie de l'Islam*, 2nd ed., vol. I, p. 931.

[3] Sauvaget, *Esquisse*, p. 468.

[4] On the coffee trade, see my book, *Artisans et commerçants au Caire au XVIIIème siècle*, vol. I (Damascus, 1974), pp. 107–157.

[5] Act I, sc. 3: quoted in J. Sauvaget, *Alep* (Paris, 1941), pp. 200–201.

[6] Paris, *Histoire du commerce de Marseille*, vol. V, pp. 383, 416.

[7] Quoted by J. Jomier, *Le Mahmal* (Cairo, 1953), pp. 218–19.

[8] A. Raymond, 'La population du Caire, de Maqrîzî à la Description de l'Egypte,' in *BEO* 28 (1975): 212. See also A. Raymond and G. Wiet, *Les marchés du Caire* (Cairo, 1979).

[9] Trécourt, *Mémoires sur l'Egypte*, ed. G. Wiet, (Cairo, 1942), pp. 24–25. I estimate that the population of Egypt in 1798 rose to about 4,000,000 people.

[10] L. D'Arvieux, *Mémoires* (Paris, 1735), vol. VI, pp. 411, 417–18.

[11] Paris, *Histoire du commerce*, vol. V, p. 416.

[12] See my articles 'La localisation des bains publics au Caire, au XVème siècle,' *BEO* 30 (1979) (Mélanges H. Laoust II), and 'Cairo's Area and Population in the Early Fifteenth Century' *Muqarnas* 2 (1984). I call Qāhira the Fatimid foundation, *intra muros*; the southern district spreads beyond bāb Zuwaila and is limited, on the west, by the Halīj (Cairo's canal); these western district spreads beyond the Halīj.

[13] See my articles, 'La localisation des bains publics,' and 'Les fontaines publiques du Caire à l'époque ottomane,' *Annales Islamologiques*, XV (1979).

[14] 'Alī Pasha, *Hitat* (Būlāq, 1306/1888) 20 vols., vol. III, 63–64. For this question, see my article 'Le déplacement des tanneries à Alep, au Caire et à Tunis,' in *Revue d'Histoire Maghrébine*, nos 7–8 (1977): 195–197 (hereafter 'Le déplacement des tanneries').

[15] See my article 'Essai de géographie des quartiers de résidence aristocratique,' *JESHO* 6 (1963).

[16] See 'Les fontaines publiques du Caire.'

[17] Sauvaget, *Esquisse*. My map of the extension of Damascus during the Ottoman period is drawn from Sauvaget's maps VIII and X.

[18] Sauvaget, *Alep*, maps LXII and LXX, from which our own map is drawn. See D'Arvieux, *Mémoires*, IV, 434–36: A. Russell, *The Natural History of Aleppo*, London 1794 (map); J. G. Barbie du Bocage, 'Notice sur la carte de M. Rousseau,' in *Recueil des voyages* (1825), vol. II, 194–244; K. al-Ghazzī, *Kitāb Nahr* (Aleppo, 1342H) 3 vols., vol. II, *passim*; National Archives of Damascus, *daftar* Aleppo, 961–963H, 995–999H.

[19] For the history of those *waqf*, see Sauvaget, *Alep*, 214, 216–7, 263–265; Ghazzī, *Nahr*, vol. II, 47–52, 112–115, 117–123, 515–522; Muhammad Tabbākh, *I'lām al-Nubalā*, vol. III, 180, 181, 191, 202–206, 213–214.

[20] 'Le déplacement des tanneries,', pp. 193–95.

[21] See my article 'The population of Aleppo in the 16th and 17th Centuries according to Ottoman Census Documents,' *IJMES* 16, (1984).

[22] J. A. Williams, *The Monuments of Ottoman Cairo*, Colloque international sur l'histoire du Caire, pp. 453–63; M. Rogers, s.v., 'Kāhira,' *Encyclopédie de l'Islam* 2nd ed., vol. IV, pp. 454–61.

Muhammad Ali and Palmerston

EVERYONE knows the political and diplomatic motives that caused Palmerston to thwart Muhammad Ali—the British attachment to Greek independence, the fear of Egyptian control of both routes to India, the threat he constituted to the Ottoman Empire, Britain's buffer against Russia. Less attention has been paid to the economic motives that underlay Muhammad Ali's expansionist policies and that led ultimately to the Palmerstonian reaction that cut Muhammad Ali down to size.

During the last decades of the 18th century the alliance between Egypt's rulers and merchants had strengthened noticeably.[1] The trend towards rationalization of agriculture directed towards an export economy was apparent. A number of the so-called innovations Muhammad Ali and his supporters carried out in Egypt were in fact a continuation of 18th century trends and were developed in response to definite pressures by vested interest groups in the country. Undoubtedly Muhammad Ali's genius forced the pace, but he could not have controlled the Egyptian economy without the support of vested interests, especially among the military and bureaucratic elite and a few select mercantile groupings.

Muhammad Ali sought to parallel in Egypt the lines of development of British industry—whether consciously or unconsciously. In order to capture a share of the world markets he planned to spread his hegemony over potential markets, and utilize their raw materials at one and the same time. These markets were Egypt's immediate neighbors, Sudan, Syria, Arabia and the Red Sea. Once all these territories had been major outlets for Egyptian trade, but fairly recently that domination had been lost through the influx of cheap western goods.[2] Since Egyptian goods could not compete economically with western goods, Muhammad Ali planned a series of wars of colonial expansion in order to recapture these markets and their abundant raw materials necessary for his industries, and to impose a system of tariffs that would give him free rein to keep out competitive commodities. In the process, and as an adjunct to his wars, he also built up a powerful navy. These steps normally should have turned Egypt into an industrial power at the core of a local market that comprised the Ottoman empire, the Eastern Mediterranean and the Red Sea regions. But they did not, and a major reason was British opposition.

The Pasha had early realized that the path to maximum profit through commerce lay in displacing as many middlemen as he could in favour of himself and his retainers. The first victims were the Egyptian tax-farmers, the *multazims*, who controlled the country's agricultural wealth, and many of whom were Muhammad Ali's opponents. He ousted the old *multazims* and redistributed the land among his family and supporters. The next step was to control the agricultural surplus of the peasants by instituting a series of monopolies forbidding the sale of specific crops to buyers other than the government appointed agents, and at a price fixed by the government. Traditionally there existed a number of Ottoman embargoes against the sale of cereals and vegetables outside the confines of the empire; Muhammad Ali implemented the terms of the embargo as far as private merchants were concerned, but allowed his agents to export the proscribed crops outside the empire.

Once agriculture was controlled the mercantile and commerical sectors followed. In time the Pasha became the largest indigenous merchant and monopolized the sale of all the export crops of the country like grain, indigo, flax, cotton. His first coup was in grain sales to the British in Malta in 1810–1813, when grain was needed for the Peninsular army. Reputedly in 1810 the Pasha made a profit of some three million francs.[3] By 1812 he was described as the richest pasha in the Ottoman empre and allegedly was setting aside 20 million francs a year,[4] certainly an exaggeration. A monopoly of textiles followed: cotton, wool, flax and silk. An Ottoman embargo on the export of silk outside the empire existed, and the Pasha could certainly have obtained a similar embargo against cotton, but he did not attempt to do so, and acted as he pleased, much to the anger of Ottomans and Europeans.

From 1816 Muhammad Ali started to industrialize the country, beginning with one of the oldest of Egyptian crafts, textiles; this he transformed from cottage industry production into that of large-scale mills. By 1828 he had thirty cotton spinning and weaving mills with 1,960 mule jennies, and 1,750 looms, plus seven bleaching establishments. The new mills employed 30,000 workers. By 1830 the annual output of cotton yarn reached 2,500 tons, much of which was exported to Trieste, Leghorn and Turkey. Output of cotton cloth was over one million meters. Woven goods were exported to Syria, Arabia and the Sudan. Import of British textiles was limited to high quality cloth. Furthermore the Pasha's agents in France, England, Malta, Naples and Venice were ordered to sell Egyptian linens and calico textiles in Europe 'on an experimental basis'. In all Egyptian controlled territories orders were given restricting imports to 'protect' local industries.[5]

Expansion of the acreage of cotton, especially the long staple variety reccently discovered, became a main purpose of the agricultural reforms. Although fluctuations in the harvests and the price of cotton were commonplace and in consequence caused dislocations in the local economy, in periods of good harvests cotton contributed up to one quarter of the total agricultural revenue, and also one quarter of Egypt's export earnings. In

1838 some 238,833 cantars were exported at a value of £716,670 or $15 per quintal, in 1845, 344,955 cantars were exported.⁶

The cotton goods produced in Egypt were of inferior quality compared to British cotton goods, but they were able to hold their own. Indeed, by 1840 it was estimated that Britain was importing 12–20% of Egyptian cotton and cereals, and by 1850, by which time Egyptian industries had been dismantled, that figure went up to 50%. Egyptian competition became a definite source of worry to British officials, at a time when cotton profits were diminishing in England.⁸

The Pasha realized that a large profit could also be made by shipping in his own ships; he therefore organized an Egyptian merchant marine. Using the same logic as an Onassis or a Niarchos, and recruiting their forebears, he shipped in his own lines, reaping a double profit.

The monopoly network set up in Egypt aroused the ire of the European mercantile community since it radically cut into their export profits. In the past the system of capitulations that prevailed in the Ottoman empire had given foreign merchants preferential treatment over indigenous ones, because they paid a lower customs duty on exports and imports. With increasing western industrialization the Egyptian import market had become flooded with cheap western goods, and the export market was largely controlled by western merchants who could outbid the local ones because of their larger margin of profit. The new policies followed by the Pasha undermined that position of advantage, except for a few hand-picked agents such as the Englishman Samuel Briggs. The Pasha disregarded the capitulations when it suited him and set up protective tariffs of his own. He sold to chosen merchants and set the sale price. All consular reports of the period of whatever nationality fulminate against what they called an 'iniquitous' system of monopolies that bid fair to destroying foreign mercantile interests—and local ones as well. In short the Pasha cornered the market and sewed it tight. He bought at his own rates, sold at his own prices, on occasion even underselling himself; he shipped in his own lines and disregarded injunctions from suzerain and foreign agents alike, thereby frustrating foreign middlemen and their commercial enterprises in Egypt.

At first the British government saw no need for action, since Egypt was an insignificant country, and they needed the Pasha's grain to feed the army in Portugal. Canning in 1825 even pointed out the right of the Ottomans to prohibit the export of any article they pleased,⁹ the implication being that the Egyptian Pasha was free to do as he saw fit, so long as his suzerain allowed him to. The position was soon to change when Muhammad Ali overstepped the limits of his little kingdom and began to expand politically and economically into British spheres of interest.

His first opportunity for a coup outside the Egyptian borders affected the Red Sea and its trade. The Red Sea had always been a Muslim enclave.

Throughout the 17th and 18th centuries the Dutch and the British had tried to break that monopoly of Red Sea trade and shipping but with little success; virtually no one penetrated north of Yemen. British mercantile interests and shipping nevertheless continued to covet the Red Sea route and its trade; by the development of steam navigation in the 1830s the whole Red Sea question gained a new dimension and raised the need for coaling stations. The East India Co. wanted Aden, but Muhammad Ali controlled part of the littoral and his navy controlled the Sea thereby frustrating British mercantile interests. The Egyptian conquest of the Hijaz in 1818 allowed the Pasha to monopolize the Red Sea along with Egyptian trade, and the following year he extracted tribute from the Imam of Yemen in the shape of a yearly supply of 20,000 bahars of coffee, the most lucrative trading commodity in the area.[10]

That year the British East India Co. sent ten naval vessels to blockade Moka when the governor allegedly insulted the British resident. The ships evacuated the port only when the Imam had signed a treaty setting British customs dues at 2·25%, 1% lower than the dues being paid by the French. Istanbul, annoyed by the incident, ordered Muhammad Ali to occupy all the Red Sea ports as far south as Aden;[11] he did not only comply but after conquering the Sudan (1820–22) the Egyptians came to dominate the African shores of the Red Sea through their occupation of the ports of Suakin and Massowa and were later to rouse the alarm of the Cabinet in England with rumours of further expansion in the area.[12]

The Morean campaign of 1825 was the first tangible hint that there was more to British antagonism towards Muhammad Ali than mere strategic considerations.

To European eyes the battle of Navarino, October 1827, when the joint Egyptian–Ottoman fleet was sunk in the bay by the combined navies of Britain, France, Austria and Russia, seemed a straightforward attempt on the part of the Allies to support the Greek movement for independence, and prevent supplies from reaching the Ottoman armies in the Morea. Admiral Codrington who was in charge of the Allied fleet was given vague orders from London but more specific instructions from Stratford Canning, British Ambassador at the Porte. Canning told Codrington that he was to act by fair means if possible, but '. . . when other means are exhausted, by cannon-shot'.[13]

Codrington obeyed the famous 'cannon-shot' letter literally, and was later made a scapegoat by the establishment who denied having any such intentions. However, that letter was presumably the reason why four so-called friendly powers blockaded the Egyptian–Ottoman fleet in the bay of Navarino and 'accidentally' sunk most of it when a shot was fired in the vaguest circumstances. Apologies were offered the Ottomans for the 'untoward event'. Yet the Allies continued to impose a naval blockade on all Egyptian–Ottoman shipping attempting to reach the area, and the Egyptian army which was planning to attack the islands of Hydra and Spezia just before Navarino, was forced to withdraw from the whole of Morea on pain of starving through lack of supplies.

In Egyptian eyes, had Ibrahim Pasha retained control of the Morea, as there is every indication he could have done, since he had soundly beaten the Greeks, the Eastern Mediterranean would have become an Egyptian lake. Control of the Mediterranean had in fact been part of Muhammad Ali's plans. From 1811 when he first organized his navy, the Pasha had constantly invited Greeks to settle in Egypt; born in Kavala, he admired their many entrepreneurial talents. A number of Greek trading families, the Tossizza, Zizinia, Casulli and Anastasi, had settled in Egypt and cooperated closely in the Pasha's financial enterprises, and in the process became extremely wealthy. Other Greeks manned the rapidly growing Egyptian navy and merchant marine. Ten years later the Pasha could rightly boast of having the 'most magnificent fleet' in the Muslim world.[14] Meanwhile he turned a blind eye to the activities of the Greek revolutionaries who were raising money in Egypt to finance their rebellion. The bulk of the money for the rebellion had come from the insular Greeks of Hydra and Spezia who came to control almost all the commerce from the Black Sea to Egypt, and used their proceeds to finance the war of independence. When those funds ran dry they took to outright piracy and disrupted all neutral trade in the area. The famous 'klephti' out of Hydra and Spezia, like Canaris and Miaulis, The Cat and the Canary, as they were familiarly called, represented an important fighting arm that even threatened Muhammad Ali's palace in Alexandria with a fire-ship. Had Muhammad Ali's forces under Ibrahim managed to occupy Hydra and Spezia, which was Ibrahim's goal prior to Navarino and the direct cause of Navarino, then Greek shipping, sailors and technical know-how would have been added to the rapidly growing Egyptian fleet and the Pasha could have monopolized the trade of southern Europe and the entire Eastern Mediterranean. Navarino was as much an economic triumph for western trade as a political triumph in favour of the Greeks.

The loss of a fleet of 81 ships was a blow to Ottomans and Egyptians, but especially to the Egyptians since the Pasha had equipped the entire fleet and paid for supplies, ammunition and repairs, but as he wisely wrote to his agent in Istanbul 'It is better to conclude peace now with easy conditions and busy ourselves with regaining our strength and putting our forces together'.[15] He was philosophical about his loss because he had other cards up his sleeve. Within a few years he had restored his navy, using local labour rather than the more costly European shipyards; a Frenchman, Cérisy, was appointed head of the new shipyard.

The post-Napoleonic era had seen an influx into Egypt of French military and civilian experts in search of a livelihood. Their technical training was put to good use in laying the foundations for Egyptian industries, in training the army and in carrying out plans for extensive irrigation projects. The French government with interests in North Africa, and in 1830 with a large colony in Algeria, effected a rapprochement with Egypt. Between them these two countries potentially controlled the entire Mediterranean, and could balk British interests at will. Throughout that period France's main opponent was Britain, and when French consuls copiously reported on the activities of 'nos ennemis' in Egypt they specifically meant the British consul and British mercantile groups.

Egyptian policies thus were not only to threaten British economic well-being but were also to bring it into conflict with the Powers—Russia at one time, France at another.

After the Morean fiasco, Muhammad Ali, who never wasted time wringing his hands, planned his next move, into Syria. At one time the Sultan had promised him Syria in return for his services in the Morean campaign, but when that promise evaporated along with possession of the Morea, the Pasha took matters into his own hands. In 1831 Ibrahim, at the head of an army, invaded Syria on a spurious charge of punishing the governor of Acre for an imagined slight. We know from Muhammad Ali's private correspondence that from his first decade as governor of Egypt he had coveted Syria. In 1811 he had even requested it from the Porte, to be soundly rebuffed. He needed Syria for economic and strategic reasons. It was rich in export materials like wood, oil and silk; it had a sound trading framework that stretched from Europe to Asia; it had a large population; and it provided a natural buffer zone between suzerain and vassal. Past rulers of Egypt had from time immemorial sought to extend their frontiers into Syria.

Once Ibrahim had conquered the whole of greater Syria within the brief span of two years, it was inevitable that he should pursue his advantage beyond Syria, across the Taurus mountains into Anatolia, as far as Konya, and manage to shake the foundations of the Ottoman empire.

Palmerston, who was Secretary of State for Foreign Affairs four times—from 1827–1829, 1830–1834, 1835–1841 and 1846–1851—was one of the few British statesmen who had a sound knowledge of economics. He had not forgotten the economics he had learnt with Dugald Stewart. Their lesson, what is more, had been dinned in by Napoleon's blockade as well as by Madison's denial of American markets to British goods. Britain's need for foreign markets was palpable. The British also complacently reflected that it was good for backward people, who would be improved by the 'general influence of our commerce'.[16] For multiple reasons, Palmerston, therefore, was a convinced free trader, determined to hold onto markets such as the Ottoman empire where, thanks to the Capitulations, Britain could export cheap western goods, and have easy access to India as well.

Palmerston frequently reiterated his view that England was a commercial nation, a practical nation, one that acted only when British interests were at stake, 'We do not go in for chivalrous enterprises or fight for others as the French do' he said.[17] Equally he was a strong believer in interference in the internal affairs of other countries should British interests call for it '. . . if by interference is meant intermeddling, and intermeddling in every way, and to every extent short of actual military force; then I must affirm that there is nothing in such interference which the laws of nations may not in certain cases permit'.[18] He was to put both these principles into practice against Muhammad Ali and Egypt.

Palmerston's second term of office, 1830–1834, coincided with a critical period in British internal and external affairs. In the 1830s the British economy was beset by economic stagnation and labor unrest. The rate of profit had declined and most obviously in the case of cotton—the commodity that had caused England's industrial boom—this rate had fallen from one shilling in 1812 to 3.75d in 1830.[19] Unrest was also rife over the Reform Bill which was thrown out in October 1831 by the House of Lords, but passed in May 1832. While all this was happening the country was on the verge of revolution;[20] serious violence broke out; there was a run on the Bank of England; Wellington's government fell.

Abroad, five major international problems loomed large and drove out all thought of British intervention outside Europe: the question of the Greek frontiers, the Belgian revolt against the Netherlands, the Russian invasion of Poland after the Poles declared their independence, further events in Italy and Portugal. Each one of these issues directly threatened British security and fully occupied her administration. But by 1833 Ibrahim had Syria under his control.

At the time of the Napoleonic wars, Egypt had been a negligible rival. Indeed, necessary as an ally because its corn was indispensable for the army in the peninsula. But by the 1820s when Muhammad Ali began to formulate ideas for an export economy fortified by Egyptian interest groups, it dawned on British exporters that here might be an industrial rival at the core of a market important for Britain—the Ottoman empire, the Red Sea and the Eastern Mediterranean. Here was a Pasha getting economic power and profit into his own hands, setting out on conquests that would widen the scope of his monopoly, who was ready to snap his fingers at the Capitulations. Palmerston had been vaguely aware of Muhammad Ali's growing importance and especially aware of the damage his protective tariffs were causing British trade. He denounced these tariffs in Parliament and said that they should 'extend to the principle of commercial monopoly the same condemnation which had been pronounced . . . upon the principle of political monopoly'.[21] In a letter to Ponsonby, British Ambassador in Istanbul, Palmerston voiced a further fear that the Egyptian ruler might acquire 'the command of Mesopotamia down to the Persian Gulph. This would certainly follow if he had the pashalik of Aleppo; Acre alone or even with Damascus added to it would not give him the command of the Euphrates'.[22] But with so many pressing European and insular commitments on the front burners Palmerston shoved the Eastern problems aside for the time being. The Sultan's pleas for assistance against his encroaching vassal fell on deaf British ears for the navy had been committed to Portugal and the Netherlands, and had no ships to spare for Turkey. Sultan Mahmud was forced to turn to the Russians and in 1833 to reach an accommodation with Muhammad Ali.

The Ottoman appeal to Russia was the cry of a sinking man, which by then Sultan Mahmud seemed to be. His armies had been defeated. Ibrahim had crossed the Taurus and advanced to Konya; he was within marching distance of Istanbul, with nothing to prevent his advance to the capital. The Sultan had turned to the British government for help and had received nothing but platitudes. Palmerston was not willing to offer the Sultan any military assistance, but contented himself with making suggestions for rejuvenating the empire through a series of reforms at the hands of European experts—which was precisely what Mahmud had been trying to do over the past decade. None of this advice was worth a regiment to the Sultan, who in desperation had turned to his traditional enemy, Russia, which offered him a defensive alliance in 1833—the treaty of Unkiar Skelessi—in return for a secret clause that opened the Dardanelles to the Russians in time of war and closed them to everybody else.

At first Palmerston believed that Muhammad Ali could be contained by diplomatic pressure exercised during the Turkish–Egyptian peace negotiations. Once the Russians became involved, and had an army solidly ensconced in Ottoman territory Palmerston could justify action in terms of *realpolitik*—dismemberment of the Ottoman empire, a consequent European war over the spoils, direct confrontation with Russia, loss of British economic supremacy in the Levant and the Mediterranean—that is, he could rationalize, even justify, diplomatic intervention in political terms. He therefore put forth the claim that Muhammad Ali had 'the best understanding with Russia'.[23] To this ridiculous allegation the Pasha could only retort that he had not yet grown senile.

At first Palmerston's reactions to Egyptian expansion were almost complacent. To his brother in Naples Palmerston could write, in 1833, 'His [Muhammad Ali's] real design is to establish an Arabian kingdom, including all the countries in which Arabic is the language. There might be no harm in such a thing in itself, but as it would necessarily imply the dismemberment of Turkey, we could not agree to it. Besides the Turk is as good an occupier of the road to India as an active Arab sovereign would be'.[24] But as that expansion progressed his tone became harsher. Not only were the Egyptians troublesome in the Levant but the previous year, following a mutiny on the part of some Egyptian regiments in the Hijaz, Egyptian troops followed the mutineers in Yemen and established hegemony over the entire Red Sea littoral from Suez to Bab al-Mandib. Strong rumors circulated that Muhammad Ali meant to go beyond the straits and establish himself outside the Red Sea. In 1837 Palmerston remonstrated with the Egyptian government through Consul Campbell and warned that such a move would not be 'well looked upon in England or in India'.[25] The Pasha hastened to assure Palmerston that he had no such ambitions, but suspicions concerning his motives had come alive, and compounded growing British hostility towards him.

The Pasha not only wanted the pashalik of Aleppo but he also wanted the sancaks of Antalya, Alaya and Cilicia and the island of Cyprus. Furthermore he would also have liked Tunis and Tripoli.[26] These territories, well beyond what Palmerston imagined the Egyptians wanted, would have spread the hegemony of Egypt over the southern and eastern Mediterranean and given it control over the trade routes from the Levant to the major European ports of southern Europe. North African territories were to replace the Morean territories in the scheme of things. The Pasha by now was the ruler of a naval power wanting wood for its ships, which came from the heavily forested regions of Cilicia, Antalya and Alaya. Copper for lining its vessels came from Tokat. Cyprus, which in 1825 had been granted to the Egyptians in return for its pacification, was necessary as a naval base, and a strategic point for guarding access routes to the Levant—the same reasons as caused Britain to covet and acquire it later on. Muhammad Ali had indeed planned to acquire Mesopotamia as Palmerston feared.

To British relief the Ottoman–Russian Treaty of 1833 had halted Ibrahim's advance towards the capital. Ibrahim had realized that he could do little to the Ottomans with Russian troops camped on Ottoman lands. The only option was to go for a peace negotiation and retain the territories he had conquered. To British chagrin, the Sultan conceded to the Egyptians most of the territories they had asked for.

For a while the Treaty of 1833 seemed to bring peace to the area. As governor of the new territories, Ibrahim, who had to cope with Ottoman intrigues in Syria, was not sanguine. He predicted that sooner or later he would come to blows with the Ottomans, and in spite of their German-trained army he would defeat them and march into Konya, if not Istanbul.[27] In any case he had his hands full with Syria. His father, in pursuit of his grand design, had imposed on Syria the same monopolistic system he had in Egypt. The Syrians, though accustomed to monopolies, were also expert in evading them by means of practices the Ottomans were too weak to stop, and Syrian Christian merchants had developed an extensive compradorial network with the European consuls-cum-merchants. The Egyptians were more efficient and their monopoly system threatened to destroy that network and to wipe out the vested interests that had grown up during the past decades within the mercantile community. Where the Syrians were being sucked into the western industrial system as suppliers of raw materials and compradors, the Egyptian Pasha was attempting to set up a core industrial system of his own on the eastern Mediterranean. Syria, naturally, objected and the fires of its discontent were fanned by British and Ottoman intrigues. The Ottomans incited malcontents to rebellion and the British supplied them with arms through Consul Woods. Palmerston made sure that the bill for the weapons was paid by the Ottomans.

The aging Pasha would have like an alliance with Britain, but Britain could see no advantage in either breaking up the Ottoman empire or in safeguarding and nurturing a potential rival. Quite the other way, the British could get much more out of dominating a weak sultan who was no rival to British economic supremacy, and who facilitated their economic domination of his empire by granting them the Treaty of Balta Liman in 1838.

This treaty was to be a nail in the coffin of all monopolies within the Ottoman empire, including Egypt. The Ottomans, who had practiced a monopoly system for a long time, agreed to revise that system in the belief that it would be more adverse to Muhammad Ali's interests than theirs, and would bring him into direct confrontation, even conflict, with the European powers.[28] The treaty dealt with two separate elements; abolition of monopolies, and a new customs tariff. Ironically enough the Pasha, whose finances by 1838 were in bad shape because of the continuous drain on his resources through wars, industrial and irrigation projects, had been forced to abandon some of his monopolies, and in due course might have returned to a system of free trade.[29] The negative aspects of the treaty as far as he was concerned were its clauses dealing with customs tariffs rather than with monopolies.

By its terms the treaty admitted all foreign goods into the empire with a 3% duty and a new *ad valorem* interior duty of 9%. All exports had a 3% export duty plus a new interior duty of 2%. Internal taxes on imported goods were abolished. Palmerston claimed that in the long run the abolition of monopolies would increase the revenues of Egypt and the Ottoman empire, presumably through increased traffic, 'though it may for the moment paralyze Muhammad Ali's scheme of finance'.[30] The principles of Balta Liman when applied in Egypt later allowed European merchants free rein in the market, and through the Capitulations, in time, gave them virtual control of that market. Secondly, the terms of the treaty encouraged an influx of British goods into the area which, being cheaper, killed off any infant industries that had been set up, since they could not as yet compete. Raw materials became exported in large quantities and at lower prices than heretofore. The end result was that local industries were killed off, because divested of protected tariffs, and the country's economy became inevitably geared to being a supplier of raw materials to the west and an importer of finished western goods. Egypt thus became reduced to the position of a poor and dependent participant in the European world market, a position mitigating any pretensions at economic independence let alone political hegemony over the eastern Mediterranean, the Levant or the Red Sea.

Muhammad Ali who had realized the consequences which lay in applying the terms of Balta Liman within his territories, refused to abide by it, much to the anger of the Powers. As Ibrahim had expected, the Ottomans attacked again in 1839 and once more Ibrahim defeated the Ottoman army, in the battle of Nezib, in spite of its German training.

After Nezib extra demands were made. Ibrahim's notions of 'secure boundaries' towards the east expanded to include Diya Bekir and Urfa from whence the Ottoman army had crossed the Euphrates to attack his position. Ibrahim determined that his future boundaries should be the entire frontier between Anatolia and the Arab provinces south of the Taurus. Such control would also given him dominion over northern Iraq, and both Tigris and Euphrates rivers. Urfa was important because of its proximity to the desert and to the Bedouin tribes who remained a potential source of sedition and a thorn in his flesh. He had previously suffered from Arab uprisings incited by the Ottomans in Hauran, in Aintab, and in the Kurdish mountains. The only means to stamp out future sedition in these territories would be to place them under his direct control.[31] The territories claimed by Ibrahim were of prime strategic importance vis-à-vis the Ottoman armies, but they were also economically valuable in themselves, lying on the trade routes from east to west, and constituting a potential stepping stone south in Mesopotamia.

By Palmerston's standards this was too much. An Egyptian presence in northern Syria was a direct threat to British interests, since it clearly presaged an impending takeover of Iraq and the Persian Gulf. To make matters worse an Englishman, Chesney, had a project for putting a fleet of steamships on the Euphrates which would connect by direct railway to Alexandretta, thereby offering a route from the Persian Gulf to the Mediterranean as an alterantive to going through Egypt and the Red Sea.[32] With Egyptian forces in control of the Red Sea and in control of the Euphrates and Aleppo as well as the Mediterranean coastline, the whole project would fall under the domination of Muhammad Ali, so that both routes to India would lie under his control, and the trade of the Levant would be entirely dominated by the Egyptian monarch and his forces. The Ottoman Sultan was a much better bet than Muhammad Ali; he could be controlled and contained as 'Grand Elchi' Canning had clearly shown with Mahmud, let alone with his sixteen-year-old sucessor. The Pasha on the other hand seemed to act either independently of all constraints, save his own interests, or was, Palmerston chose to believe, under the influence of a power inimical to England, and rival in the Mediterranean, France. For all these reasons, the Pasha having won the war against the Ottomans was forced to lose the peace through British initiatives.

The Ottomans, whose old sultan was dead and whose new ruler was a young boy, had prepared a message conceding all the Egyptian demands. But Palmerston rallied the Powers, even Russia; all but France responded and ordered the Ottomans to leave matters in their hands. France on the other hand was in favor of Egyptian demands, since they aided French policy. Palmerston believed that he could force the French government into joining with the other powers especially since Louis Philippe's position was none too strong and he feared a *coup d'état* that would oust him. Palmerston, however, failed to rally Thiers, who was determined to bring about a showdown with Britain over Egypt.

From this time, 1839, Palmerston's tone about Muhammad Ali changed completely and became virulent '. . . the Sultan is the sovereign and though he may have been the aggressor [since he first attacked Ibrahim's forces] still he has right on his side. There was no *treaty* at Kutahya. There could be none; the parties there were a sovereign and a rebel— no treaty can be made between such parties—there was indeed an agreement, and the Sultan conferred certain governments upon Muhammad and Ibrahim. But those governments were given during pleasure, and the Sultan had the right to resume them'. He added 'that it was for the advantage of every Power in Europe except Russia that the Sultan should be able to reassume what he then conferred.'[33] In another letter he wrote, as though his conscience were troubling him, '. . . there is no question of fairness towards Mehemet . . . a robber is always liable to be made to disgorge'.[34]

In another communication to Granville he wrote, 'For my part I hate Mehemet Ali, whom I consider as nothing but an ignorant barbarian, who by cunning and boldness and mother wit has been successful in rebellion . . . I look upon his boasted civilization of Egypt as the arrantest humbug; and I believe that he is as great a tyrant and oppressor as ever made a people wretched'.[35]

Other 'rebels' against the Ottomans might be supported, it was not the principle of 'rebellion' that exercised him, but the policies of that rebel. The person of the rebel must be discredited along with his policies in British eyes to justify what was untoward interference in Ottoman–Egyptian affairs. From being a ruler, Muhammad Ali was demoted into a rebel, a robber and an ignorant barbarian, 'a waiter at a coffee shop'.[36]

Muhammad Ali had given British economic interests far too many jolts. In the late 1820s he posed a threat with his projects for cotton development and the expansion of his fleet, and Navarino was the riposte. In the next decade he continued to be a source of worry in the Eastern Mediterranean and the Red Sea with his potential control of shipping, commerce, and his protective tariffs that were closing markets in the face of British goods at a time when new markets were desperately needed. He controlled both routes to India which was an added acute economic threat, and his projects seemed to favor France as his main ally and thus served to undercut Britain's strategic and economic position even further. Egypt was teeming with French experts of every sort and France was making bellicose statements. The British government had good reason to fear that an alliance between France and Egypt would dominate the entire Mediterranean and squeeze England out of the Sea.[37] Politically Muhammad Ali's projects could bring France and England to another war. Notwithstanding these French gestures, Palmerston believed that the French government would not go to war with England for the sake of Muhammad Ali. The crux came when the Ottoman navy defected to the Egyptian side.

In spite of a split in the British cabinet between men who feared war with France and men who admired his firmness, Palmerston decided to risk a gamble. Muhammad Ali was ordered to withdraw his forces from Syria and given an ultimatum. Allied ships bombarded the coastline in the Lebanon: allied forces were landed in Beirut signalling a Syrian uprising. The French government made violent pronouncements in support of the Pasha but finally did nothing. Later Louis Philippe said, 'M. Thiers est furieux contre moi, parceque je n'ai pas voulu faire la guerre. Il me dit que j'ai parlé de faire la guerre; mais parler de faire la guerre et faire la guerre sont deux choses bien différentes.'[38] When the British fleet appeared outside Muhammad Ali's bedroom window in Alexandria, the Pasha realized he was beaten. He could have battled it out to the last man, but without French support he decided the wisest policy was to cut bait, and concentrate on making Egypt a hereditary kingdom for his family. Ibrahim's army returned to Egypt, some on British ships, and the grand design evaporated. The treaty of 1841 which he was constrained to accept stripped the Pasha of all his conquests and left him the hereditary pashalik of Egypt according to the Ottoman law of succession. Without protective tariffs and a captive market Egyptian industrialization came to a grinding halt, and Egyptian economic efforts henceforth became directed towards turning the country into an export market for agricultural produce. Muhammad Ali's plans had been foiled and Palmerston's gamble paid off handsomely.

Notes

I owe a deep debt of gratitude to John S. Galbraith (UCLA) and Elizabeth Monroe (St. Antony's Oxon) for their invaluable advice and pertinent criticism of this paper. Part of the research for this paper was carried out under a grant from the Social Science Research Council (1975), a UCLA Academic Senate Grant (1975), and a grant from the American Research Center in Egypt (1976).

[1] See excellent work by André Raymond, *Artisans et Commerçants au Caire au XVIIIème Siècle*, Beirut: 1973, and forthcoming work by Peter Gran, *Indigenous Origins of Egyptian Capitalism*, Austin.

[2] Raymond, *op. cit.*, passim.

[3] Vice-Consul Drovetti's report for the month of June 1812 in Edouard Driault, *Mohamed Aly et Napoléon: 1807–1814*, Le Caire: 1925, p. 187 for an account of the sale of 40,000 ardebs of 98,800 hectolitres of wheat.

[4] *Ibid.*, p. 203.

[5] E. R. J. Owen, *Cotton and the Egyptian Economy: 1820–1914*, Oxford: 1969, pp. 45, 47. Also Ali al-Giritly, 'The Commercial, Financial and Industrial Policy of Muhammad Ali', in Charles Issawi, ed., *The Economic History of the Middle East: 1800–1914*, Chicago: 1966, p. 389. Mustafa Fahmy, *La Révolution de l'Industrie en Egypte et ses Conséquences Sociales au 19ème Siècle: 1800–1850*, Leiden: 1954, pp. 21–27, Amin Sami, *Taqwim al-Nil*, Cairo: 1928, II, p. 501.

[6] Owen, *op. cit.*, pp. 40, 73.

[7] *Ibid.*, p. 81.

[8] See J. Bowring, *Report on Egypt and Candia*, P.P., vol. xxi, p. 1 for comments made by Consul-General expressing 'mis-givings' about Egyptian competition, p. 35.

[9] Quoted in M. Sabry, *L'Empire Egyptien Sous Mohamed Ali et la Question d'Orient*, Paris: 1930, p. 86.

[10] Abdel Hamid el-Batrik, 'Egyptian-Yemen Relations: 1819–1840' in P. M. Holt, *Political and Social Change in Modern Egypt*, Oxford: 1968, p. 282. A bahar is equivalent to 222 lbs., 6 oz.

[11] H. Dodwell, *The Founder of Modern Egypt*, Cambridge: 1961, p. 61.

[12] *Ibid.*, p. 84.

[13] Pierre Crabitès, *Ibrahim of Egypt*, London: 1935, p. 80.

[14] *Ibid.*, p. 84.

[15] Egyptian State Archives, *Mutafariqat*, Muhammad Ali to Nejib Effendi, 13 Rabi II, 1243.

[16] Donald Southgate, 'The Most English Minister . . .', New York: 1966, p. 144.

[17] Jasper Ridley, *Lord Palmerston*, London: 1970, p. 145.

[18] Ridley, *op. cit.*, p. 117.

[19] E. J. Hobsbawm, *Industry & Empire*, London: 1977, p. 76.

[20] Ridley, *op. cit.*, p. 104.

[21] Herbert C. F. Bell, *Lord Palmerston*, London: 1936, I, p. 340.

[22] Bell, *op. cit.*, p. 181.

[23] F. S. Rodkey, 'The Attempts of Briggs and Co. to Guide British Policy in the Levant in the Interest of Mehemet Ali Pasha: 1821–1841', in *Journal of Modern History*, V, 1933, p. 342.

[24] Evelyn Ashely, *The Life & Correspondence of Henry John Temple, Viscount Palmerston*, London: 1879, II, p. 145.

[25] Batrik, *op. cit.*, p. 287.

[26] Egyptian State Archives, *Sham 9*, Ibrahim to Muhammad Ali, 13 Ramadan, 1248. Abdin 243–85 Rustum 2.245.

[27] *Ibid.*, Abdin 242–155 Rustum 2.225, same to same, 19 Shaban 1248, also *Sham* 16, 8 Rabi Awal, 2255.
[28] Harold Temperley, *England and the Near East: The Crimea*, London: 1936, p. 32.
[29] Owen, *op. cit.*, p. 57.
[30] Henry Lytton Bulwer, *The Life of H. J. Temple, Viscount Palmerston*, London: 1870, II, p. 285.
[31] Egyptian State Archives, *Sham 16*, 12 Jamad Awal, 1255.
[32] Temperley, *op. cit.*, , pp. 94–95.
[33] Bell, *op. cit.*, p. 295.
[34] *Loc. cit..*
[35] Temperly, *op. cit.*, p. 89.
[36] Ridley, *op. cit.*, p. 209.
[37] Remusat had declared that France '. . . meant to establish a new second-rate maritime power in the Mediterranean, whose fleet might unite with that of France for the purpose of serving as a counterpoise to that of England', Ashley, *op. cit.*, I, p. 391.
[38] *Ibid.*, p. 392.

George Antonius, Palestine and the 1930s

I

I WANT to try and say something about George Antonius—as a person and as a political thinker. My talk will be in no sense biographical, though it has often struck me, while writing it, what an admirable subject for a biography George would be. But at least there may be some prolegomena for any future biographer. Nor, though I have included 'Palestine' in my title, will there be any attempt to define George's attitude to the Palestine problem. That would require far more serious and systematic research than I have been able to undertake. Palestine and the 1930s simply provide the spatio-temporal setting for what I have to say about George.

During the period when I knew him—from 1933 till 1936, indeed till 1939—he and Katy were living at their very beautiful house on the outskirts of Jerusalem, Karm al-Mufti, though, of course, he was also constantly travelling, in the Middle East, Europe and the U.S.A. With John Richmond they were my closest friends in Palestine—indeed in one letter at a moment of particular misery in 1935 I remarked that, without them there, life in Palestine would be unendurable, and I spent more time at Karm al-Mufti than anywhere else (apart from my own successive homes—the *ain* at Jericho, Tantur, the Austrian Hospice, Government House, Ain Karim).

At this point I must be briefly autobiographical and explain how I came to be in Palestine during the years 1933 to 1936 and what I was doing there. I took my finals—Greats—in June 1932 and left Balliol after four years, with no idea what to do next, apart from a strong desire to see something of the Middle East and the Arab world (I had already wandered in Greece and Albania). The only way of doing this appeared to become an apprentice archaeologist. The most obviously available Middle Eastern archaeologist prepared to take on totally inexperienced unpaid apprentices was Professor John Garstang of Liverpool University, who was then excavating at Jericho. So I signed up to work at Jericho, arriving, after a month's pleasant wandering in Cyprus, on December 26th 1932. Here I found John Richmond, whom I had known slightly at Oxford. We became close friends, linked partly by common distaste for Garstang's ideas and methods and common love of Arab civilisation and language—though John was a very capable, and I very incompetent, archaeologist, and John already had a working knowledge of Arabic, of which I was then ignorant—so he was my mentor. From my three months experience at Jericho I learned one useful lesson—that Bronze Age archaeology was not for me. Fortunately though, thanks partly to the nepotism which is the one unchanging characteristic of

British and academic life, my kind godfather, J. A. Smith, Waynflete Professor of Metaphysics, helped me to a Senior Demyship at Magdalen, ostensibly to work on the history of Roman Palestine.

This I attempted to do for the next seven months (January to July 1933), reading Josephus, visiting Transjordan, the Hauran and the Jebel Druze, and the cities of the Decapolis and the early Christian churches of Northern Syria. I returned gradually to England in August having acquired many friends (including George and Katy Antonius), a smattering of Arabic, a love of the country and a longing to return.

But how? If I couldn't be an archaeologist I would have to try to be a colonial civil servant. Posts in the Palestine civil service were rare, but it seemed possible that one might soon be coming up. Meanwhile, I failed, somewhat to my annoyance (but on good grounds I'm sure), for a second time at All Souls, taught briefly in unemployed units in West Cumberland, and had a very happy time standing in for John Stocks teaching philosophy at Manchester University, almost deciding that Manchester and philosophy were more desirable than Palestine and Arabic—but not quite. So when blessed nepotism worked again—and I was interviewed by my cousin-by-marriage, Ralph Furse (known to history in other connections) and offered a job in the Palestine Secretariat, starting in May, 1934, I was overjoyed at this prospect of return. I even believed, naively, and tried to convince my less naive father, that I could do some good.

The next two years from May 1934, when I returned to Palestine, till June 1936, when I was expelled from Palestine, were a complicated period in the country's history and in mine. They were also the period when I knew George best—and, fortunately, for which his reports in the Rogers file are relatively full. Palestine history I will leave till later. As regards my own, most of the time I was working in the Secretariat in the gloomy building just opposite the Damascus Gate.

But, by an odd historical accident, I also had two short exhausting, fascinating spells as Private Secretary to the High Commissioner, Sir Arthur Wauchope. In 1934, and at the very end of my time, I worked for about two months as Acting Assistant District Commissioner, Haifa. At the level of ideology I was moving, as most of us were at this time, 'forward from liberalism'. But, like Ho Chi Minh (to compare small with great) it was by way of radical rationalism that I came to Marxism—and in this first stage of my political education the objective historical situation and George were my main educators.

During this period I was gradually becoming conscious of the nature of imperialism. Hitherto I had thought of modern Western imperialism as roughly comparable with Roman (as I had been brought up to think of it)—unattractive, oppressive, but possibly in some sense 'civilising' and reformable from within—some sort of use might be made for it. During the eight months which I had spent in England I had been mildly exposed to Marxist ideas, mainly through the influence of a dear friend, Derek Kahn. But essentially I had not got further than Kant with a dash of Hegel. Indeed, on my return to Palestine I rapidly became not a fox-, but a jackal-hunting young man, buying a horse for £30 and riding out through the beautiful orange groves in early dawn with the Ramleh Vale (Master, Chief of Police, Spicer). It took me the next twelve months or so to discover the characteristics of Western imperialism in general, and British imperialism in particular, which others had discovered before me—the destruction of the established peasant economy; the alienation of land to immigrant colons; proletarianisation and the growth of unemployment; the emergence of shanty-towns; the imposition of an oppressive alien bureaucratic apparatus; the stimulation of communal rivalries and conflicts (behind the myth of 'preserving the balance between communities'); striking bargains with the collaborators and imprisoning, exiling or killing the revolutionaries; the intellectual corruption of the colonial ruling class through their absorption of imperialist and racist stereotypes. On such points I don't think George and I differed markedly at this time, though he would not have expressed his views in quite this way. It was when we came to discuss the strategy of liberation that differences arose, once in a crude way (influenced by what little I had begun to read of Palme Dutt, Hook, Strachey, Brailsford and the like) I had begun to accept some kind of Marxist analysis—believing that the anti-colonial revolution must mainly be made by the workers (including of course the valid anti-Zionist elements among the Jewish workers) and peasants in alliance with the petty bourgeoisie.

It was during this period of transition that I first made contact with the Palestine Communist Party. It is difficult to date this at all precisely, though Musa Budeiri's excellent history of the PCP has helped me to reconstruct the chronological framework. It was, I think, through association with Magnes, President of the Hebrew University—and a common concern for hunger-striking Party members imprisoned in Jerusalem gaol—that I was able to visit them, or some of them, though the Prison commandant didn't at all like the idea. I have a very clear memory of this, my first prison visit. Twenty or thirty Party members caged in a small room—Arabs, Muslims and Christians, Jews, Armenians. I was deeply impressed. I don't remember what we talked about—they of course were naturally reluctant to talk to a bourgeois-looking young British colonial officer. But this seemed to me the first firm evidence that this kind of anti-imperialist united front in which I had come to believe was objectively possible. And though I did not actually join the Communist Party till I returned to Britain in September 1936—immediately after the Battle of Cable Street, in fact—this was, so to speak, my Damascus Road. Meanwhile I decided, early in 1936 perhaps, that I had better resign from the Palestine Government. How could I justify living on a salary of £400, plus various allowances, paid for by taxes on fellahin whose income was less than a twentieth of mine and who were deceived and evicted as well as exploited and plundered. But I had many hesitations—both because of friendship with Wauchope and others, strong parental pressures to fulfil my commitments for a few more years, at least, and a doubt in my own mind whether it would not be better and more sensible to stay on and work against the imperialist machine from within. I eventually wrote my letter of resignation on 10 May 1936, giving three months' notice, as was proper. Then, on the 15th. April the storm broke. The Arab rebellion began. The call for the general strike came on April 21st. I was in Haifa at this time, working under Bailey, the Acting District Commissioner. Being politically unreliable I was not sent out to read the riot act with the troops but kept in the office to concoct misleading reports on what was happening. But after a month I found it impossible to go on serving a government that seemed mainly directed to carrying out punitive raids—which it called 'searches'—against people with whose beliefs and aspirations I was entirely in sympathy. So I 'banged the door' telling Bailey I wanted to resign immediately, but also wanted to stay in Palestine indefinitely to watch the progress of the rebellion. For a fortnight I remained typing an article on the rebellion for *Labour Monthly*, my first essay in radical journalism, but then, alas, I was sent for by Bailey and told that I must be across the frontier within 24 hours. Somewhat feebly I did as I was bid—fled to Tyre, Sidon, Beirut and spent the next three months travelling and working in Syria and the Lebanon.

Luckily I have preserved some letters which George wrote to me during the summer of 1936 which are interesting for the light which they throw on the way his mind was working, and on the enormous helpfulness and kindness which characterised his relations with those who turned to him for help:—

(June 16)
I have no comment to make about the article, other than to say that I think it excellent and accurate. If you think that an Egyptian paper is the best medium, then I would advise *Al-Ahram*, because (mainly) of its wide circulation. I should like it to go to an English paper. But which? I think you could answer that question better than I can. Would the *Nation* take it?

I think it essential that it should be sent to a few honest people in political life in England. I am assuming that the species exists, though I am not familiar with it. Would George Lansbury bother to read it, or Philip Baker, or Hugh Dalton—or even the bright C R Atlee. Do you know any Quaker circle who wields political influence?

(June 23)
It is a great pity that you shd have to leave, for there are a few indispensible jobs to be done here which no one I know could do as well as you. A weekly

paper has appeared called 'Palestine and TJ', edited by 'a group of Arabs and their friends' in that earnest and plaintive tone which never fails to make a paper unreadable. How I wish you were here to guide them! This is apart from my own desire to see you.

I hear frequently from Katy, but Tutu has not written yet, although she promises to in every one of her mother's letters. . . .

I did nothing about our friend when I got back: simply ignored him, taking no steps to present my credentials. Last week I was invited at short notice to go and see him. I just went, and returned with my opinions and my feelings unchallenged—but vented.

Ormsby-Gore's statement in the House last Friday has had a disastrous effect—and rightly so. Regarded as a statement designed to deceive opinion in England, it was admirable, but as a contribution to the restoration of peace— . . . The psychological cause underlying the unrest is the loss of faith in British promises. Mr O-G has thought of nothing better, as an antidote to the loss of faith, than another (and a super-British) promise.

(*July 19*)

I feel more than usually depressed, and a bit run down. I like to think that is because I have been working hard and in loneliness, but that is probably not the real reason. The insane situation goes on, with the same destruction and bloodshed. And it goes on because two or three—not more—men lack the courage or the honesty to say what they think.

(*August 23*)

Your plan of a year in Russia does not sound to me at all fantastic; on the contrary, interesting and probably valuable. How much value it would yield in one year, to one who doesn't know Russian, depends entirely on oneself. I hate finding myself in a country whose language I don't at least read. But if I wanted to study a country, ignorance of its language would not deter me. For there are so many other things needed to enable one to understand. Language is only one of them, sympathy another. And I am not at all sure that an open mind is not more important than a fluent tongue.

If you got to Ankara or Istanbul to find out, I could put you in touch with two or three people:

1. Vedat Tör, Director-General of the Press Bureau in Ankara. An intelligent and keen little Turk, something of a poet and of a communist. Served a term of imprisonment once, but I am not certain whether it was on account of his communism or his poetry.

2. Semsettin Arif Mardin, a young Turkish diplomat with a nice intelligent wife. Was in Moscow for three years as attache in the Turkish embassy, and now at the Ministry of Foreign Affairs in Ankara. Is apt to spend the summer in Istanbul.

3. Leon Haykiss, USSR Consul General in Istanbul. A young and intelligent and very nice person. Sympathique and helpful.

I repeat these names just as an example of the range of George's connections.

I want now to try to do three things: first, to give you a few rather random impressions, memories of, thoughts about George and second, to say something about the Palestine ambiance and the people with whom George was involved (so far as I knew them) during the 1930s; finally to say something about his ideas—the way in which he saw the contemporary situation, its historical background and future possibilities.

Here is my first recorded impression (so far as I have been able to observe it) of meeting George and Katy in a letter to my mother dated May (?) 16th. 1933 from Tantur. It is, I'm afraid, jolly rather than accurate:—

> This last week was mildly social—a moonlight picnic by the Dead Sea ... then the evening after a 'small dance' which, as there was a great deal more talk than dancing, I enjoyed, given by rich Syrians called Antonius, a man with rather the manner of a young fellow of All Souls and a mysterious profession of controlling governments—travelling expensively around, interviewing Amirs, Sultans, Grand Rabbis and Secretaries of State—and opening all their eyes. His wife has a social sense—and the exquisitiveness of her small late food almost rivals Aunt Helen's [my godmother Helen Sutherland]—platefuls of truffles and asparagus-tip sandwiches ...

And here is a small extract from my first letter from Katy, written a week later:

> Karm al-Mufti, May 23rd–33   Dear Mr. Hodgkin ...
> I'd love to go to the pictures with you one night—the 1st. house and we will eat sausages at the Vienna or German Cafe. Please let's do this picture and supper show 'en camarade'. I was very sorry the hats frightened you last Thursday—there were very few people and they were mostly Richmonds ...

Here is another impression of George writing more than a year later in a letter to my brother Edward, dated August 15th, 1934, during my Private Secretary period:—

> ... Jerusalem has been enriched for me by the return of Perowne and Antonius. The latter you remember talking passionate politics and not eating at the Maison Basque [a rather grand restaurant in Dover Street where I had my farewell lunch]. He is even more charming here than in England—because in England there are more people rather like him whereas here there are very few—no one that I have ever met that so admirably combines the passion of the Syrian patriot with the lucidity of the Cambridge don in stating his patriotic beliefs ... It would be a jolly good thing for the Arabs if they had some more people equally clear-minded to put their case: as he says, the Arabs do lose from having no Englishmen practically competent to understand their point of view, and no Arab competent to express it ...

Much of the world flowed through Jerusalem at this time. I seem to have taken those visitors whom I particularly approved of to lunch with George and Katy (they never seemed to complain of this exploitation of their hospitality). When Tom Boase turned up in July 1933 (and he, John Richmond and I later did a wonderful Syrian expedition together) I say—after trying to show them round—'I am very bad at the antiquities of Jerusalem. However I made up for my ignorance by taking him to lunch with the Antoniuses'.

On (I think) the 6th. September 1934 Isaiah Berlin turned up.

Writing on September 10th. I say:—

> I like having Isaiah here—he came three or four days ago—I have been trying to find good company for him—but they are mostly Jews that I find. Arabs (apart from George Antonius who had lunch with him yesterday) would either be too rude at him or too stupid for him. He speaks Zionist opinions (without quite calling himself a Zionist) and I try to answer with British official opinions (without in the least calling myself a British Official), and as we neither of us claim to be expressing our own sentiments it is very amiable and pleasant. . . .

One characteristic of George's of which one was immediately conscious was his wit. It was a very pleasant, gay, but at the same time critical, mocking kind of wit. Since his later relations with the Palestine Director of Education, Humphrey Bowman, with whom he worked as Assistant Director from 1921 to 1927, were troubled it is nice to find Bowman quoting in his diary for the 24th. September 1922 this lighthearted Baedeker-like guide to the journey by car from Haifa to Beirut which George had composed for him:—

> Leaving Haifa at say 1 p.m. by way of the sea-shore the traveller passes Acre at about 1.40 and then proceeds along what is perhaps the worst road he has ever driven on, past the remains of the old aqueduct, past the village of ez Zib and on to Ras al Nakura (2.30)—a kind of Beachy Head, which commands a good view of Acre and the coast-line. There he will have to exhibit his passport. The road now enters French territory and almost immediately begins to improve until, five minutes later, the traveller will find his temper returning and his equanimity restoring. But not for long, for presently he has to stop again and exhibit himself and his passport to a not unpleasant French sergeant. The traveller would be well advised to take off his hat as he enters the room, and to address the bureaucrat as 'Monsieur'; nor should he miss the opportunity of examining the ornaments on the walls of the room by sidelong glances over the bureaucrat's shoulder, for on the walls of that room he will find a characteristic collection of things that have made France what she is: great but rather common . . .
>
> He will now proceed along a comparatively first-class surface, and his speed will probably rise to 50 miles an hour, but not so fast that his discovering eye would fail to see a hillock to the right, the elegant columns of a pretty Roman temple. Proceeding (3.15 p.m.) along a road which now skirts the sea and now turns inland from it, he passes Tyre at a point almost a mile away from its

> outskirts. But a little before he does so, he may or may not be held up at a little quarantine station—a small hut with a dirty yellow flag and a yellow rather dirty little doctor with a marked tendency to familiarity. From Sidon to Beirut the scenery becomes a little more interesting. The traveller will, among other things, pass (but alas! not see) Djoun, the residence of Lady Hester Stanhope. . . . Soon he enters Beirut, a town of dirty squalid streets, bereft of all charm, and ends up on the Burg, outside Nairn office, at 6 p.m.

It was typical of George to write such an essay when asked for advice about a journey. One finds him constantly carrying out works of supererogation, well beyond the limits of ordinary kindness, in this way. When Bowman's first wife dies very suddenly in Jerusalem while he is on leave in England he goes out of his way to attend a memorial service for her in London. He is constantly seeing people or arranging for people to be seen across Alexandria—or Egypt—using his family network for the purpose.

George had, of course, a remarkable range of friendships. One was conscious of that at the time. So many interesting people one met at or through Karm el-Mufti. What Bernard Wasserstein calls Katy's 'Salon'. Katy's more Jerusalem (and Cairo) -centred universe was distinct from, though overlapping with, George's more cosmopolitan, pan-Arab, world. I particularly remember Vincent Shean, author of *In search of History* (who had visited and written about Abd el-Krim, President of the Republic of the Rif), Robin Furness, Oriental Secretary in Egypt, later Press Officer in Palestine (with whose niece, Diana, I fell in love, and was scolded by Katy for my inconsiderate behaviour), Abdul Rahman Kayyali, who was my kind doctor and friend in Aleppo in the summer of 1936, of whom I then wrote:

> His travels, with Clayton and elsewhere, during the 1920s had already helped George to develop his wide international network of friendships and relationships. During the 1930s his work with the Crane Foundation led to their further expansion, especially within the Arab world. A fascinating diversity of people appear in the pages of his reports and letters to William Rogers over the years—Seyyid Ziauddin Tabatabai, the former Prime Minister of Iran and secretary of the standing executive committee of the 1931 Jerusalem Islamic congress (which promised much but achieved little), Ismail Sidqi Pasha, the Egyptian Prime Minister, Nuri Pasha of Iraq; Jamil Mardam and the right wing of the Syrian National Bloc; Saadallah Jabri, Dr Abdul Rahman Kayyali and Ibrahim Hanano of the mainly Aleppo-based left wing; King Feisal, with whom George had several long conversations in Baghdad in 1933, his elder brother Ali and his younger brother Zaid, as well as, of course, Abdullah of TJ; Shakib Arslan; Gibb, Massignon, Mallion, Snouck Hurgronje, Denison Ross, Père Anastase 'the greatest of living Arabic lexicographers', Louis Fischer, Walter Lippmann, and so on.

One very important quality of George's of which I was not adequately aware in the 1930s—indeed have really only begun to understand reading through his reports during these past weeks—was his genius for mediation. One has the impression that George was always mediating beween somebody and somebody, and not infrequently involved in several tasks of mediation at the same time. As he from time to time remarks, he was constantly being sought out as a mediator. He did not himself seek the role, for which he was admirably equipped by his essentially rational way of looking at the world and belief in the rational solution of problems, the lucidity of his reasoning, his Henry Jamesish sensitivity to the undertones and overtones of a complex situation, his imaginative power of grasping, and identifying himself with, conflicting points of view, the wit and lightness of touch of which I have already spoken.

How and when did George first become involved in mediation? This is a question which it ought to be easy to answer. He was certainly already a very skilful practitioner by 1925 when Gilbert Clayton persuaded Bowman and the Palestine Education Department to release him for the Ibn Saud Mission. Thereafter he was to become more and more involved in mediating operations, as his reports to Rogers of the Institute of Current World Affairs, where he was Senior Associate, show. In his 1932 reports he mentions being asked, while in London the previous November, 'by a group of public men who take a special interest in the Near East, and who were considering the ways and means of initiating negotiations of wide international scope, with a view to securing better prospects of peace in these disturbed countries' if he would be prepared to act as an 'unofficial negotiator'. Nothing seems to have come of this group, one of many such well-intentioned bodies of which, over the years, most of us, I am sure, have had experience. He was also being asked by Magnes, President of the Hebrew University, and some of his friends to cooperate with them in their attempts to secure a basis for understanding between Arabs and Jews.

Of more practical value at this time was his intervention in the affairs of the Supreme Moslem Council. He explains that he had been 'invited by a Moslem notable to use my good offices in the matter of a crisis which had arisen in the ranks of the Supreme Moslem Council and had split the Council into two parties. Having satisfied myself that both factions did in fact desire my mediation', he goes on, 'I set to work, and for nearly a fortnight devoted several hours a day to the task of finding a way out of the deadlock. My efforts were sufficiently successful to enable the contending factions to get to work together again, and this unity has been maintained to the present day.'

A longer and more complicated involvement was in the affairs of the Orthodox patriarchate. The quarrel here was over the election of a new Patriarch of Jerusalem. Hitherto the Patriarch and their synods (the members of which they appointed) had been Greeks, whereas the great majority of their clergy and flock were Arabs. George was called on to use his good offices partly, of course, because he was himself a member of the Orthodox community. (It is interesting, by the way, to know that in spite of Katy's objections he had insisted on a religious wedding in an Orthodox church in Paris as well as a civil ceremony. When Katy asked him why, he said he wanted to be 'properly married'. Katy argued that there was a lot to be said for being improperly married because it made the matrimonial knot easier to untie.) But as well as being a distinguished member of the community George was also on good personal terms with members of the Synod (which was split between two rival candidates), with Patriarch Meletios in Alexandria, and with the Orthodox community in the Levant. And he was friendly with officials in the government, especially the District Commissioner for Jerusalem, who would be involved in the affair.

George regretted the decision of the lay community to take the matter to the courts, though he could understand it. As always, he was able to see both sides of the question. As an Arab nationalist he sympathised with the lay community; as a reasonable man, experienced in the give and take of politics and government, he realised that the sentiment of nationalism was not always enough. 'I have tried to impress upon my friends on the Executive Committee of the community,' he wrote, 'that good order, discipline, and financial soundness are as important assets, to say the least, as Mixed Councils, Arab bishops, and so forth.' As he said, the issues were so involved, and feelings were running so high, that even getting the issues down 'to wieldy proportions' was going to 'require the exercise of a great deal of time, labour and patience'. Labour and patience were qualities George could always command; time, on the other hand, there was never enough of.

I have to emphasise that these were all examples of people asking George to do something, not of his initiating anything. He was the exact opposite of a busybody. The sort of thing which he did take the initiative in were big intellectual enterprises like the Arabic lexicon or an Institute of Arabic Studies. It was only occasionally, when a particularly glaring political gap presented itself, that he was moved to intervene. For example, when, on a visit to Syrian and Lebanon at the end of March 1932, he found that M. Chauvel, Chief of the Political Cabinet of the French High Commissioner, had never met Riad Solh, 'by far the most influential nationalist figure in Beirut'—an omission which he rightly considered astonishing—he offered to introduce them to each other; an offer which they were both happy to accept. It was on this same journey, incidentally, that he was asked by Christopher Lumby, staff correspondent of *The Times* in the Middle East, to recommend a stringer for Beirut—a good example of the small, but not unimportant, personal service that George was always being called upon to provide.

Thereafter he remained very much involved in Syrian and Lebanese politics—not directly as a negotiator, perhaps, though the fact that he was the confidant of Arabs of every political colour as well as of the French must have meant that he was much more than a listener. His main contacts at this time were with the so-called Moderates, led by Subhi Barakat, and with the Nationalist group whose 'leadership is in the hands of three of the most powerful personalities in Syria, Saadallah Jabri, Dr Abdul Rahman Kayyali, and Ibrahim Hanano'.

This is not the place to discuss George's role in the 1939 round-table conference on Palestine. That would involve me in a consideration of his attitude towards the whole Palestine problem, and as I said at the beginning that is too big a subject for me to embark on in this lecture. But as we have been looking at George as a negotiator and conciliator some mention must be made of this occasion, which was in a sense the culmination of his achievements in this role.

Nobody at that conference had a more arduous task. On arrival in London on January 27, as a member of the delegation of Palestine Arabs and secretary of that delegation, he learned that the British government were hoping he would agree to act in addition as secretary-general of the united delegation of the six Arab countries represented at the conference. This, as he said with a good deal of understatement, involved him in 'the important and somewhat onerous duties' of coordinating the work of the six delegations, 'acting as a channel between them and the UK delegation, organising the keeping of their records and eventually the custody of their archives, with all that would mean of translation to and from one language to the other'. Pressure on George to accept this additional task came not only from the British government but also from many of the leading Arab delegates, notably Nuri Pasha, and he found himself, as he described it, 'sliding into the secretarial functions by the sheer pressure of the work to be done'. He was unanimously adopted as their secretary-general by all six delegations.

That was not to be the end. Two more appointments were to come his way as the conference progressed. One was to serve on the Anglo-Arab committee set up by the conference to examine Britain's wartime pledges to the Arabs. There were four other Arabs, and three British led by the Lord Chancellor, on the committee, but George was undoubtedly the most important person on it, as it was thanks to the recent publication of *The Arab Awakening*, and the texts of the McMahon–Hussein correspondence which were there printed for the first time, that the committee was set up. As Albert Hourani said in the second of these lectures: 'It was largely because of his advocacy that the British members of the committee admitted that there was more force to the Arab contentions than had appeared hitherto, an expression which came as near as any great government does to agreeing that it had been mistaken.'

The other appointment was to what was called the Committee on Policy—a smaller group set up in an effort to speed up the work of the conference when, not surprisingly with nine British and thirty Arabs, delegates were found to be too thick on the ground and too much time was spent in translating. The Policy Committee consisted of three from the British side and one each from the six Arab delegations, plus George.

As he wrote to Rogers after the conference was over: 'As you can imagine, these various functions gave me more to do than I could possibly cope with alongside of the day-to-day business of running the central office. In addition to the sessions of the plenary conference and of the Committee on Policy, there were frequent meetings of the united Arab delegations, for which I had to prepare the agenda, keep the records of the proceedings, and give effect to the decisions. A good deal of my secretarial duties,' he concludes, 'that is to say, those which could be without loss postponed, remained neglected. . . . ' On top of it all he was ill for much of the time. He caught a chill and was laid up in bed, though his doctor generously allowed him, as he told Rogers, 'to get up to attend meetings of the conference'.

A footnote to the conference proceedings. Katy turned up in London as a member of a delegation of Palestinian women, and proposed to stay in the same hotel as the rest of the women delegates. George would have none of that, but carried her off to the flat he was staying in.

II

Now something about the people with whom George was involved in the 1930s. First, Arthur Wauchope. He was very unlike my idea of a general. I know too little of his particular Scots liberal background, except that his family used to live in my cousin Mary Cowan's house near Dalkeith, Newton House, until, so she tells me, they moved to somewhere bigger and better. Music he loved especially, which was a bond with the cultural life of the Yishuv, of course—Helen Bentwich and the performers who could come and play quartets and quintets at Government House. Painting and sculpture too, which was a link with Eric Gill, in Jerusalem to carve the capitals for the pillars in the courtyard of the Rockefeller Museum—and with Helen Sutherland, whom he very nicely invited to stay with us when I was acting Private Secretary and she was on her way to Kenya. And poetry—a bond with me. Admiration for Islamic architecture and decoration gave him a certain access to Arab civilization too.

Essentially Wauchope was a tremendous romantic, in the sense that he expected reality to conform with his idea of reality. Applied to the Palestine problem which, when I knew him, was his personal preoccupation as well as his job, this meant a touching but quite serious belief that it could be solved by the establishment of good personal relations between himself and the

Mufti (representing the forces of Arab nationalism) on the one hand, and Ben-Gurion, representing the forces of Zionism or the Yishuv, on the other.

Like other mild dictators I have known—Kwame Nkrumah and Lord Lindsay of Birker—Arthur Wauchope was a good deal influenced in his political judgements by his likings. He liked Ben-Gurion; he liked Shemarya Levin even more. He didn't like Shertock (Sharett) much—a somewhat pert little man—whereas Ben-Gurion seemed to smell of the old Narodniks and Dostoievsky. (He wasn't devoted to Weizmann either, but he was a bit rare, whereas with Ben-Gurion and Shertock of the Jewish Agency he was in constant contact.)

And he liked the Mufti—I'm not sure why. To me the Mufti seemed a slightly sinister character, so cat-like in his appearance and movements. As the Mufti didn't talk English Wauchope had to communicate with him through interpreters—who?—Ihsan Hashim, his Arab private secretary, sometimes, I suppose. But I suppose this is where George came in a great deal too.

It is clear from George's reports to Rogers that he was excited by Wauchope's appointment and attached much importance to their conversations. Their first meeting was on January 19 1932, when George was invited to dinner at Government House 'and we sat up till midnight talking of affairs of Palestine and neighbouring countries'. This was the first of many such meetings—there were seven in the first four months of 1932, which consolidated what George called 'an association of increasing scope and cordiality'.

George says he kept a record of their talks, though it should be said that he didn't reveal their substance to the Institute or, as far as I know, to anyone else. He had very strict notions about the impropriety of revealing confidences. He gave me good advice after I too had left government service and was trying to write something about the Palestine situation: 'I think the only thing that matters is that one should not make use of information revealed *solely* in one's official capacity,' he wrote. Presumably Wauchope kept a record too. It shouldn't be difficult to recover these, though unfortunately I haven't yet.

It would be interesting to know as much as possible what they said to one another. From George's references it seems that it was partly to do with the historical background to the Palestine problem—Hussein, McMahon, Sykes–Picot, King–Crane and all that—but partly also to do with contemporary politics—for example, the Legislative Council proposal, and how far the British were prepared to go in the direction of self-government.

Given George's belief in mediation and the possibility of rational solutions, and Wauchope's charm and natural affection for a fellow civilized being (King's and the Scots enlightenment) it is not surprising that they should have got on well together. All the more distressing for George—for both, no doubt—when their relationship broke down, after the outbreak of the Arab rebellion in 1936, and George felt that by his policy of repression Wauchope had betrayed their common assumption—the justice of the Arab claim to independence. On August 23 he wrote to me: 'I am shocked at the last turn events are taking here. We seem to be drifting towards real civil war. Billig's murder [Billig was a nice lecturer at the Hebrew University] was a tragic example of the insanity prevailing in this country: the most harmless, likeable person one could wish in this land of hatred. Meanwhile the Govt's faith in prestige continues, as far as I can see, unabated.'

Two statements about Wauchope in that useful thesis on the Palestine mandate during the Wauchope period by G. Sheffer are, I think, incorrect. One is that he didn't take the Legislative Council plans seriously and wanted an excuse to suspend the whole operation. My remembrance is rather the reverse—that he exaggerated the importance of his very jejune proposals. I remember a weekend when we were working on Legislative Council arithmetic of a familiar kind—so many Arab Muslims, so many Arab Christians, Jews, Europeans, elected members, nominated members—all that number-juggling that is an essential part of colonial Legislative Council making. My remembrance is that the power of this Legislative Council would have been so restricted in respect of everything that really mattered—immigration, land sales, police, and internal security—that they would have had little to offer even the most right-wing Arab nationalist. But I'm sure Wauchope took them seriously.

Likewise the mounting oppression of Jews in Germany from 1933 on was certainly a factor—though not of course the only factor—pushing Wauchope into his very expansionist policy in relation to Jewish immigration—which became by 1936 such an explosive factor.

Of course Wauchope had a temper, and could be oppressive—oppressing particularly those who looked as though they expected to be oppressed, like Pudsey, the Director of the Public Works Dept. Poor Pudsey—with a name suggesting that he went in last for Yorkshire second eleven. H.E. would write sharp minutes in the file: 'Pudsey should have the new Post Office/Barclays Bank/The Haifa marshalling yards, ready the day after tomorrow, as promised in his letter to Sir John Chancellor of 2.4.29. If not, he will explain reasons for delay.' Poor Pudsey.

Poor Dawe (Director of Agriculture), another of the oppressed. Saddest for me were H.E.'s continuingly bad relations with Austen Harrison, a dear friend, the causes of which were never wholly clear to me. But the face of each darkened when one talked of the other. It was all to do, in origins, with Government House, which Austen built and H.E. lived in and thought had defects which Austen ought to have remedied. Austen was naturally a sensitive artist who didn't like criticisms which he thought irrelevant or improper. I don't know that this conflict was ever reconciled.

Those best at handling his demands, pressures, grumbles, directives, were those who had a way with them, who gave the appearance of producing desirable results, whatever they were actually up to. Like Andrews, Development Officer, assassinated in 1937, and Keith Roach, Northern District Commissioner—both histrionic characters in their different ways—spellbinders.

The morning parade
The royal barouche (H.E.'s Rolls) arrives, flying its Union Jack, H.E., ADC, and I inside. I have the red box with files H.E. has read—or hasn't—lots of little bits of paper with his thoughts on various subjects. 'Now, Thomas, what's my programme for this morning?' I rummage. H.E. smiles benevolently. Here it is, thank God: '11 a.m. Dawe. 11.30 Men of the Trees, Pirie-Gordon. 12 Husain Khalidi, mayor of Jerusalem, acting DC in attendance.' 'Now, Thomas, just find my notes about the Jaffa Gate—what is Johns up to there?' Oh dear! I saw them such a little time ago. And what are all these bits of typescript? Top secret reports from Domvile, and secret service, go to no one but me. 'You'll be losing them in a moment—don't worry.' H.E. is in a gay and chaffing mood.

Out we get. The sentries at the Secretariat present arms. H.E. smiles at them—stops for chats on the way up the stairs and down the passage. First he must have Hall with him. I get the lady to bring her boss while I rummage in the red box so as to meet the next three demands for bits of vital paper.

And so the day begins. 'What's the little man like today?' 'Rather chirpy, I'm glad to say.' It ends, with luck, with pleasant talk of love, life, poetry, music, after snoozing through a dinner party for 30. The ADC is mildly bored, but the loyalties of the Seaforth Highlanders keep him going till bedtime, and H.E. doesn't like to stay up after 11 p.m. as a rule.

No denying it gives one a sense of power, this Private Secretary business, driving in the Rolls with a red crown on blue ground instead of the Union Jack—though unlike Christopher Eastwood I never go so far as to have blue facings on my dinner-jacket, as a Private Secretary should.

Before moving on from Wauchope I would like to quote from one or two of the letters which he sent me in the summer of 1936, when I was in the process of leaving government service and, as it turned out, Palestine. It was not an easy time for either of us,—that he should have written as he did shows better than anything else what a nice man he was.

May 25,
My dear Thomas,
I gather from Nurock that you are now anxious to resign and leave the service without delay.

In your earlier letter you said you were willing to leave it to Govt to decide when your resignation should take effect, and I had hoped you would continue your duties till your successor arrived.

I gather now you feel you cannot serve Govt usefully any longer. You will appreciate the fact that by leaving Govt when Administrative work is greatly increased by the first duty of all Government in all capitalistic states, namely the maintenance of good order, you embarrass Govt and throw extra work on your colleagues.

However, if you tell the C.S. that you feel you can no longer perform your duties here with any real advantage to Govt, I shall accept the fact and your resignation.

I agree with you that differences in political opinion need not interfere with friendship, and I hope very much you and I will meet again when we are both living in happier conditions than either of us are at present.

There is of necessity much sadness for you and for me: but that is unimportant compared to the general affliction throughout the country today; and that again is less important than the suffering and bitterness that I fear will come tomorrow. I feel I have more chance of lessening this by serving within Government, you feel the opposite. That difference though acute need not end friendship or regard.

I write in haste, but I wanted you to understand my position just as you have made clear to me your position.

> Yours very sincerely,
> Arthur Wauchope

Four days later:

In this wicked world it is difficult to live outside the capitalist system.

I do not know whether you feel drawn to the Society of Friends—as you know, they have decided to work within the C. system.

For the last 6 years I have been interested in their work of assisting people to go back to the land.

The only 2 schemes I know worked on a non-capitalist basis are certain Jew settlements here,—the 2 young ones mentioned on p 4 of enclosed pamphlet. . . .

Finally:

I look back on the months you worked with me here with nothing but pleasure and memory of happy hours. Bless you my dear Thomas—a French woman once said of me Arthur, coeur de chrystal. I do no deserve that. I believe you do.

It is not surprising that a person who could write letters like those should have believed that political problems could be solved through personal relationships.

J. Harthorn Hall, Chief Secretary during most of my time there, was no histrionic spellbinder. But he is well known to history—a somewhat boring character I thought, with a wife described as 'easy on the eye', H.E. needed

Hall, as every prophet needs an efficient bureaucrat to interpret his utterances—a Pompidou to his De Gaulle.

The rest of the Secretariat were a mixed lot. Moody, Assistant Chief Secretary (Acting C.S. from time to time), a poor fish. I had an embarrassing interview with him when he sent for me having found an anti-imperialist poem I had written lying around. It was, I had to agree, very rude about the British bourgeoisie. But why did I always have to leave this evidence of my rejection of the values of my class and order lying so conspicuously around?

Another corner of this later period of my Secretariat life (roughly coinciding with my return from our great Bethlehem to Sinai expedition in December 1935 and January 1936 with Edward and Prudence Pelham) was my effort to organize the Secretariat clerks, messengers etc in a study group which should also be a trade union and an expression (of a modest kind) of Arab–Jewish–Greek–Armenian etc unity against British imperialism. Derek Kahn (or someone) sent me Klingdor's *Clerical Labour in Britain* as a guide to this kind of political work—a very useful book. Later—in and after the war—I came to know Klingdor as a wonderful lecturer and writer on art history, in North Staffs, Burlesdon and elsewhere, and I told him how much I owed to this other early work of his.

Others—Max Nurock, a brilliant historian from Trinity College Dublin, with whom I had a very happy relationship—a kind of Zionist opposite number to George. He taught me much about administration—how to keep a tidy desk, make the files move around. He had a contempt for most of his colleagues. According (I think) to Wasserstein, everything that happened in the Secretariat was known the same night to the Jewish Agency through Max. Well, naturally he didn't tell me about that aspect of his activities, and I suppose I never realised how in the case of someone like Max the commitment to Israel-in-the-making went vastly much deeper than any commitment to the British colonial service and the mandate.

As for the actual opposite number of Max Nurock, Ruhi Bey Abdul Hadi, he was everything one would expect an old-fashioned Ottoman official to be—polished, gentle, restrained in the expression of his opinions, evasive, with strong moral principles when moved—despised by Max for idleness, he certainly didn't want a heavy workload. He was valuable to H.E. because he knew most of the personalities in the Arab/Islamic world, not in the context of nationalist politics as George knew them, but in the context of family ties, old friendships, connections within the old order of Ottoman society. It was a comfort to have him about during my last very unhappy month in Haifa after the outbreak of the Arab rebellion. Why he was there I can't remember—but we went about together a good deal. He shared my misery over the brutality of the repression and knew more than I did about what was actually going on.

D. C. Thompson, with whom I shared an office to start with—a sweet character—'Balliolensis Balliolense' he said, when he gave me a beautiful edition of Catullus, Tibullus, Propertius—regretted somewhat by the colonial ruling class since he (like nice James Cullen) had married a native—not a Palestinian native, true, but a Cypriot native, and are they not also a troublesome and treacherous coloured people? Thompson was not terribly hard-working and didn't mean to be—in fact I see I described him as 'a diehard, talks a lot, hates work, smokes a cigar every day after lunch, a thorough bureaucrat'—a rather unhappy character, who made this noble end when the King David Hotel was blown up, as all will remember.

And Shaw—a nice smiling chap. His was the office dealing with Transjordanian affairs, which I was in too for a time, and which had the big map of Palestine and Transjordan hanging on the wall with, in the middle of TJ, the splendid legend 'This part of the map is ten miles too far to the east'. Shaw was the person Wauchope always turned to for advice on TJ's problems (he was High Commissioner for TJ too of course). He had all those exciting *orange* files (TJ confidential and secret; Palestine ones were yellow) about the delinquencies and problems of Abdullah and offspring, Tallal, Naif.

Here it is tempting to quote from a letter written by me in July 1934 from Government House describing a visit by Abdullah and family:

> I write from among princes. Abdullah has just arrived and has been excitedly describing to H.E. his adventures, how he saw over the Humber factory, how he went to the House of Commons and sat in the Distinguished Strangers gallery and got a wave from Sir Herbert Samuel, how he went to the aeroplane display at Hendon and watched men coming down from aeroplanes in parachutes and had to hide his eyes till the parachutes opened; how he went to Edinburgh and was met by the Lord Provost, & to Peebles & stayed at the best hotel: he told all this like a boy of 14 just back from Wembley, trying all the time to think what was the next most exciting thing that he had seen: he had a beautiful childish power of description—especially when he began to imitate the aeroplanes & the fizz of the bombs they dropped hitting the ground: he had brought presents for H.E. in the proper oriental way—photographs of himself in striking attitude, cigars, tuffets, and (his best present) an iced cake in the shape of a mosque from McVities—to remind H.E. of the Dome of the Rock whenever he ate it I suppose—but unfortunately the dome had been smashed completely on the way, and the walls of the Rotunda were badly caved in on the east side. Abdullah travelled with Fuad Pasha, his (I suppose) adviser, an agitated man who was meant to do the interpeting but always just forgot the English word which he wanted at the critical moment . . . He also had a Chamberlain (he had left Palestine as a personal servant but came back a Chamberlain I suppose because Abdullah decided when he was in England that his suite would look better with the addition of a Chamberlain) . . . The little Amirs had come to meet him here

the night before and were rather bores—great bores in fact—they wore swords and spurs and one heard them rattling at the far end of the passage, like Punch ghosts, before they came into the room. The larger one had been to Sandhurst so had at least the merit of talking English and was moderately friendly: the smaller could only snigger (in Arabic) behind his hand. They played hide and seek with their father along the passages till midnight—or that was the sound they made at anyrate—and were up at half past four in the morning to have the Koran read aloud to them by Dad. All this is fun but it uses up time and wears H.E.'s temper.

George's circle

Humphrey Bowman needs to be mentioned here because of having been so much part of George's circle in the early 1920s, till the great Farrell row, about which much has been written, and no doubt Bowman had a bad conscience. ('I wrote to congratulate George on his CBE,' says Bowman pathetically, 'but he sent me only a formal acknowledgement'.) The story is a sad one, reflected in the Bowman diaries. He was a kindly, snobbish, bumbling, Polonius-like Old Etonian, who had directed education in Iraq and the Sudan before he came to Palestine. He was always kind to me and I was always getting into trouble with him, and Nora, his second wife, was a very helpful, sympathetic person. He had good stories about the past— Ronald Storrs as Governor of Jerusalem, going round the Old City, talking Armenian to the Armenians, dining out and admiring his host's carpet, ordering it to be rolled up and taken back home—apocryphal, one imagines. He liked intelligent Palestinians, like Fawzi Ghusseini and Anwar Nuseibeh— very paternalist, not to say colonialist, in his attitude, as most of his generation of course were. But I was fond of him in my earlier period, when we went some good walks together, down the wadis to the Dead Sea. But the breach with George remained, understandably, irreparable, I'm afraid.

Two of the older generation who were close to George were Sir Michael McDonnell, the Chief Justice, and Ernest Richmond, Director of Antiquities—two devoutly Catholic families, sharing many of George's criticisms of British policy, though from a different political standpoint. McDonnell was eventually forced to resign because of judgements which failed to conform to the Melian definition (justice equals the interest of the stronger) and so embarrassed the military regime. His wife was a dear friend of Katy's, a sweet and rather beautiful woman, reminding me somewhat of Conty Sitwell.

Ernest Richmond I loved, partly for his own sake, partly for John's. A good relationship was early established when he came to visit us at Jericho, and I was living in that little house beside the ʿAin. We shared a bottle—or two—of good burgundy for lunch, cooked by my very dark hued cook, and I reeled back to the tell at about 3 p.m., terribly late for the afternoon stint and capable only of sleep in the hot sun. Of course, one of George's early works was a Guide to the Haram, and this would have been a special link with Ernest, who knew more about the Haram and the Dome of the Rock than anyone. He and John taught me much about those great works, and so did Cresswell, when I got onto him.

Our relationship no doubt was easier because I thought of myself as something of a Catholic at this period, influenced by Hopkins and Martin D'Arcy, whose lectures on Thomas Aquinas I attended in my last year (he read The Leaden Echo and the Golden Echo beautifully). Influenced too by Maritain and neo-thomism, and Eliot's literary criticism, which I found fascinating (never loving him much as a poet), thinking the Benedictine mass at the Dormition a marvellous show, reading my missal. And of course, involved in long and constant discussions with Eric Gill (with David Jones one didn't discuss that sort of thing much). And John Richmond and I (as he says) naturally influenced one another when we were living together, at Ain Karim especially.

Stewart Perowne. How can I talk of dear Stewart? After George and John Richmond my dearest friend in Jerusalem—when he was there. With what I called too Oscar Wildean love of witty epigram, to which there was no possible reply—'Verdi's Othello—so much better than Shakespeare's'. He would have liked to be Hereditary Prince Bishop of Worcester, but, alas, such things are more difficult to fix nowadays; so, like many of us, did something quite different.

Let me add one or two remarks as a framework for these memories of Palestine in the years 1933–6—the political climate within which George and I lived our different interesting lives.

I have just reread my 1937 *Labour Monthly* pamphlet, *Who is Prosperous in Palestine?*, for the first time for 40-odd years and must immodestly admit that I am surprised how good and perceptive it is—for one who had only come to Marxism 12 months earlier. It reads particularly well on land sales, evictions and proletarianisation of the Arab peasantry, I thought. But as a general explanation of the historical roots of the Great Arab Rebellion, and the three demands around which the struggle was organised—
1) The stoppage of Jewish immigration
2) Legislation to prevent the further sale of Arab land to Jews
3) The establishment of an independent democratic government
—it seeems to me not at all bad.

And my argument that British imperialism needed the Arab–Jewish conflict as a justification for preserving—or trying to preserve—its domination over Palestine for strategic and military purposes has been nicely borne out by Shaffer's work on the PRO material. It owed much to many discussions with George, or course, particularly on the historical side, Lawrence and all that. Immodestly again I was pleased to find that it was written in a good hard-hitting pamphleteering style—that is our inheritance from the Levellers. Hugh Foot, then ADC Nablus (whom Wauchope regarded, rightly, as Palestine's only intelligent administrative officer) liked it, I remember—'You must meet my radical little brother, Michael. He shares many of your ideas,' he said. So I did. It seems to fit too with the two Palestinian books that I have recently read that have impressed me most: David Hirst's *The Gun and the Olive Branch* and Musa Budeiri's *The Palestine Communist Party, 1919–1948*.

But on two fundamental points I was sadly in error.

I greatly exaggerated the possibilities of Jewish workers and agricultural colonists—some at least of them—liberating themselves from Zionist ideology and identifying themselves with the struggle against British imperialism. To be honest this was partly because Palme Dutt, editor of *Labour Monthly*, who commissioned the pamphlet, was leaning on me somewhat heavily, I seem to remember, to produce something that would be true, but the kind of truth that could give as much encouragement as possible to the anti-Zionist comrades in London, Manchester and elsewhere. So, if read carefully, you will see that, like the book of Isaiah, there are really two hands at work, one more optimistic, one more grounded in the evidence. (However one finds in Musa Budeiri that these hopes were shared at this time also by the leadership of the PCP.)

The other major error was not to anticipate Israel or rather to regard a Jewish state as a Jabotinskian revisionist plan, seeing Ben-Gurion and the Histadruth leadership as essentially the instruments of British imperialism, not its ousters and inheritors. I never grasped that the British, by crushing the Great Arab Rebellion, cleared the decks for the establishment of a new and far more efficient imperialism. David Hirst sums it up well—

> But the real striking force, the real instrument of 'gun Zionism', was in the hands of David Ben-Gurion, the rugged pioneer. And the seeds of the real, essentially Jabotinskian triumph—the swift, sharp transition to Jewish statehood in a land without Arabs—had already been sown in the British defeat of the Great Rebellion.

Did George grasp this vital point before he died? I would love to know.

III

In his essay on Religion and Politics in *The Chatham House Version* Professor Kedourie claims that Antonius 'shared the belief that Islam and the Muslims ought to have the primacy in Arab nationalism'. He quotes from a letter of George to Mohammed Rashid Rida in which George says that Abdul Rahman el-Kawakabi was working towards two fundamental and related aims, 'the revival of Arab nationality through the revival of Islam, without which the Arabs can have no life'.

Kedourie implies that remarks like this indicate a rather pathetic betrayal of loyalties: In the past 'loyalty did not extend beyond the community (of Orthodox Christians). . . . But now religion suddenly seemed a badge of servitude. Membership of the Arab nation had a price—which Muslims, being the majority and the rulers did not have to pay. It meant the abandonment of communal organisation and the defiant assertion that religion was a strictly private affair'.

Were George and all the others who felt like him trying to jump on a political bandwagon, to abandon their friends and ingratiate themselves with their masters? Was he perhaps, as some, like Christopher Sykes, have implied, hypnotised by the Mufti? Or even—a more sinister interpretation—influenced by what Kedourie calls 'the fashionable anti-semitism' of his 'patron Charles Crane'?

To anyone who knew George these speculations must be ridiculous. For him to say that Islam was a life-giving element in a revived sense of Arab nationality was as much of a truism as to say that the Arabic language was another vital element in Arab civilization. And the Arabic language and Islam are of course inseparably entwined.

George was profoundly convinced that, as he put it in his annual report to the Institute for 1935, 'the extent of the Arab contribution to human progress is still imperfectly understood'—that the two main periods of contact between the Arabs and Europe, in the early centuries of Islam when the influence was mainly from east to west, and in recent times when the influence was in the other direction, both needed much more study. He believed that language was the chief barrier to understanding: 'If I were asked to name the most important of those reasons [why scholars and scientists were unaware that 'the most original and valuable productions of the Middle Ages were those which were expressed in Arabic'] I should unhesitatingly point to the widespread neglect, among the historians of science and general culture, of the study of Arabic.'

Hence his enthusiasm for the idea of a technological lexicon of Arabic terms, to which he devoted a great deal of his time, and for his concept of an Institute of Arabic Studies which would coordinate the efforts 'of a band of scholars and scientists who, in addition to a mastery of their particular branch of learning, will have acquired proficiency in the Arabic language'.

The notion that George was ever a narrow propagandist on behalf of the Arabs in general, or the Palestine Arabs in particular, or even of one particular section of the Palestine Arabs, is commonly held but completely wrong. His vision was much wider than that of most of his critics. He was, as has been seen, a negotiator, a reconciler, and not just because he was good at negotiating and reconciling but because his background and instincts lifted him above parochial disputes and made him aware of much bigger and more important areas of human prejudice and ignorance.

George saw the awakening in the Arab world as leading to inevitable—and probably irresistible—demands for closer unity between regions which had, in many cases, been artificially created and artificially kept apart by foreign imperial interests. This was one theme of his book. Not that he was ever an easy optimist about the chances of political cohesion among the Arabs; optimism was perhaps even harder in the 1930s than in the 1980s. Diversity as well as unity were the twin guides to his ecumenical approach, as they must be for any sensible man.

In a letter sent to Rogers soon after he started working for the Institute he wrote: 'I make a point of holding periodic interviews with leaders and public men in this country, and of meeting those of other countries who happen to be visiting Palestine. I regard this as the basis of all my work in the field. It takes up a great deal of my time. Although these countries form part of one great family, and are united by the closest ties, yet in point of local and immediate problems they present a picture of great diversity; so that each country has, up to a point, to be studied as an entity in itself.'

As a precis of his views about unity it is perhaps worth quoting part of a longish letter which he wrote to my brother in October 1937. Edward had by then been working for a year as a leader writer on the *Manchester Guardian* and had written to George about some article about the Arab world he was due to write. It was typical of George's kindness and thoroughness that, although as he explained he had secluded himself in a Hertfordshire cottage in an attempt to finish off his book as quickly as possible, he should have taken the trouble to send a very full answer.

(Memorandum on Arab unity sent by George Antonius to Edward Hodgkin on October 30, 1937. The covering letter from Little Hadham, Herts, states that he has taken this 'little cottage' (Saddler's Cottage) 'in the hope of finishing off my book as quickly as possible'.)

The idea of Arab unity is inherent in the movement for Arab national regeneration, which arose out of the purely cultural revival (*circa* 1850).

In its early and indeed in all its pre-War stages, the national movement was essentially non-regional: the battle-cry was not 'Syria for the Syrians' or 'Yaman for the Yamanis', but rather 'Back to the Arab life and forward to freedom from non-Arab domination.'

It was only after the War, that regional tendencies began to manifest themselves, largely due to the variations in the regimes set up in various parts of the Arab world: real independence in the Peninsula, short-lived mandate in Iraq, die-hard mandate in Syria, virtual dictatorship in Palestine; and partly owing to the partitioning imposed by Great Britain and France. These gave free scope and encouragement to the play of selfish localism and to the individualism and lack of corporate spirit which is at the root of the Arab character. Nevertheless, the general sentiment throughout the Arab world is still strongly in favour of unity.

Unity does not necessarily mean federation on the American or any other Western pattern. The essentials of unity as desired by Arabs are: unification of education, abolition of artificial barriers (customs, passports), development of economic ties, freest possible cultural intercourse etc.

That sort of unity is generally and strongly desired, and it seems as though nothing could stop it. It is the reflection of a state of mind common (though not always to the same degree) to all the Arabic-speaking countries; and its strength is in direct ratio to the level of cultural development as between one country and another (e.g. strongest in Egypt and Syria, least strong in Sudan and Morocco) but present everywhere.

But when it comes to the political aspects, divergencies are revealed—most notably in the case of Egypt which 'walked out' of the Arab national movement as far back as the '80s and developed a nationalism (anti-British occupation) of her own. What with that, and with the problems created for Egypt by the new Italy, Egyptian politicians are chary of identifying themselves too openly or too deeply with the Arab aspirations. But the cultural forces making for unity (as against political federation) and the forces inherent in the religious Islamic ties are driving Egypt (willy-nilly) towards rather than away from the Arab ideas.

The case of Syria and Lebanon is a special one, made special precisely by differences in cultural development, viz. great activity of French and other Western schools in the Lebanon during 2nd half of XIXth century, which gave Lebanese generations a different outlook—non-Arab and predominantly Frenchified. This tendency has been greatly intensified since the War by the deliberate policy followed by France in the Lebanon, viz. to encourage separatism and foster the doctrine that the Lebanese were not Arabs but Phoenicians! . . .

In the opinion of many people (of whom I am one) the separatist tendencies of the Lebanese Christians (the Lebanese Moslems who are if anything more numerous than the Christians are hotly in favour of union with Syria) are bound in course of time to be swamped by the tide of the growing sentiment—growing all around them—for Arab unity. But that might take a long time.

Another aspect of George's thinking was the somewhat Tolstoyan one that it is often the small and seemingly irrelevant facts which can have a fundamental influence on events rather than the big and dramatic ones. This comes out clearly in a letter which he wrote to Rogers of the Institute in January 1933 in which he described the fall of the Sidqi government in Egypt. The crisis, as he explained, 'had its origins in a trivial murder case'. But 'to the student of political science the crisis affords an interesting lesson in the value of institutions, and more particularly institutions established in eastern countries on western patterns. It is said that the destinies of nations are shaped in equal measure by accident as by design. The Badari incident [the trivial murder] is a case in point.' He described the absolute control the Sidqi government had obtained over the country—the press muzzled, parliament packed with its supporters, the goodwill obtained of Palace, residency, the European communities and the foreign press. 'It may almost be said that every vestige of material power was in their hands.'

> Then an accident occurred, trivial in its beginnings, which all but brought the edifice to the ground. A very subordinate official in an obscure and remote hamlet had been murdered some twelve months ago. The case had passed through the usual routine of courts and tribunals; and, like many other similar cases, was well on its way to liquidation and oblivion. Owing to a hitch, however, in the working of the judicial machine, it went automatically to the Court of Cassation. And there an opinion was expressed on one aspect of the case, which shook the edifice of government down to its very foundation.

George listed the consequences of this trivial accident—the cabinet fallen and reshuffled; losing thereby three of its most active members; the self-confidence and sense of immunity of thousands of tyrannical officials shaken; the discrediting of those, including the British High Commissioner, who had long been told of the abuses that were going on but had not listened. He said he wouldn't be surprised if in the next few months Sidqi was superceded and there was a new High Commissioner—and by the end of the year both these prophecies had come true, though perhaps not wholly as a result of the Badari incident.

In a not so Tolstoyan way George was very conscious of the part played by individuals in the direction of events and of the failures, the disasters, which could be attributed to a faulty understanding of human or national psychology. In one of the letters to me from which I have already quoted, written three months after the start of the Arab general strike, he wrote: 'The insane situation goes on, with the same destruction and bloodshed. And it goes on because two or three—not more—men lack the courage and honesty to say what they think.' And in another of these letters he spoke of 'the psychological cause underlying the unrest' being 'loss of faith in British promises'.

Three years earlier, after he had come back from a visit to the now theoretically quite independent Iraq—and practically independent too, as he conceded—he compared progress in that country with the lack of progress elsewhere, particularly in Egypt and Syria. 'It has,' he wrote, 'taken Egypt some 40 years of autocratic British tutelage and ten more years of internal autonomy to reach her present administrative freedom. Whereas in Iraq the same process has taken only 13 years. This shows, once more, that in a nation's evolution the factor of time is by no means constant; that what counts is not so much the time spent in acquiring experience, but rather the manner in which this experience is acquired in relation to the contemporaneous movement of ideas.'

As for the French argument that Syria would have to pass through the same stages as Iraq, 'However right this premiss may be in logic, in reality it amounts to a fallacy. For it overlooks the force of the movement of ideas and of the psychological changes which this movement has engendered'.

I think that at this period George may have been over-impressed by what seemed to him the contrast between the hopeful newly independent Iraq, and the apparently hopeless cycle of repression and revolt in Syria and Lebanon, and so led him to ascribe too many of the ills of colonialism to differences in the psychology of colonial nations.

George's approach to the writing of history was important. He anticipated the upside-down style of historiography—the history of peoples rather than of governments. Although of course a lot of *The Arab Awakening* is about governments, the significant message in it is that national movements can be kept alive in difficult times by small groups, often acting independently of each other. It also shows George's appreciation of oral tradition as a vital source for national history.

I have tried to describe George Antonius as I knew him. It will be seen that this is not altogether the same person as is beginning to appear in books written about the Middle East between the wars by people who did not know him or his work at first hand. The picture already emerging is of a talented and cosmopolitan Egyptian who, after leaving Cambridge, took service in the Palestine government, but who resigned in pique after an Englishman had been promoted over his head and turned to Arab nationalism instead. This chip on his shoulder made him susceptible to the specious charms of the Mufti, whose blind adherent he became, just as his own specious charms were later to convert Europeans and Americans to the Arab point of view, for which he was a paid apologist.

This is of course a totally false picture. Far the most important thing about George Antonius is that he was a patriot, and for the same reasons that people like Mazzini and Kossuth were patriots. There is a tendency today among American, and American-inspired, political scientists and historians to deny the existence of genuine patriotism among the peoples of Third World countries—apparent patriotism has to be explained as a reaction to being passed over for jobs or for some other humiliation; these people didn't *really* want to be independent. What George admired about Kawakabi was that, as he said, 'he practised what he preached; putting patriotism above distinction of creeds'. George was certainly charming, civilized, rational, cultured, and all the rest of it, but always a patriot first and last.

Cairo Memories

I HAVE reached the age when I can look back half-a-century with some chance that vividness of memory will not fade too quickly. I think back to a childhood in the late 1920s and early '30s, to an adolescence on the eve of World War II, and to a youth and maturity spent during the War years and followed by an awareness of lesser wars, some on my own doorstep, others further afield. The one conscious thread through the turbulence of our times has been the sense of recurring upheaval and of the alienation which has beset most of my generation.

Most of my life has been spent in Cairo, where the chance of birth made me aware very early of the infinite complexity of a city crowded with people of vastly differing backgrounds, rapidly changing class structures, and heterogeneous cultural values. The experience of living in Cairo was—and probably still is, though to a lesser degree—one of constantly coming to terms with change, constantly reinventing ideas which had been invented quite frequently before, and of starting afresh with political and social passions which echo those of past and forgotten generations. For a sense of the historic past carried forward is not relevant in situations where the present is always invented as if from scratch, with the enthusiasm of spontaneous discovery. Cairo, the physical place, the changing metropolis, with its protean forms of vanishing communities and social strata, is ever melting, ever taking on new shapes.

The Cairo of my childhood in the early 1930s was one of three converging cities. The first was middle-class and residential, with nervously centrifugal tendencies, moving out of the traditional residential quarters of Abbassia, Ezbekia, Helmia and Moneera, to the relatively new ones of Heliopolis, Zamalek, Garden City and Giza. The old Italianate–Ottoman-style houses laden with stucco were soon turned into insalubrious flats, schools and office buildings. The new houses, built mainly by French, Italian, and local Jewish architects (for whom the '20s were bonanza years) tended to imitate the 'Modern Style' of Paris and Marseilles. These new houses were defiantly grand, but hardly ever had much of a garden attached to them. Almost abutting on the tree-lined pavements, they lacked the privacy which characterised a Parisian *hôtel particulier* or an opulent London town-house. Besides, however costly and grand they might have been, they were relatively small and in no way comparable to any of the stately houses of Europe in size or number of rooms. With this new pretentious architecture came a plague of cabinet-makers and agents for reproduction antique furniture from Paris, London, and Milan, all vying with each other to fill spacious halls with imitation Hepplewhite, Sheraton and Scottish Baronial from the workshops of Majorel, Jansen, Maple's and Heal's. Yet, strangely, the emphasis was on furniture and statuary (especially in bronze). The walls often remained bare, except for the occasional imitation Flemish tapestry. A taste in paintings was rare—it was certainly more common among the Levantine cotton-brokers of Alexandria.

The second city was the commercial centre, consisting of a triangle of three tree-lined streets—Kasr-el-Nil, Soliman Pasha, and Fuad. Here were the department stores (guarded by the moustachioed Albanian doormen, in their fustanella and high boots) which had emerged from the hinterland of crowded medieval Cairo, round the Mousky, Atab, and Azhar. And here the French and English bookshops, the tea-rooms and Parisian-style cafés (of which Groppi's has alone succeeded in gaining a small measure of cosmopolitan fame) mingled with fashion boutiques, milliners, art galleries, clubs for the well-to-do, banks, court photographers, motor-car showrooms, antique shops and jewellers (as distinct from the goldsmiths who remained in the medieval city). The Europeans, rich Egyptians and Levantines of any class did their shopping here, conducted business in offices, sipped coffee in cafés.

Separating this area from the older city was the Royal Opera House, with its traditional winter seasons of Italian opera and *Comédie Française* repertory. This bastion of Western culture, on the marches of the commercial centre, was (apart from the cinemas) one of the few venues where Europeans, Levantines and Egyptians mingled freely. They found a common language in opera, and the alexandrines of Racine and Corneille were familiar to the ears of middle-class Egyptian wives brought up in the largely French-speaking convent schools.

The third city was nomadic. Like amoebae regrouping, it wandered from the narrow alleys of the area between the Citadel, the Azhar and Abbassia, to the outskirts of Shubra, Zeitoun, the island of Roda and the loose conurbation of Giza behind the Zoo.

The lower-middle class lived here, its true roots in the countryside; and also the small shopkeeper class, gradually being dispossessed by the growing Levantine commercial houses, the impoverished *ulema* of the Azhar, and the lower rungs of the clerical hierarchy in the Ministries. In tenements, with minimum standards of sanitation, safety and comfort, the future bureaucrats and nationalists, revolutionaries and intellectuals, dictators and emigrants to Canada and the Arab countries were born. Their families had been atomised, reduced in collective awareness, by their severance from the large tribal families of the villages or the intense local loyalties of patriarchal families in the multi-storeyed courtyard houses of the medieval city. Moreover, the mobility of government employment, the obligation to move from one provincial posting to another, had reduced home to a congeries of iron beds, primus stoves, bulky brass saucepans and washbasins, and hard divans which doubled as beds for the children.

A glimmer of hope in all this squalor was the possibility of acquiring an education at one of the state schools. Elementary schooling in the Koranic *kuttab* was almost free, but the fees in state schools were not low; somehow, by scraping and sacrifice, the lower-middle-class family was able to provide this one luxury, for the male children at least.

This was the city as I knew it—protean, shifting its various centres, plunging from the heights of opulent peace to the miseries of overcrowding and strident noise with breathtaking suddenness. It struck out in various directions. South, where Maadi provided a substitute for London suburbia or a flattened-out Indian hill-station. North, on the edge of Shubra, where Mohammad Aly had built a palace, and a shanty town of depressing squalor spread out tentacularly, with no sanitation, little electricity, less drainage, and few distractions, except for the annual visit of an Algerian circus, patronised by Farouk, Prince of Upper Egypt, and his four young and beautiful sisters. To the East, the City of the Dead lay hushed and desolate. To the West, the poor of Giza were already spilling into the fields around.

The European communities, jealous of their national specificities, turned their backs on the tinsel brilliance of Alexandria, yet all melted into the one 'Frangi' identity for the Egyptians around them. Perhaps the largest group was the Italians, concentrated in Cairo, Alexandria, and the Canal Zone, unlike the Greeks who filtered into the provincial cities and villages. The Italians of Egypt enjoyed a Golden Age in the 1930s, with a class structure which rose from the semi-proletariat of garage mechanics and chambermaids to the intellectual aristocracy, centred on the Mixed Courts and the Vittorio Emmanuele Hospital, and the very rich architects, builders and bankers.

Fascism was taken much more seriously in the Italian communities overseas than it had ever been in Italy proper, and the Italians in Egypt were no exception. There were Fascist youth parades in the main streets of Cairo throughout the winter months, and the streets of Boulak, behind the Leonardo da Vinci Art Institute, echoed to the strains of *Giovinezza* as the young *Balillas* and *Giovane Italiane* marched to their community schools. In those days Fascism was still guiltless of its race laws, and in Cairo a few of its most enthusiastic supporters happened to be Jewish. Throughout the '30s the Fascist Party established splendidly appointed Sports Clubs and Stadiums, homes for the aged, summer holiday camps in Italy, and winter excursions to Libya and Somalia. The rare anti-Fascists were frightened into silence; they withdrew to the safer precincts of Masonic Lodges and the nascent Left-wing movements. One memory of Fascism triumphant is a box at the Opera filled with corpulent lawyers in black shirts; another is of a

Youth Festival in the Ala Littorio club near the Pyramids, with Egyptian peasant children chanting 'Duce, Duce' in unison with the Italian children inside the club.

Then came 1940 and the total and irreparable collapse of the Italian community. Overnight, the men were hauled off by the British to camps in Fayed and Ismailia. The women were left to make do as well as possible with no legitimate source of income, and all Italian property was placed under sequestration. Nothing remained except lonely housewives, a timid anti-Fascist movement scorned by most of those who were left, and a number of Italian Jews opting for British and sometimes Egyptian naturalisation papers. The deserted schools, hospitals and clubs were taken over by British and Egyptian bureaucrats. This was the end of the largest European community, other than the Greeks, whose Egyptian associations went back to the days of Mohammad Aly and even beyond.

The Greeks of Cairo could never claim the brilliance and opulence of their Alexandrian counterparts. There was no Cairene Cavafy, nor any of those merchant princes whose patronage had animated so much of the Alexandrian scene. Our Greeks were more down to earth, more immediately functional, less Durrellian.... Like the Italians, they formed a stratified social community, which rose from the semi-proletariat to the very rich, and consequently they were able to live among themselves, speaking their own language as a self-sufficient society, with their own clubs, services, and political passions.

While the Greeks of Alexandria were torn by the conflicting loyalties of the Metaxian and Venizelist persuasions (this especially among the refugees from Anatolia and some of the well-to-do Phanariots), the Greeks of Cairo were more inwardly oriented, more concerned with their own dissensions in local businesses and church affairs. The Cairene Greek press was like a parish journal, full of local news and obituaries; the Alexandrian Greeks launched into considerations of world dimensions. When the War came, and with it the German occupation of Greece, the Government-in-Exile was established in Cairo; but all the political upheavals, culminating in the Naval Mutiny, took place in Alexandria.

Yet, withdrawn and self-sufficient, cut off from cosmopolitan Hellenism as well as metropolitan Greece, the Cairene Greeks had their immortal longings too. They had their hour of glory in the War years when Cairo became the home of George Seferis, Elli Papadimitriou, Sophocles Venizelos, the pianist Gina Bachauer, and the novelist Stratis Tsirkas. Lesser luminaries from the local community also had their day. Such were the blind concert pianist George Themeli; Charalambos Pelarinos, a mute, inglorious philologist, trained in Germany, who wrote a grammatical commentary on the whole of Dickens, wandering from café to café; Avlonitis, a gifted classical guitarist, who changed his name to Abloniz in order to give the impression that he was as Spanish as Segovia; Theokari de Comnène, a naturalised Frenchman, claiming descent from the Byzantine Emperors. De Comnène was the headmaster of the French *Lycée* and private tutor to the young Prince Farouk; on the occasion of every Royal Princess's birthday he published a congratulatory sonnet in the purest Parnassian manner, on the front page of one of the French daily papers.

A memorable publication of the pre-War and War years was the weekly magazine of the Egypt–Greece Friendship Society. Edited by Stavros Stavrinos, it came out in French, and provided some of the earliest translations of Cavafy, Sikelianos and Palamas. In its pages can be found short articles by E. M. Forster, Bonamy Dobrée, Robert Graves, André Maurois, Jacques de Lacretelle, Henri Peyre, and many other distinguished visitors to Egypt. At that time, French was considered the only language to use, especially in cultural reviews such as the monthly *Revue du Caire*, the *Revue des Conférences Françaises en Egypte*, and most of the learned journals.

My next foreign community is not the French but the French-speaking—a complex diversity of people, cutting through race, community, nationality, and religion. To be French-speaking in Cairo before the 1952 Revolution was to belong to a group of people who felt themselves deeply rooted in Cairo as a place, and probably believed that their lives would be spent in that city until death disseminated them to their various cemeteries, distinguished only by religion or religious rite.

This rootedness did not imply a sense of belonging in any way to the world of culture, politics, and religion which informed the rising nationalism of the Egyptian middle classes. To be French-speaking was to think of Cairo as home, but to believe that Paris was the navel of the world. You could be French-speaking and yet feel patriotic, regardless of your origins; but as the shift of your intellectual loyalties became more of a habit, you gradually lost touch with these origins. This is what happened to a few Egyptians in the 1930s and '40s, but also to many local foreigners. Resistance did come, however, from such embattled communities as the Armenians and the Cypriots, whose attachment to a national language for nationalist reasons made them, at most, bilingual.

Nevertheless, the social circles of the Mixed Courts, where justice was dispensed in French by Scandinavian, Italian, German, American and British judges, belonged essentially to this French-speaking world. The banks and cotton houses, the vast majority of foreign schools, the Catholic missions in Egypt, the nascent Fuad the First secular university, the Royal Family (apart from King Fuad himself, who preferred Italian), the Egyptian plutocracy (both Moslem and Coptic), the Masonic Lodges, the department stores, the Suez Canal Company, the majority of the press (including the editors of Arabic papers), the eligible young girls of all communities who expected brilliant marriages, the habitués of the tea-rooms and restaurants, the young cinema industry, the legal profession, the better-class brothels, the hotels, the tram and métro inspectors, the learned societies, the Antiquities Service, and naturally the French community itself—all were French-speaking.

The cinemas showing films in English would occasionally provide Arabic, Italian, Greek and Armenian translations of the dialogue on revolving scrolls on either side of the screen, but the sub-titles were in French. 'La Littérature égyptienne d'expression française' soon grew to sizeable proportions, which required the services of a number of local publishing houses. For some of the more gifted, the lights of Paris shone brightly, and their work rolled off the presses of the *Mercure de France* or the Librairies Stock and Flammarion. Few attained the glory of a Gallimard imprint, but there was certainly enough coming out of Egypt to engage the pens of literary critics from Jules Lemaître and Anatole France onwards. There was genuine talent in the writings of Prince Haidar Fazil, Elian Finbert, Wacyf Boutros Ghali, Mohammed Zulficar, Ahmed Rassim, Georges Cattaui, Joseph Ascar-Nahas, and Nelly Vaucher-Zananiri. But the true wealth of creativeness was only to come, ironically, in the 1940s, with the twilight of French culture in Egypt, in the work of Georges Henein, Albert Cossery and Edmond Jabès, who became *émigrés* in Paris.

Yet there was a strange malaise in all this literature, written with an eye to a Parisian audience, often prefaced by a successful French writer, sometimes noticed in Parisian literary journals, lavishly praised in the Cairene French-language press, but sadly limited to a first edition and a number of presentation copies. The second-hand bookshops of Cairo are full of them, bearing inscriptions to long-dead, indifferent wives of wealthy cotton-brokers and State Under-Secretaries.

This loose, almost classless, community of the French-speaking was to die a slow death in the years between 1948 (the first Palestine War) and 1956 (the Suez War). Today nothing is left of its past pretensions, hopes, and modest achievements. Already, during the 1940s, there had been a profound shake-up of the community in the wake of the Fall of Paris. The Metropolitan French were sharply divided into two opposing camps, the pro-Pétain faction and the Free French. The situation was compounded by King Farouk's refusal to withdraw recognition from the Vichy representative, whom he used to invite to duck shoots which were also attended by Lord Killearn, the British Ambassador. As political passions tore at the heartstrings of the French, breaking up marriages and cutting families in two, the marathon of French culture was taken over by the local French-speakers, mostly Jewish and Syro-Lebanese Christians. These were largely Free French in sympathies: the Jews for obvious reasons; the Syro-Lebanese with reservations, but ultimately persuaded by de Gaulle's promises of independence for Syria and Lebanon.

In this French-speaking world the Jews of Cairo had pride of place. By nationality they were, for the large part, divided into three categories: ex-Ottoman, thereby becoming Egyptian or stateless; French, by virtue of their North African origins and the naturalisation opportunities of the *Loi Crémieux*; and Italian, rapidly becoming French, British, or stateless, because of the promulgation of the Race Laws in Fascist Italy. One thing they all shared was the French language, and the overwhelming majority of people working in the French-language press were Jews.

This was also true of the membership of the French cultural centres, such as the *Amitiés Françaises*, the *Amis de la Culture Française en Egypte* and the *Atelier*; the daily grind of their foreign cultural activities continued doggedly throughout the 1940s and '50s, when English culture seemed to be reserved for the British and Commonwealth Forces in Egypt. French was the language in which catalogues of artists' exhibitions were written, French for the programme notes of the concerts given by the Palestine Symphony Orchestra (largely composed of Central European and German Jews), French for the early Zionist appeals in Cairo, for the Hebrew lessons given by young enthusiasts, for the Catholic Scout Movement, for the neo-Thomist discussion groups, for the discussions in the bourgeois intellectual groups spawned by the *Amicale des Anciens Elèves du Lycée Français*, leading to that congeries of mutually hostile Marxist groups struggling for a foothold in Egyptian politics. The apostles of early Egyptian Marxism were French-speaking Jews, who were also generous promoters of the arts; their inability to communicate rapidly and correctly in Arabic was one of the main reasons for the collapse of their influence and the gradual 'Egyptianisation' of the Communist movement in Cairo. Not that this new development was calculated to strengthen or unify the warring groups, but that is another story....

With Zionism looming, the fate of the Jewish community was sealed. Timid attempts were made by some rich and important Jewish families to dissociate themselves from Zionism, or else to reconcile Egyptian public opinion discreetly to the emergence of a Jewish state in Palestine. The Cattauis, Hararis, Mizrahis, Rolos, and Mosseris tried in vain to stem the tide of militant anti-Zionist nationalism, but their voices were drowned, for they addressed themselves to a minority of increasingly helpless pashas. They had at best an almost non-existent place in Egyptian public life (as distinct from the world of trade and banking); they had a poor command of Arabic; they had remained aloof from the tidal wave of Egyptian nationalism (unlike the vast majority of the Copts, some Karaite Jews, and a small but intellectually distinguished number of Syro-Lebanese); and they spoke French.... Having thrived under the British dispensation they remained loyal to it and had not thrown in their lot with Egyptian nationalism and the Arabic language after 1919, the one date when minorities had to stand up and be counted. To the extent that some of them had Zionist hopes, these were sufficiently clear-sighted to realise that a break was bound to take place between themselves and the teeming nationalism around them.

The Syro-Lebanese Christians, who spoke French with equal fluency, *had* retained a link with Arabic. The Arabic press was largely Syro-Lebanese Christian, and the movement of ideas was conducted bilingually. They had penetrated the government bureaucracy and held positions of influence in the banks and commercial houses; they were woven into the fabric of Arabic cultural life. *Emigrés* from an atmosphere of Ottoman intolerance to a relatively relaxed and stable Egypt, they regarded Arabic as the symbol of an oppressed and revolutionary culture asserting its independence from Turkish. Their presence was immediately felt in the literature of ideas, in debates about tradition and modernism, in the theatre, the music-hall, the emergent cinema, and the less well-documented shadow world of translators, speech-writers, ghost-writers and secretaries which provided much of the international dimension of the Egyptian national movement. They were, *par excellence*, communicators and transmitters, discreetly preparing texts and formulating proposals for politicians locked in mortal negotiation with the British. They also played an important part in the translation of the codes of law and the jurisprudence which was the foundation of the Egyptian national judiciary. This was no mean achievement in a country struggling to become accepted in the family of nations.

There is a sense also in which their ability to construct bridges between cultures, their availability as interpreters of ideas from one world to another, and their genius for innovation brought upon them some of the onus attending on being almost alien. The Muslim Syro-Lebanese merged into the world of Islamic tradition and discourse, but the Christians maintained a precarious position between two worlds—with an impeccable command of Arabic, they kept one eye cocked on the fashions and ideas of Western Europe and America, and were never able quite to overcome their reputation as outsiders. They, too, had to join the swelling ranks of emigrants from Egypt after the Second World War. Perhaps the final test of belonging was Islam (although this did not apply to the Copts), or speaking Arabic (although this did not apply to the Syro-Lebanese Christians or to countless poor Jews and Armenians in the back streets of the Azhar quarter).

One cannot speak of a composite English-speaking world, formed of many different communities, in quite the same way. The British were a self-sufficient community, mainly professional and middle-class. Happily oblivious of the nationalist rumblings beneath them, they led, before the War, peaceful and sedate lives, with a certain quality of living which distinguished them from other communites in Cairo. Not for them the cultural centres, the fashionable lecture tours, and the brashness of visiting

French music-hall artistes. Their pleasures were simpler: gardening in Maadi and Zamalek, flower shows, circulating libraries, antiquarianism, amateur theatricals (crowned every year by a performance of Gilbert and Sullivan at the Royal Opera House), and polo at the Gezira Sporting Club, played by the officers of cavalry regiments garrisoned at the Kasr-el-Nil Barracks (a site now occupied by the Nile Hilton Hotel, the sometime Arab League, and the sometime Arab Socialist Union). At the time of the summer solstice they joined the migration to the north. Yet, whereas the pashas and rich Levantines went to Alexandria, whence the Messageries Maritimes or Lloyd Triestino bore them to Marseilles or Genoa *en route* to European spas, the English would go to Port Said and board a Bibby or P. & O. liner bound for Tilbury and family reunions.

They were bankers and judges at the Mixed Courts, accountants, insurance brokers, dentists, inspectors and advisers in Egyptian Government service, schoolteachers, police officers, clergymen and retired military personnel. They read the *Egyptian Gazette* or *Mail* every day and *The Sphinx* over the week-end, tracing with self-gratification the gyrations of their small society in club and garden party. When homesick they would go to the Turf Club and read week-old papers brought from Britain by sea-plane.

My earliest recollections of the British in Cairo are of parades and fanfares: a searchlight tattoo on the polo grounds at Gezira in honour of Edward, Prince of Wales; air shows at Almaza Airport on every Armistice Day, with poppies raining from the sky; church parades in Garden City. These were indeed a sight to warm every true British heart. First, there was a changing of the guard outside the Residency; then, from the wrought-iron gates with the monogram of Victoria Regina picked out in gold, the High Commissioner's black Rolls-Royce slowly emerged. On either side of the slow-moving car rode a detachment of the King's Horse, their mounts caparisoned and champing at the bit; bringing up the rear marched a battalion of the regiment in garrison. I remember the swirling kilts and pipes of the Black Watch drawing the really large crowds. The procession, led by officers of the Egyptian Mounted Police, progressed to the small Anglican cathedral church of St Mary's (now a Greek Catholic parish church), where Bishop Gwynne of Cairo and Khartoum, attended by Archdeacon Johnson, would be waiting in chasuble and alb to receive the High Commissioner at the church door. What splendour, after Divine Service, when the High Commissioner returned to his Rolls parked in the little square outside, accompanied by the portly Bishop and met by the massed bands of the garrison! It was a world of ceremony sufficient unto itself, and the patriotic certitudes of Bishop Gwynne's sermons gave his congregation a sense of permanence and destiny.

The high moment of the year was the King's Birthday when the High Commissioner took three days to hold his reception in the beautifully proportioned Residency Ballroom (now a Visa Section divided up into plyboard cubicles). On the first day came the Judges (Holmes, Blake-Reed, Murray-Graham, *et alii*), the Ministerial Advisers, the knighted residents (Gregg, Russell, Campbell, Spinks, Keown-Boyd and Rolo), the Anglican clergy, visiting celebrities and the diplomatic staff. On the second there were the irrigation inspectors, the agricultural experts, and the higher ranks of the police force (mostly Levantine Beys, with a sprinkling of British pashas). And on the third, the lesser breeds without the Law, the so-called P.I. (Public Instruction), consisting of (mainly Welsh) schoolteachers in the State education system, some members of the Fuad the First University staff, as yet untouched by the fashionable radicalism of the '30s: Robert Graves, Bonamy Dobrée, Creswell, Scaife, but perhaps not Malcolm Muggeridge or Bryn Davies; then the Cypriots, the Maltese and the recently naturalised Jews.

The British community took a mercifully unconscionable time to die. First, it went into a sort of discreet hibernation period between 1936 and 1939, when nationalist riots occurred with disturbing frequency. Then came the War, and the emergence of an entirely new, largely male British community in uniform, with its own ENSA shows, NAAFI stores, and short-lived literary reviews such as *Personal Landscape* and *Salamander*, its own popular press modelled on *Picture Post* and *Lilliput*, its own dance bands, its own academics in Intelligence Units—and its own feeble gesture of friendship towards the Egyptian intelligentsia (then teetering on the brink of pro-Nazi sympathies), calling itself, quaintly enough, the Brotherhood of Freedom. This is the world pictured in post-War English fiction with a Cairene setting, by Evelyn Waugh, Olivia Manning, Robert Liddell, and P. H. Newby.

The new nomadic population had little to do with the old residents, who felt that their patriotic duty was accomplished in working for the '"Kumangetit" Fund Millième per Plane Club' (whose members gave a donation whenever a German plane was officially declared destroyed) and for the British Red Cross, with occasional tea parties for the Eighth Army wounded. The old community was dying, its children sucked into the War, its security shaken by anti-British riots and the crippling infirmities of age. They held on as long as possible, after the burning of Cairo, after the fall of the King, after the Revolution; but the final blow came, for them as well as for many many others, with the Suez War in 1956.

Yet the English language survived. It survived among the children of rich Egyptians and Levantines brought up by English nannies, among the rich Presbyterian Copts of Assyut attracted by the more clement weather of Cairo and the chances of social life in a capital, among the boys who had been to Victoria College and the English School, among the pupils of Graves, Dobrée, Scaife and Bryn Davies, who had gone on to take PhDs in

England after the '50s, among the upper echelons of the Egyptian Civil Service, who had probably done some graduate work in English and, in a few cases, had brought back that brave breed of British wives, cast up on the wilder shores of love. English survived, but it did not bear the same fruits as French. There was no Egyptian Naipaul. No Egyptian political leader or Cabinet Minister before the present decade, except for the unfortunate Amin Osman Pasha and a Regent, Aziz Izzat Pasha, had been to an English school. French schools had, on the other hand, produced a sizeable minority of Egyptians in politics: four Prime Ministers—Rushdy Pasha, Ziwer Pasha, Sedky Pasha and, not so long ago, Wing Commander Aly Sabry—and a dozen or so Cabinet Ministers. English was a relative late-comer in the movement of translation from the Western languages into Arabic, and the typical library of a cultured Egyptian in the '30s would have contained few books in English compared with the book-shelves of French classics, Anatole France, Homer, Shakespeare and Goethe in French, Gustave Lebon, Paul Bourget, Gabriel Hanotaux, the inevitable *Vie de Jésus* by Renan and countless productions of the French specialised law publishers.

The Cairene Egyptian élite of politicians and members of the professions were mainly people who had achieved distinction the hard way, through slow promotion in the judiciary or the civil service, or through involvement in the political upheavals which culminated in the 1919 Revolution. As élites went, it was deeply coloured by nationalist politics and by a variety of defiant stances adopted towards the British occupier. To achieve distinction was to occupy ministerial position, at some time in one's life. It did not matter really how gifted one might be as a writer, journalist, academic, surgeon, or person of wealth. The yardstick of success was political involvement and the achievement of Cabinet office, however briefly. Few pashas could resist the passion for politics, and the looseness, the almost occult nature, of the British hold on power in Egypt gave the impression that emulation was the true spur to success.

One day, perhaps, a computerised study of obituaries will yield some information on the continuity of transmission from the élites of the 19th to those of the 20th century. *Ulema*, Mameluke families, and the entourage of the Royal Family may have provided some lines of transmission; but the overwhelming majority of Egypt's pashas beween the two World Wars and right up to the 1952 Revolution were shining examples of social mobility.

Once pashadom was achieved, a certain channelling into clubs became *de rigueur*. The Wafdist pashas were members of the Saadist Club, a picturesque Italianate–Moorish structure, where argument, loud rhetoric, and no less loud backgammon reigned supreme.

All the other pashas, whatever their social origins, belonged (or tried to belong) to the Mohammad Aly Club. Unlike its Alexandrian counterpart, it was an attempt to reproduce the formality of the St James's in London and the *Interallié* in Paris. The cuisine, both Ottoman and French, was of the best, and its Italian chef was so good that throughout the War the British spared him the misery of a concentration camp. Bridge was the game encouraged among older members and billiards among the younger. Here princes, pashas, some rich Jews and a small number of British knighted residents mingled in an environment of hushed splendour, dominated by one of the most interesting collections of 19th-century Orientalist painting in existence.

King Farouk did not set foot in this club, although his father had been a frequent visitor. He preferred another establishment, the Royal Automobile Club, where the membership was younger, of both sexes, and the décor less grand: the dominant game here was poker, played for very high stakes. There was a hint of fast living in this club, which also had links with the horse-racing world, and it was generally felt that though its members might be rich or ambitious, they would never achieve much distinction in the political arena. In its heyday, however, it served as a staging post for Egyptians and Levantines in a hurry to take part in the growth of Egyptian industry. Round the poker tables, where fortunes were made and lost, boards of directors were being formed right up to the early '50s.

When did the bell toll for this evanescent world? Nobody can really tell. With the first Palestine Campaign, in 1948, the writing was on the wall, but all who were not Jewish, and many who were, did not pay it any heed. The second warning came with the burning of Cairo in 1952, but again it seemed impossible to take these matters seriously. Here was a society which could not exist elsewhere in quite the same way, and the idea of emigration was alien to most of its members. The Suez War changed all that, and the palpable sign was the occupation, almost overnight, of the flats and houses of the departing 'enemy aliens' in Zamalek, Garden City and Maadi, by a new class of Egyptians. The new class had been growing for some time, rediscovering the world for itself, as the nationalist pashas had before. Down with the old Pharaoh, up with the new! An élite of jurists, politicians, bankers and doctors was replaced with breathtaking speed by one of technocrats, officers and PhDs of every description. There was, naturally enough, a lost generation of budding statesmen and intellectuals, who might have carried on from the pashas, if the monarchy had remained or if a liberal republic had succeeded it; however, this generation seemed to be anaesthetised by the rapid unfolding of events, looking on helplessly as Nasser and his élite propelled the country into a complex world of deadly seriousness and *Realpolitik*.

Today a vast expanse of tenements, high-rise buildings, bursting sewage, traffic jams, broken pavements, impressive flyovers and self-assertive posters forms the townscape of Cairo, but occasionally one's mind moves back to that city of flowering jacarandas, rose gardens, and colonial or Italian-style villas. An Arabic sentence spoken with slow deliberation, Turkish words mingling with Arabic, the music of the open-air cinema intervals—Tino Rossi, a Souza March, the Lecuana Cuban Boys. . . . An abandoned yo-yo, the taste of mastic in the ice-cream, the casual mention of Dunlop (that almost mythical *bête noire* of Egyptian civil servants in the '30s), the guttural French still surviving in a song by Dalida, the blaze of bougainvillaea, the deep-throated agony of a song by Um Kulthum, the world-weary slapstick of a Naguib el Rihani film, the clashing cymbals of a liquorice-sherbet street-seller, the mild fun of a Colonel Jarvis satire, the haunting, mournful call of the stone-curlew—memories of that kingdom of illusion rush into the mind, borne on a host of echoes from the past.

Ernest Bevin and Palestine

I HAVE two excuses for standing here this evening. The first is that I am one of the very few people in the room who met George Antonius and talked, or more accurately listened, to him. We met twice in 1939, during the Anglo-Arab conference of that year at which the force and persuasiveness of his advocacy obliged the British Government to modify their previous interpretation of the promises made to Arabs and Jews during the First World War.

My second excuse is that it so happened that I joined the Eastern Department of the Foreign Office and was put at what the Americans would call the Palestine desk almost simultaneously with the general election of 1945. Palestine was one of the new Secretary of State's most constant preoccupations during the next four years; for three and a half of those years I remained in the same position, and when I was not away at United Nations meetings in New York or Paris I spent much time in his room.

The Labour victory in the election of July, 1945, was warmly welcomed by the Zionist leadership. The Party appeared to be firmly committed to supporting the establishment of a Jewish State in Palestine, and it was expected that the Foreign Office would go to Hugh Dalton, who at the Party Conference a few weeks earlier had proclaimed support for Jewish immigration 'without the present limitations' to establish 'a happy, a free and a prosperous Jewish State in Palestine'.

Attlee himself had not finally made up his mind on the allocation of offices in the Cabinet he was about to appoint, and he knew that Bevin wanted the Exchequer. So when King George VI, after commissioning him to form a Government, asked who he had in mind for the Foreign Office, he replied that he had been considering Dalton. The King asked him to think carefully about this, and suggested that Bevin would be a better choice. Attlee reflected on this until the following afternoon, when he decided to switch Dalton to the Treasury and give the Foreign Office to Bevin.

This was a disappointment for the Zionists, and there was worse to follow. One consequence of the contrast between what they had hoped for and expected from a Labour Government and what actually followed was the growth of the idea that Bevin was antisemitic. Bevin was sixty-four when he became Foreign Secretary, he had been a prominent national figure for three decades, and his antisemitism had not been discovered during that time. The fact is that there was a clear distinction in his mind between the Jewish people and the Zionist movement. And he came to believe that the sympathy to which the Jews were so richly entitled by the suffering they had endured in Europe since 1933 was being exploited—not necessarily in their own best interests—by the Zionists. 'We cannot accept the view', he told the House of Commons soon after taking office, 'that the Jews should be driven out of Europe and should not be permitted to live again in these countries without discrimination and contribute their ability and their talent towards rebuilding the prosperity of Europe.'

Just as he would not accept that Jews were necessarily Zionists, so he recognised that Zionists were not necessarily Jews. I once felt obliged to draw his attention to a telegram which arrived from Washington a few minutes after he had taken a decision, in which the Ambassador, Lord Inverchapel, set out arguments against what had been decided. Bevin waved it aside. 'Don't take any notice of 'im', he said, ''e's a Zionist.'

He certainly resented the methods by which the Zionist lobby sought to influence British policy—'his policy' as he considered it to be. The pressure they exerted through the White House aroused his anger more than once, though he accepted it as more legitimate than their efforts to make use of his own Cabinet colleagues to undermine his position; Dalton and Cripps, and intermittently Creech-Jones, were among those subject to their influence. Bevin not only resented their efforts on his account; he also, with his lifelong feeling for the underprivileged, felt that he had to discount the effect of the multiple vehicles of Zionist propaganda by comparison with the vastly smaller resources and less sophisticated presentation of the Arab case.

At the outset his approach to the Palestine problem was conditioned by long years of experience as a trade union leader in the conduct of industrial negotiations. It is characteristic of industrial disputes that they are almost invariably settled by a compromise. It may take a considerable time, but in the end the requirements of labour and management arrive at a point of equilibrium, and production is resumed. It was natural that the conflict of Arab and Jew in Palestine should initially present itself to Bevin as a problem with similar characteristics requiring similar skills for its solution. This, I think is the explanation of the statement, which in retrospect seems so reckless, and which he made in the House of Commons in November 1945: 'I will stake my political future on solving this problem.' He repeated it in almost identical words at a press conference on the same day.

The use of the first person singular in this statement was typical. He thought of the foreign policy of the Attlee Government as *his* policy, and in fact his relationship with the Prime Minister was such that he was not far from wrong in doing so. I once expressed anxiety to the Secretary of the Cabinet, Sir Norman Brook, about the chances of Cabinet endorsement for a proposal the Foreign Secretary was about to put forward. 'You needn't worry,' Brook said, 'all Ernie has to do is to wave his fat hand over the table and say "I won't 'ave it", and that's the end of the matter.' Attlee explained his readiness to yield the lead to Bevin on questions of foreign policy in somewhat unflattering terms: 'You don't keep a dog and bark yourself.' Bevin was sometimes as casual as the Prime Minister in expressing what was in reality their profound mutual reliance and respect. I remember him hesitating to despatch a telegram and eventually saying 'Better show it to the Prime Minister. 'E's funny sometimes.' But when a group of Ministers, dissatisfied with Attlee's leadership, planned to remove him and put Bevin in his place, their candidate brought the conspiracy to an abrupt halt with a simple question: 'What's Clem ever done to me?'

I had an insight into Bevin's attitude to his Cabinet colleagues when I was called in one Sunday morning to draft a message that he wished to send to the American Secretary of State. Normally this would have reached him through my superiors in the Office, but on Sundays—at any rate on this Sunday—they were not there, so I took it to him myself. He read it carefully, then picked up his pen and went back to the beginning. I watched him pausing five or six times to cross something out and write an amendment in his almost totally illegible hand. Then he signed the text and pushed it across his desk to me. I was surprised to find that in fact he had made only one change. Wherever I had used 'I'—normally one of his favourite words—he had struck it out and substituted 'His Majesty's Government'. He waited for me to take this in, then he said: 'I haven't been in trade unions all my life, my boy, without knowing when to say "My Executive".'

Of course his egoism and his formidable self-confidence were among the qualities that endeared him to his officials. What Government Departments value most highly in their Ministers is the ability to override opposition in Cabinet. And while this was far from being the only basis for the affection in which he was held, without it he would not have been, with possibly one exception, the Foreign Office's best-loved Minister in modern times.

Returning now to Palestine, I have suggested that Bevin was not uninfluenced on the one hand by exasperation with the pressure tactics of Zionism, and on the other by his growing conviction that the Arabs had had a raw deal. But he was not a man to base policy on emotions, and it is time to enquire how he related this problem to his major preoccupations and his overall political strategy. At the end of 1945 Britain was the only European power of consequence west of the Soviet Union. As such she carried major responsibilities for the revival of Europe itself, for the future of European dependencies in Asia and for what was already perceived by Western leaders, if not yet by their public opinion, as the threat of Soviet expansion. In all these fields, maintenance of the special relationship with the United States was an imperative necessity. In one of them, the containment of Soviet pressures, relations with the Arabs were of crucial importance. If Bevin had not been constantly aware of that, the Chiefs of Staff would not have let him forget it for long. 'Any solution of the Palestine problem', as they told the Cabinet in one of many similar representations, 'must ensure the retention of the goodwill of the Arab world'.

The participants in the debate over the future of Palestine to whom the greatest attention was paid were thus not the Arabs of Palestine or the Zionists inside and outside Palestine, but the American Government on the one hand and the independent Arab States on the other. Their conflicting pressures set limits to the mandatory power's freedom of action and imposed on it a measure of neutrality which sprang less from the merits of the case than from calculation of the balance of external forces. Paradoxically, the effort of the British Government not to act in Palestine in such a way as to alienate the Arab world should have been in the context of the increasingly evident Soviet threat to western interests, as much an American as a British requirement. It was indeed seen in this light by many of the officials in the State Department, notably by the wise and experienced Loy Henderson, Director of the Office of Near Eastern and African Affairs. There is no evidence, however, that President Truman was impressed by this consideration. Neither, it must immediately be added, was Truman emotionally or intellectually committed to the Zionist cause. His attitude is best summarised in the remark he once made that it would help if both the Mufti and Rabbi Silver were thrown into the Red Sea. Intrinsically the question of Palestine does not seem seriously to have engaged his interest. He had, I think, a genuine sympathy for the recent tragedy and the current plight of the Jews in Eastern and Central Europe, which inclined him to accept without much questioning the solution proposed by the highly organised Zionist lobby, deeply entrenched as it was in the Democratic party and occupying key positions in the White House. But the cement which bound the President to the lobby was its influence on the funding of the Democratic Party and on a significant proportion of the electoral vote in New York and certain other States.

It was Truman who gave the impetus to Bevin's first attempt to find the solution to which he had committed himself.

Less than three months after the end of the European War Truman was pressing Churchill to lift the existing restrictions on Jewish immigration into Palestine. He returned to the charge when Attlee became Prime Minister, proposing the immediate issue of 100,000 immigration certificates (the existing rate was 18,000 a year). It was in response to this communication that Bevin, early in October, hit upon the idea of involving the Americans in a joint study of the problem by a Committee which would make recommendations to both Governments. By the time news of this proposal reached the Foreign Office, it had already been endorsed by the Cabinet, and our forebodings were irrelevant. Accepting Truman's starting point but not his conclusion, the terms of reference suggested by Bevin envisaged first an examination of the position of the Jews in Europe, and secondly a study of the possibilities of re-settlement in Europe and of emigration to countries outside Europe, 'including the United States'. There was no specific mention of Palestine, and when Lord Halifax suggested including one Bevin refused. Inevitably these terms of reference did not survive examination in Washington, whence a draft returned with the primary emphasis firmly on Palestine. This had finally to be accepted, though an attempt to exclude any reference to non-European countries other than Palestine was successfully repelled, at the cost of abandoning any reference to the United States.

This exclusion remained a sore point with Bevin. He told the Labour Party Conference in 1946 that the American demand for the 100,000 immigrants 'was proposed with the purest of motives. They didn't want too many Jews in New York'—an example of his rather curious persuasion that it was not necessary to keep as careful a guard over his self-expression on party as on more official occasions. This particular indiscretion was added to the evidence for his alleged anti-Semitism and drew a fierce protest from the two Senators for the State of New York.

The Anglo-American Committee disappointed Bevin's hopes that it might lay the foundation for an agreement between the two Governments on the way forward. That its report was anodyne and insufficiently constructive was to some extent his own fault. For at a lunch he gave for the twelve Committee members (six British and six American) he told them that if they reported unanimously he would do his utmost to see that their recommendations were put into effect. This prospect gave the Committee a bias towards the sacrifice of controversial views in the interest of unanimity, which effectively ruled out any proposals for definitive constitutional decisions. The report explicitly ruled out a Jewish State, an Arab State and partition, leaving the British Government to continue indefinitely to administer the Mandate which it was by now their strong desire to terminate. The Committee made a number of proposals including—a necessary concession to the American members—the immediate authorisation of the 100,000 immigration certificates to be 'awarded as far as possible in 1946'.

Contact between the two Governments to consider their policy in the light of the report was pre-empted by Truman in a public statement endorsing the proposal for the 100,000 and adding that he would give careful study to the other recommendations. The Prime Minister thereupon declared that His Majesty's Government could not agree to decide on one recommendation before they had determined their response to the report as a whole. And that was virtually the end of the story of the Anglo-American Committee.

It was not the end, however, of the attempt to secure American support for an agreed policy in Palestine. A few weeks later, in the summer of 1946, an official American delegation, led by Ambassador Henry Grady, arrived in London for consultations with their British opposite numbers headed by

Sir Norman Brook. Once again the representatives of the two countries reached agreement, and once again Truman was to decline to associate the United States Government with their conclusions. This was hardly surprising, since the plan on which the group had agreed was one which the Colonial Office had had in stock, so to speak, for some time. It involved a system which was known as Provincial Autonomy, under which a Jewish and Arab province would be created and would exercise limited powers under a central government still administered by the British High Commissioner. It thus fell short of partition, and was held to possess the merit that, in the light of its operation over a period of years, it would be possible to determine which of two long-term solutions would be the more practicable, partition into two independent States or the creation of a single bi-national State.

The attempt to devise a policy which could be put into effect with the active support of the United States had thus broken down. This was at the end of July, 1946. Seven months later, in February 1947, the British Government announced their inability to solve the problem unaided, and invited the General Assembly of the United Nations to decide what should be done. It is to this interval that we must look if we wish to know what Bevin himself believed would constitute a just and reasonable outcome, what he might have done if he had had a free hand. In the first place, the records show that he returned more than once to the idea that, if Palestine was partitioned, the Arab area could not be left to stand on its own but should be united with Transjordan. This was what eventually happened in 1949, but in Bevin's eyes it was very much a second-best. He regarded partition as a desperate remedy, he believed—rightly—that it would outrage and antagonise the Arab world, and he also believed—wrongly—that it would be rejected by the United Nations.

He therefore rejected partition, and at the end of this period produced what is known as the Bevin plan. The Bevin plan has been too lightly dismissed in most of the accounts published hitherto. Following as it did soon after the scheme of provincial autonomy and having certain features in common with that, it has been regarded as a variant, a minor revision without much significance. This impression has been combined with doubts as to whether Bevin was in fact its author, or whether it was simply one more ingenious but anonymous product of the Whitehall machine. This impression at least I can dispel, in the light of an experience which I believe could be paralleled by a number of the officials who worked with Bevin in these years. He sent for me one morning, and said he had been lying awake since five o'clock thinking about Palestine, and had had a number of ideas which he proceeded to outline, in no particular order like the pieces of a disassembled jigsaw puzzle. As with his impromptu speeches, however, which were bafflingly obscure to anyone listening too carefully to the language, the general intention behind what he was saying was luminously clear. Finally he told me to 'go away and see if you can make a memorandum out of that'.

Logically speaking he started from the proposition that, in the words of the memorandum, 'His Majesty's Government are not prepared to continued indefinitely to govern Palestine themselves merely because Arabs and Jews cannot agree upon the means of sharing its government between them.' He therefore proposed to set a limit of five years to the continuance of British responsibility and to use that period for the development of self-governing institutions, both local and central. Locally there would be administrative areas with an Arab and Jewish majority. But the originality of his concept, differentiating it from the various earlier plans for partition or provincial autonomy, was that he was thinking not of one Arab and one Jewish area but of several which would not necessarily form two contiguous blocs, and consequently would not point towards partition. I like to think that this idea was put into his mind by someone well known to many of us, Musa Alami. They met in September, 1946, Bevin was impressed by him, and the record of their conversation quotes Musa as saying that 'a series of communes might give both communities the protection they needed without splitting the country'. At the centre the High Commissioner would appoint an Advisory Council with Arab and Jewish members but also with representatives of 'labour and other organised interests'. This was an idea Bevin had cherished for some time. He refused to believe that it was necessary to treat the Arab and Jewish communities as monolithic, or to accept that as the country developed there could not be alliances of Arab and Jewish groups based on a community of economic interest.

Jewish immigration would continue for two years at the rate of 4000 a month, thus providing an intake very close to Truman's 100,000. Thereafter the rate at which it continued would be decided by the High Commissioner in consultation with his Advisory Council, or in the last resort by arbitration.

At the centre, there would be a gradual introduction of Palestinians into an Executive Council, and after four years elections would be held for a Constituent Assembly. If agreement could be reached between a majority of the Arab and a majority of the Jewish representatives an independent State would be established without delay. In the more probable event of disagreement the Trusteeship Council would be asked 'to determine future procedure'.

With its target of a unitary State and therefore a State with an Arab majority, combined with the guarantee of a limited initial Jewish immigration and minority rights to be defined in the constitution, Bevin's plan was in essence a return to the White Paper of 1939, since regarded by the Arabs as the high-water mark of their influence and by Zionists as their gravest setback in the decades of negotiation with the mandatory power. If few people appeared to understand this at the time, one who did was Ben Gurion, who denounced the proposals as 'a complete retreat from the provincial autonomy plan in the direction of the White Paper of 1939'.

It is reasonably clear, therefore, what Bevin had in mind when, in presenting his plan to the Cabinet, he claimed that its outstanding merit was 'that it is the only one likely to be supported by either of the two directly interested parties'. He believed that the acquiescence if not the positive support of either the Arabs or the Jews was an essential precondition for the approval of any settlement by the United Nations. And the military advice he was receiving was that no solution could be imposed against the hostility of both peoples. Accepting this logic, he had in fact decided to see whether he could persuade the Arabs to accept a solution which, while obviously falling short of Palestinian demands, would provide the basis for a general understanding with the Arabs.

On the day following a preliminary discussion of these ideas in Cabinet, Creech-Jones, probably after a night of anxiety over the distance the Government was travelling away from his own earlier views and the Party's preelectoral commitments, wrote a paper noting that Bevin's proposals were 'in diametrical conflict with the undertakings given by the Labour Party, prior to its assumption of power, regarding the development of the National Home', and declaring that partition was 'the only reasonable solution'. Three weeks later, however, he was accepting joint responsibility with Bevin for a powerful statement of the case against partition written by Norman Brook.

These exchanges took place in January and February, 1947, in the interval between two sessions of an Anglo-Arab conference held in accordance with an undertaking, dating back to 1942, that the British Government would not commit themselves on the future of Palestine without first consulting the interested parties. As this pledge required, the Jewish Agency was also invited to the conference but declined to participate unless the principle of partition was conceded in advance. It was at this time that the Jewish Agency, while maintaining its claim to a Jewish State in the whole of Palestine, agreed in practice to discuss what they defined as 'a viable Jewish State in an adequate area of Palestine'.

Their condition was refused, but arrangements were made for the Foreign and Colonial Secretaries to have separate meetings with the Zionist leadership. It was at one of these meetings that Bevin observed that in his opinion the Balfour Declaration was the biggest mistake of British foreign policy in the twentieth century. I have a vivid memory of the words, and of Bevin and Creech-Jones sitting side by side in the conference room of the Colonial Office. I cannot remember precisely who was on the other side of the table, but if I have identified the meeting correctly in the records, the audience Bevin chose for this confidence included Ben Gurion, Shertok, Nahum Goldman and Aubrey Eban.

In a somewhat less dramatic form, Bevin again expressed his feelings about the Balfour Declaration and its consequences in a speech in the House of Commons a few weeks later. The mandate, he told the House, 'provided for what was virtually an invasion of the country by thousands of immigrants, and at the same time said that this was not to disturb the people in possession.' And in the same speech he said of the Arab case against partition: 'If it is wrong for the Jews to be in a minority of $33\frac{1}{3}$ or 40 per cent in the whole country, what justification is there for putting 360,000 Arabs under the Jews? What is your answer to that? I have no answer to that.'

The Arab States, however, rejected the Bevin plan. What would have followed if they had accepted it is an interesting speculation. In the first place, Bevin was not entirely consistent in his opinion of what could be achieved on the basis of acquiescence by one party only. At one of the meetings with the Jewish Agency he is recorded as saying that 'His Majesty's Government would in no circumstances consider enforcing a solution on either party'. And this was certainly the position adopted by the British Government after they had transferred the responsibility for decision to the United Nations. I am not convinced, however, that with Arab acquiescence in his grasp, Bevin would not have been strongly tempted to ask the United Nations to endorse his plan rather than throw in his hand. In a paper apparently dictated by him about this time he said: 'I am satisfied that we could get sufficient support in the U.N. if we went forward with the idea of an independent unitary State.' He probably drew a distinction between imposing a settlement of purely British origin and acting as the instrument for implementing a United Nations resolution.

The wording of the Cabinet conclusions, at the meeting which authorised presentation of the Bevin plan to the two parties, supports this interpretation. It is there stated that Bevin and Creech-Jones would report 'whether in their judgement these proposals were likely to meet with any substantial measure of acquiescence from either of the two communities in Palestine, and would then invite the Cabinet to decide whether His Majesty's Government would be justified in bringing the scheme into operation on their own authority pending the negotiation of a trusteeship agreement'.

I therefore think it can be accurately said that the Arab rejection in February, 1947, was for Bevin the decisive turning point. It brought him firmly into line with Attlee, who had been attracted from the outset by the idea of abandoning Palestine, and indeed had sometimes advocated withdrawing altogether from the Eastern Mediterranean, whereas Bevin had worked to maintain our strategic position while reducing its moral and material cost.

It also brought policy in Palestine into conformity with decisions which were being taken at the same time in relation to other British responsibilities. The decision to refer the question of Palestine to the United Nations was virtually simultaneous with the notice given to Washington that Britain could no longer carry the burden of supporting the independence and security of Greece and Turkey. And the withdrawal from India, also announced in February, was to follow a few months later.

This was a winter of severe financial strain and restrictions on the living standards of the British people. A substantial reduction of overseas responsibilities was an inevitable consequence, and so far as Palestine was concerned it met a popular demand. From October 1945 onwards the mandatory administration and the armed forces had been confronted by a campaign of terrorist action spearheaded by two small paramilitary groups, the Irgun Zvai Leumi and the Stern gang, which had been independently active earlier but which were now accorded the collusion of the Zionist leadership. Their most dramatic exploit occurred in July, 1946, when they blew up the wing of the King David Hotel in Jerusalem which was occupied by the government secretariat, causing the death of nearly a hundred British, Arab and Jewish officials. This tragic event and other outrages on a lesser scale led to a growing desire in Britain to be rid of a responsibility whose advantages were less apparent than its hazards. The revulsion of feeling reached its climax a year later when two British sergeants were hanged and booby traps placed on their bodies. As Michael Cohen writes in his admirably objective volume on this period: 'History would seem to indicate that the IZL's draconian methods. . . . were decisive in transforming the evacuation option of February 1947 into a determined resolve to give up the burdens of the mandate by August of that year.' These events certainly played some part in the withdrawal from Palestine, just as the Arab rebellion of 1936–38 had played a part in the decision to adopt the policy of the 1939 White Paper. I cannot remember, however, or find in the documents much evidence of their effect on Bevin himself, whose decisions continued to reflect longer-term considerations.

The decision to refer the question to the United Nations did not, at this stage, necessarily involve a British withdrawal. As Creech-Jones told the House of Commons, 'we are going to the United Nations setting out the problem and asking for advice as to how the Mandate can be administered'. In accordance with this request a special session of the General Assembly appointed a U.N. Special Committee on Palestine (UNSCOP) with instructions to report back in time for the regular session in September. It was the UNSCOP report, with its majority recommendation of a form of partition highly favourable to the Zionists, that finally persuaded the British Government that there was no acceptable alternative to the decision, towards which they had been drifting, to abandon Palestine.

The announcement of this decision to the United Nations, on the 26th

September, was accompanied by the statement that Britain was not prepared to be the instrument for giving effect to proposals which were not agreed by both communities. As it was evident that the majority report was the only one which had any chance of endorsement by the Assembly, and that it would be actively resisted by the Arabs, the implication was plain that other means would have to be found if it was to be implemented. The mandatory would withdraw its administration and its armed forces at an early date.

It is not easy to remember exactly what we in the Foreign Office thought would be the consequence of this decision. To begin with we doubted whether the Assembly would succeed in taking any decision whatever with the required two-thirds majority. This scepticism, based on what was becoming the almost automatic opposition of the American and Soviet Delegations, and secondly on the known sympathy of a number of neutral States for the Arabs, was not unreasonable. We should perhaps have foreseen that on this issue the primary aim of the Russians would be quite simply to remove the British presence from Palestine, and that in United Nations terms this could only be done by lining up the votes of the Soviet bloc with the Americans. But we were not prepared, partly because our relations with the State Department hid the possibility from us, for the pressure tactics, organised from the White House to the dismay of the Department of State, which caused certain Delegations to change in plenary session the votes they had cast in Committee. Without this switch by such client States as Haiti, Liberia and the Philippines, the Resolution might still have failed despite Russian support.

The passage of the Resolution recommending the partition of Palestine and the creation of a Jewish State seemed at the time to be a historic event. In fact it probably made very little difference. What was decisive was the British decision to withdraw.

Resolutions of the General Assembly are recommendations only; they have no legislative force. But the United Nations was in its infancy in 1947, and this was not clearly understood. Moreover the immense effort which had been expended by all the interested parties between April and November, the excitement in the public galleries, and the walk-out of the Arab delegates after the vote, leaving Zafrullah Khan in the rostrum prophesying doom, all combined to create the impression of a turning-point in history.

It was followed, however, by a period of absurd confusion, resulting largely from the continuing failure of communication between the White House and the Department of State. It was evident to the latter that in the absence of any provision in the Resolution for enforcing its proposals, and with the imminent departure of the British, armed conflict in Palestine was a certainty. Three months later, therefore, the Americans proposed that the Resolution they had successfully carried through the Assembly should be suspended, and that another special session should be convened to consider putting Palestine under a temporary trusteeship. They were presumably unaware that on the previous day Truman had given a personal assurance to Weizmann that the United States was still firmly behind partition. He followed this up on the 23rd April with a further undertaking that the United States would recognise the Jewish State which was due to be proclaimed at midnight on the 14th May. But the American Delegation, sitting in the Assembly in New York at midnight Jerusalem time on that day, was stunned by the news that this had actually happened.

It should by then have been evident to all concerned that the ultimate decision on the future of Palestine would be determined not by votes in the United Nations but by the balance of forces in the country itself. Fighting was already in progress when the British army sailed away, and it continued—with interruptions during periods of truce called for by the Security Council—until *de facto* frontiers were settled by armistice agreements in 1949.

During this period Bevin made two attempts to influence the character of the territorial settlement. Both were based on his reluctant acceptance of the inevitability of partition.

The first was to encourage King Abdullah to carry out his intention of incorporating into Transjordan as much of the territory allocated to the Arabs by the General Assembly's Resolution. The second followed from the decision taken by the Assembly, on the day following Truman's recognition of the State of Israel, to appoint a Mediator without binding him to seek a settlement within the terms of the partition resolution. The Mediator was Count Bernadotte, who was assassinated later in Jerusalem, but not before he had proposed an exchange of territory which would have given Israel an additional area in Galilee in return for a part of the Negev which would have restored direct land communication between Egypt on the one hand and Transjordan and Iraq on the other. This, in view of Britain's military commitments to the three Arab countries, was also a British interest of appreciable importance. Bevin and the American Secretary of State, now General Marshall, agreed to work for the endorsement of these proposals, but they were overtaken by the campaign for Truman's re-election, in the course of which the President rallied the Jewish vote by undertaking to support modifications of the partition resolution only if they were acceptable to Israel. Once again a plan was derailed by the ambivalence of American policy. It must be admitted, however, that it would probably not have succeeded in any event.

The direction of Bevin's sympathies in the Palestine conflict is beyond doubt. It had little to do with specific feelings about Arabs or Jews, but a great deal to do with the egalitarian principles which had developed through his experience as a trade union leader and which guided many of his political attitudes. He was exposing his deepest feeling about Palestine when he told Ambassador Douglas in 1948 that 'the fundamental difficulty over Palestine was that the Jews refused to admit that the Arabs were their equals'.

But, as I have tried to show, his personal feelings had a limited influence on his decisions, and in any case the balance he tried to hold was dictated not by the conflicting claims of Palestinian Arabs and Jews but by wider international considerations. He had two fears: on the one hand that Britain's involvement in Palestine would poison the relationship with the United States on which the entire structure of his policy depended; and on the other that Arab goodwill, necessary if the eastern approaches to the Mediterranean were to be protected against the threat of Soviet expansion, might be alienated.

He held this balance successfully, if sometimes precariously, at the cost of following a line which looked indecisive and ended ingloriously. We are entitled to ask if he could not have done better. One alternative would have been to take the course advocated by the majority of his Cabinet colleagues with strong support on the Government back benches, and to adopt the principle of partition. This would have brought him into line with Colonial Office thinking and especially with the last High Commissioner, Sir Alan Cunningham. An argument regularly advanced in these circles was that partition was the only solution having the merit of finality. Bevin was not impressed by this unconvincing claim. I can offer no evidence for his reasons, but I am sure that his vast experience in negotiation left him in no doubt that the threat of finality was the one thing calculated to make absolutely certain that any form of partition he might propose would be rejected by both sides. In any case he was convinced that those responsible for the creation of a Jewish State would not be forgiven by the Arabs.

The other possible course would have been to accept Attlee's view that the most sensible thing to do with Palestine was to leave it. Attlee was not alone in this opinion; it was shared by, among others, Churchill who, shortly before the end of his Premiership, addressed a minute to the Colonial Secretary and the Chiefs of Staff in which he said: 'I am not aware of the slightest advantage which has ever accrued to Great Britain from this painful and thankless task.' And he publicly advocated, some months before it became the declared policy of the Labour Government, that we should lay down the Mandate. At that time Bevin did not agree. Apart from his confidence that he could solve the problem himself, he was impressed by the conviction of the Chiefs of Staff that Palestine was an important link in the defences of the Mediterranean and the Suez Canal, and thus in the protection of our petroleum lifeline. And this not in military terms alone, but in terms also of our political relationships with the Arab States.

I have had the immense advantage, and pleasure, while preparing this lecture, of being permitted to see the typescript of Lord Bullock's masterly forthcoming volume on Bevin as Foreign Secretary. It is an ungraceful return for his generosity to conclude by expressing a partial dissent from one of his conclusions, in which he contrasts the success of Bevin's policy in Europe with his lack of success in the Middle East. He had worked both for a Palestine settlement and for a substitution of treaties based on equality of status with Egypt and Iraq for the pre-war treaties which were increasingly resented in both countries as expressions of a semi-colonial relationship. He did succeed in negotiating more equal treaties with the Prime Ministers of Egypt in 1946 and Iraq in 1947-8, but in both countries domestic opposition prevented their ratification.

Nevertheless if we extend our view of his policy and its results beyond his own lifetime, I think a different conclusion suggests itself. His adamant refusal, despite American pressure, to play any part whatsoever in the partitioning of Palestine had the result that Britain emerged in Arab eyes as the only major power displaying any sympathy for their cause. As Dean Acheson put it, giving the credit to the Prime Minister: 'Attlee had deftly exchanged the United States for Britain as the most disliked Power in the Middle East.' And the Prime Minister of Iraq, speaking at a meeting of the Arab League Council in December, 1947, said that 'Britain's stand on partition had changed the position. The enemy was now the United States'. The policy was indeed designed with the purpose of making it possible to retain our strategic assets in Arab countries, and in this it was successful. Without it I do not think the Conservative Government which followed would have been able to secure the defence agreements with Egypt in 1954 and with Iraq in 1955, both of which owed much to the pattern established by Bevin in the negotiations he had conducted eight years earlier.

They were destroyed, immediately in Egypt and after a brief interval in Iraq, by the folly of Suez in 1956. What Bevin would have said to that, if he had lived to see it, is not hard to imagine. Of course the structure he tried to create and which others built on the foundations he laid would perhaps not have had a long life. But if Britain's Middle Eastern policy had not been impulsively wrenched off the course he set, it is at least possible that a steady and positive evolution might have avoided the destructive upheaval of the late fifties and the sixties. Bevin's vision was as clear in the Middle East as in Europe; but the external political forces, which helped him in Europe, frustrated him in Palestine.

Mouths of the Sevenfold Nile: Modern Egypt in English Fiction

THIS century has seen a flow of English novels and short stories concerned with modern Egypt. Even though many of them are not of intrinsically high quality, it is interesting to survey them because they reveal the different approaches which the western imagination makes use of when confronting an alien environment. One cannot claim that the English fiction that deals with Egypt forms a *genre* of its own: in fact, the works separate themselves into several distinct streams—hence the allusion in the title to Virgil's 'septemgemini ostia Nili'. These English mouths that speak about the Nile have enough in common in what they say, but also enough variety, for them to be the subject of a comparative and contrastive survey of variations in the treatment of the same overall theme.

Though the British occupation began in 1882, the line of fictional work does not start then, but in the opening years of the twentieth century. It continues today, although the occupation ended in July 1956, while the troops involved in the Suez adventure, having arrived in November of that same year, had withdrawn by January of the next. In fact, however, the works fall into discernible groupings as regards their dates, as well as in their manner—for popular and literary vogues brought it about that a large number were produced in the years around the First World War, while another cluster belongs to the period soon after the Second War.

Patchy in quality, some of them are written purely for entertainment and many show a breathtakingly cavalier attitude towards veracity: this gap between outward fact and artistic construct is itself one of the interesting features in a study of this tradition. Behind this line of fiction, and side by side with it, lies the non-fictional literature of travellers and memoir-writers—a literature of description, encounter, and reflexion which remains superior to the works of fiction. Perhaps this peculiarly English tradition of excellence should have been adhered to by those who, instead, worked hard at constructing a narrative. It seems true of Marmaduke Pickthall (1875–1936)—to whom I shall return later—that the documentary sketches in his *Oriental Encounters* are good, his short stories, where the plot element is slight and the vignette element is strong, are less good, and his novels, with their creaky structures, are least successful—though they are at their most persuasive when the story line intrudes least. The typical English novel about Egypt can be classed among C. S. Lewis's 'good bad books', bad in its use of approximation rather than exactness, its smudginess and banality, its shallow attempts at wisdom—but good where it demonstrates skilled craftsmanship, affords imaginative insights and enhances the human outlook of the reader. Let us also add that the last thirty years of Anglo-Egyptian fiction have seen the rise of 'bad good books', slovenly or quackish, with over-lofty claims, though they are the work of writers who, as one can see from other elements in the books, have a humane understanding and the artist's powers of illumination.

Something other than their exotic subject places these works in an off-centred position. When we compare them with the main line of modern fiction, with its characteristic psychological and narrative content and its strategies of image and language, they are seen to lie to one side of it. The line of fiction about Egypt started in Edwardian times, and its early circumstances perhaps fixed its distinctive directions. When the Anglo-Egyptian novel emerged, the critical view did not draw so sharp a distinction beween the adventure story and what was then called the 'psychological novel'. Gilbert Parker and Hall Caine chose the adventure story as a vehicle because Stevenson, Kipling, and others had done the same thing, and this at a time when Conrad's more subtle art was emerging out of that very genre. The unreflective, activist character of the stories and of their English heroes reflects the leisured-class reader for whom they were intended. Some of the writers were men who had taken part in the actuality of Anglo-Egyptian relations, or who had observed them at close hand. Underneath Edwardian Anglo-Egyptian fiction lie some of the main strands of English literature, colouring its vision as much as the reality of Egypt does. These strands, however, are not the ones that underlie the main fabric of good modern English fiction. One of them is the pseudo-oriental tale of the eighteenth century, with its lush setting and its picaresque heroes; another is Byron's double vision of the Orient, a sensualist's and a satirist's; another, behind the Stevensonian one, is Walter Scott's combination of adventure and documentary description, with a hero with whom the reader identifies, as he steps into a life that is alien and colourful; another is Dickens's combination of grotesque characters, genre scenes, and a mesh of destinal but implausible entanglements. Threads from all of these can be discerned in Anglo-Egyptian fiction from Gilbert Parker's *Donovan Pasha* in 1902 to Durrell's *Alexandria Quartet* in the nineteen fifties.

A precursor to them all, and perhaps a direct influence upon some of them, is the picaresque novel *Anastasius*, by Thomas Hope, published in the opening years of the nineteenth century; it is a Mediterranean novel with several Egyptian episodes, containing genre scenes, and showing some knowledge of military and political involvements in late Mameluke times. Perhaps echoing it, a century later David M. Beddoe published *The Lost Mameluke* (1913). This is a romance in the manner of Walter Scott, and, owing to their common ancestry, it is strangely similar to the Arabic historical novels of Gurgi Zaydan, the Syrian Egyptian imitator of Scott. The narrative cannot be taken seriously because of the unacceptable number of meretricious details—including the identifying of no fewer than three long-lost children—but the book is memorable for its portrayal of life in Mameluke Cairo, with political and military details, and quite particularly, for the meshing together of the attitudes of Egyptian and European, Moslem, Christian, and Napoleonic secularist. Fairly accurate knowledge of more modern Egypt is sometimes found even in fiction which has the typical story line and the superficial characterization of the novelette. The Edwardian romance of highlife continued its existence largely by shifting in media, flourishing as cinema film, and, later, as television entertainment. Egypt, as a result, figures prominently in the popular mythology of the modern entertainee. I need only mention such figures as the cunning Levantine and the sensuous oriental aristocrat and such motifs as the kidnapping in the backstreets of Cairo, the visit of the wily ill-intentioned oriental to London clubland and English country-house parties, the revived mummy who comes back to join the life of the international set.

The most celebrated of these early-twentieth-century romances is Robert Hichens's *Bella Donna* (1909), in which a sensual Egyptian villain collaborates with an English would-be murderess, and the land itself forms the background for the melodrama. *Bella Donna* is the apex of that subgenre of highlife romance which deals with luxurious voyagings upon the Nile, and which has been christened the *dahabeyya* romance. Yet even in the triteness of this novelette there is some contact with the reality of Egypt: the vignettes of Upper Egypt are pleasing, and the luxury world of the houseboat is contrasted with the honest unspoilt world of toil around Nigel Armine's tent in the Fayoum.[1] I do not know whether to accept as veracious one motive attributed to Baroudi in his seducing of Ruby: that is, that it is a way of getting back at the British occupiers of his country.

In the earlier products of the tradition of lighter books, the main Egyptian characters are almost always malevolent. A shift in the Egyptian from 'baddy' to 'goody' comes at the same time as the shift of the American Indian from 'bad guy' to 'good guy', so that today the original situation has been reversed. In the recent Canadian thriller *The Scorpion Sanction*, by Gordon Pape and Tony Asplar, not only are most of the Egyptians likeable, but the Egyptian police are even shown as efficient, though the authors have chosen to introduce a super-efficient Israeli security man as *deus ex machina*. Like other post-war entertainers the authors bring in the regulation amount of sex, which plays the same distracting role here as the discovery of long-lost children does in the Edwardian novel; the reader is made to dally in the bedrooms of the Hilton Hotel, when he would rather spend more time on the remarkably accurate and vivid scenes the authors set in the streets of Sadat's Cairo. This thriller joins one line of the more serious Anglo-Egyptian novels in celebrating the theme of understanding and collaboration; working together for justice in a country which needs it, men of goodwill live out the theme of 'East meets West'.

From some of what has already been said, it will have been deduced that the problem of veracity is a central one in these imaginative treatments. It arises particularly in connection with certain works of some quality produced by English visitors after the Second World War. A writer who steps into an alien environment, as these writers have, experiences it differently from the inhabitant. He cannot readily tell whether his experiences are representative or marginal; he ought not to decide too swiftly whether his impressions veraciously interpret the outward facts; his contacts and relationships will be fewer than an inhabitant's; the solitariness of an outsider will actively distort external realities for him. Crucially, too, not knowing the language of the host environment will throw the visitor into a solipsistic attitude. This is not to say that a novel set in such an environment must necessarily attempt to be realistic; of course a writer may choose to use his experience as the point of departure for a work of art which may be impressionistic, or expressionistic, or in some other way subjective. But while the documentary element need not be present, failure is in sight when the difference between the subjective and external veracity is obfuscated. This is not an ethical point, but one concerning the empiric relationship between the text and such readers as do have some knowledge of the alleged topic. If a subjective work is not clearly perceived as such, the knowledgeable reader expects veracity. Even if the experience behind the narrative is declaredly subjective, the author, unless he makes up his own country of the mind from scratch, and invents its own terminology, must use external data in objectifying his experience into a written work. If he falsifies and fudges, he will be considered to be a deformer of his subject. Some extremely simple, even trivial examples from Lawrence Durrell's *Quartet* can illustrate this. At one point, some characters from his presumably subjective city drive east to get to the desert. But the city bears the name of the actual city of Alexandria, and the English words *east* and *west* have fixed meanings, and common topographic knowledge tells that you cannot get to the desert by going east from Alexandria. Again, let us accept the highly unlikely political plot, in which some Copts are in secret alliance with the Zionists: within the framework of the novel, this is the outcome of the hostility between the Moslem and Coptic communitites—and yet, still within the framework of the novel, the distinction between Moslem and Copt is blurred by having the Koran recited at Narouz's Coptic funeral-wake. These are small examples of artistic carelessness, but there are more damaging ones,[2] and, contend as one may that an artefact has an autonomous existence, one can hardly fail to agree that there is something faintly silly when a reader's knowledge of the actuality is a positive hindrance to his appreciation of the artefact, and when, as so often in Anglo-Egyptian novels, mistakes in topography, names, Arabic conversational tags, and so forth, reduce an adult reader to giggles when the author intends to move him in quite other ways. And, when all is said and done, would you have reproached a sitter for a Picasso portrait if she bewilderedly failed to recognize herself in it?

All this is to say that a reading of Anglo-Egyptian fiction emphasizes the contrast between the informed and the imaginative. The less knowledgeable works tend to be by writers who have lived in Egypt only briefly, whose knowledge of Arabic and of Arab culture is slight. These may be named the Sojourners, to distinguish them from two other groups: the Indigenes, by which I mean Egyptians or resident Middle Easterners who write in a Western language, and the Habitants, by which word (echoing a French-Canadian term) I mean Westerners who have lived in Egypt, or paid it frequent visits, and have been connected with it by long term links. Looking at the different approaches, one after another, involves abandoning chronological order to some extent. In fact, there were more of the Sojourning writers in the earlier, the imperial, period, than in the later and more 'ecumenical' one, so that, paradoxically perhaps, the emphasis in this survey will proceed largely from the later period backwards to the earlier. It will turn later, but only briefly, to the Indigenes, then, more fully, to the Habitants but starts its examination with the Sojourners.

A fact which the contemporary western sensibility finds it difficult to accept is that these more ecumenical post-imperialists simply do not understand the Egyptian mind—or indeed, the non-western conscience in general—at all well, compared to their Edwardian pro-consular predecessors, even when those were disposed to be unfriendly. It is yet another case of the bleeding heart not being of particular help as an aid to clear observation and understanding, which are so often replaced today by the limp handshake of incomprehending sympathy. (Who, after all, in fact understood India better, E. M. Forster or Kipling?)

With regard to veracity and to artistic economy, there are fewer flaws when a writer acknowledges that he only knows a small corner of an alien community, and is not tempted to extrapolate from it an entire country of the mind which will overlay the real country. In his novel *The Levantine* (1952), John Sykes lays no claim to knowing the average Egyptian, and restricts his canvas to the Levantines, that is, to the community of Mediterranean but non-Egyptian residents—he speaks therefore of what has become for him a half-familiar world. In Jack Debney's recent short stories, the Sojourner's main encounters are domestic ones with Greek families such as the author knew best, with servants in such families, and with the street-life of the city.[3]

Robert Liddell knew a wider range of groupings in the universities and in society; in addition, his protagonist, Charles, responds more actively to the world around him, in two different ways. One is a sharp wit which, without distorting the picture, produces very funny accounts of the absurdities of the world of learning and the superficialities of rich living; another is the sense of pathos which detects a muted sadness and lack of fulfilment underneath the pinchbeck. The moving but never complete relationships between the Sojourner and members of the host society arise gradually through and above the humour. Liddell adopts the device of placing most of his Levantines in one novel, *Unreal City* (1952), which is set in Alexandria— here called Caesarea. In a second, *The Rivers of Babylon* (1959), the setting is Cairo, and the characters are largely Egyptians. In *Unreal City* the narrator observes the last of the homosexual love affairs of an aged Greek, Eugenides, who is recognizably the poet Cavafy, whom Liddell can only have known through his writings. *The Rivers of Babylon* winds through the comedy of Egyptian university life, and of the last months in it of English academics, before the burning of Cairo in 1952. Again, tenderness arises in the reachings-out of Charles towards his more sensitive students. This is a gentle treatment of a motif recurrent in these university novels, the failure to bridge the gap between two worlds. The work ends with the departure of the dismissed English academics—and so treats of another repeated theme in the Anglo-Egyptian novels of this period: the ending of a way of life. One after another, politically important dates are used as curtain-falls, for that is what they were in real life, both for members of the British community in Egypt, and for Egyptians with English affiliations—the dates of such events as VE Day, the July Revolution, and the Suez War.

The same mix of very comic narrative, and moments of genuine tenderness, forms D. J. Enright's Alexandria novel of 1955, *Academic Year*. The newcomer Brett, with his fresh eyes, notices the poverty and contrasting riches, which the older hands hardly note any longer. A continual shift of viewpoint makes it possible also to see Alexandria—and here I repeat the analysis of the critic William Walsh[4]—in two other ways: for Brett's colleague Packet sees in the city what is good and unique, while his friend Bacon sees what is common to all human communities. But Enright is a poet, not a novelist, and when he is free from the exigencies of story-telling, and is not writing farce, but is, instead, being poignant and wry, that is, when he is writing verse, he achieves a truer understanding of the personal dilemmas of cultural confrontation than most of the writers being considered. Enright's first volume bears the title *The Lost Abonné*: this reflects the persona that dominates it, the lonely but observant foreigner who is a season-ticket holder in that rolling microcosm of Alexandria life, the Ramleh tram. In one poem in *Laughing Hyena* (1953), 'The Beach at Abousir', the pity for the downtrodden and the helplessness of the transient intellectual are movingly conveyed, in combination with fine descriptive lines. Another poem deals with the reverse situation to Enright's, the plight of 'An Egyptian in

Birmingham'. In this dramatic monologue the expatriate recognizes the faults of his own society, but realizes that they are parts of the whole for which he longs, and remembers Egypt's cheerful bonhomie which makes misery easy to bear:

> Home is made of love and hate: the beggar's incantation
> Clamoured about me where church bells now complain;
> Tyranny ran us down in city streets, with klaxons sneering—
> Yet Freedom lounged in every alley, no man too poor
> To buy her hourly, for a broad story or a smaller coin.

In one way, the situation of the persona in this poem is identical with that of the English writers of these novels. Enright evinces a rare recognition of the workings of the imagination upon alien experience. The Egyptian visitor finds the Midlands town drab, but realizes that, when he is back home, he will represent it as magical and passionate, brilliant and exotic—that is to say, he will construct a nostalgic city of the mind:

> ...But wait, when I go home, you too, Birmingham, you
> Shall be marvellous, your fame ripple through the bazaars like a
>   belly dancer—
> A city of peril, like the shark, a city of witty Gohas,
> Your streets astream with passions, big as buses,
> Brown jinn shall squat upon your chimneys, ravage the
>   countryside—
> Your chanting pigeons, at evening, be princesses and enchanted
> When I am home, and my bored days flame up in brilliant story.

Again combining comic and touching, and reflecting upon the cultural gap, P. H. Newby's *The Picnic at Sakkara* appeared in the same year as Enright's Egyptian novel. Here, an English lecturer has difficulty in grasping the motivations of his students, and, indeed, of the entire ambience. The modernist view of individual character as unpredictable and consisting of a bundle of disparate elements has clearly influenced Newby's vision of things, but surely the Sojourner, in his solipsistic caul, has seen the environment as more mysterious and fortuitous than it really is. The cultural deafness of an intelligent Sojourner impells him to construct his own network of explanations. The plot is one long romp, funny enough, and with a muffled affection for the place, but, even more than the other products of these university wits, a limited vision results in a distorted picture of Egypt. The *tone* in particular, misrepresents the place: Egypt is not a droll place, but one with grave problems, which succeeds nevertheless in being happy—*happy* but not *comic*.[5]

It is disappointing that the fiction of college teachers should achieve so little empathy, and be so strongly concerned with the isolated visitor's problems. If there is one aspect of Egypt which may claim to be the perquisite or realm of the Sojourner, it is to be found in the Western Desert and in army camps: the Egypt of the British soldier is his own autonomous world, which he knows in a way that is entirely his. Dan Davin's *For the Rest of our Lives* cuts backwards and forward between the battle zones and Cairo as a base and a leave-town. Davin's New Zealanders turn into rootless transients in Cairo, and some scattered descriptions of the streets they wander through are the most evocative cityscapes of any in all of these books. But, paradoxically, the finest accounts of desert warfare come from a writer who cannot have known the fighting directly, since she is a woman. In her *Levant Trilogy*,[6] Olivia Manning gives us a memorable picture, not only of the fighting, but also of the chance encounters and still-born relationships among the British combatants and civilians who find themselves in Cairo and Alexandria. One weakness she shares with other such novelists: it is inevitable that the Cairo of the British soldier should be a land of hotels, cafés, and bars, and that the indigenous people should only occasionally be met with, and their roots never perceived: but there is something unsatisfactory, and, in fact, comic, about a writer's world in which encounters take place around little tables in public places, with hardly any indigenous home entered into, and a native population of single men with never a sister or mother between them.

A curious structural feature has developed in the literature of Sojourners. In some novels set principally elsewhere, Egypt is given a cameo role. There is, for example, a wonderful three-page sketch of a Sojourner's Cairo life in Angus Wilson's *No Laughing Matter* (1967). There is a longer episode in John Fowles's *Daniel Martin* (1977). Daniel and his sister-in-law pay a visit to Egypt and Syria in the final section of this long novel and, as a result, find self-realization and are brought together. Among other encounters, they meet intellectuals in Cairo suffering under the Nasserite dictatorship; in Upper Egypt they are deeply affected by the landscape and monuments. Their contact with a European scholar conveys to them an almost mystic sense of the meaning of personal pain and of historical continuity. It is a fine re-use of the old *dahabeyya* motif torn out of its thriller context. The episode is one of the most substantive in the novel, equal in effectiveness to the opening description of harvest time in England in Daniel's boyhood. It is in fact an episode which saves a sagging narrative, too occupied with the drifting emotions of a writer in the artistic ghettoes of London and Los Angeles. To a large extent, what Daniel is at last encountering in his exotic sortie is average humanity, the humanity outside of the media entertainment world: there is more than a little absurdity in this inversion of the usual theme—here a befuddled Englishman is such a prisoner of his quasi-artistic environment that he has to travel to Luxor and Palmyra to meet ordinary human beings.

The most bewildering episodic treatment of Egypt is in John Noone's *The Night of Accomplishment* (1974). Fragments of an unfinished novel about

Egypt are imbedded in another novel about an English lecturer who, like the author, moved on from Egypt to Japan, and who, in Japan, is writing the Egyptian novel. The overall theme is the destruction of being which must take place before a personality can be rebuilt, the death which must precede resurrection. But this philosophical motif is not made easy to discern in the narrative and complexity is more in evidence than subtlety. There are, however, some good descriptions of the broken-down cityscape of Nasserite Alexandria, and genre-scenes such as an auction sale at the house of a wealthy Greek whose property has been sequestrated. The protagonist shows true sympathy for the slum-dwellers: unfortunately, it is expressed in the interstices between bouts of party-going—and am I right to complain that, from time to time, there surfaces, if only in a shadowy fashion, an odd 1960s tone of high-minded perkiness? The impressive qualities of Noone's first novel, *The Man with the Chocolate Egg* (1966), a work with a contemporary domestic background, but with Biblical resonances, are not equalled in the mixed exoticism of this work. I approached the work with some trepidation: I had already recognized several friends in Liddell's *Waters of Babylon*, and myself in two subordinate clauses in Enright's novel: Noone also had been my colleague. I need not have worried: the author is courteously silent about his former academic associates, and I recognized only, in casual snatches of description, a mirror-topped table and a silver card-tray filched from my flat.[7]

Of the fiction of Sojourners in general the chief weakness is what I would call the Iceberg Fallacy: the authors' failure to realize that what they see is only one-eighth of a very large and mainly submerged whole—that Egyptian life cannot be understood with little knowledge of the Arabic language, Islam, the Arab past, and recent history. Faced with the unfamiliar, the writers fall back each upon his predecessor, that is, upon literary models rather than experience, or they cling to whatever is half-shared and half-familiar, without facing the fact that the wholly exotic is too difficult to grapple with: around their writings one makes out a bewildered buzz which echoes that of Montesquieu's Parisians' 'Comment peut-on être égyptien?'

The defects of Sojourners' literature are seen very clearly in one work which, at the same time, because of its qualities, is most rewarding to the reader: I come back to Durrell's *Alexandria Quartet*. It will have been seen that several general points I have made apply to it quite particularly. Further points may be added. Inseparable from Durrell's view that the Mediterranean way is that of liberty and self-fulfilment, while the ways of England represent inhibition and dessication, is the underlying assumption that Egypt is a land of sexual freedom. Durrell's view fails, of course, to predict either the Anglo-American sexual revolution of the 1960s, or the rise of Islamic fundamentalism. The equation *Egypt = Sex* is an objectifying of the fact that any Sojourner enjoys greater freedom of most kinds. Generations of Egyptian students in Britain, long before the 1960s, could have riposted with the contrary equation, *England = Sex*. The sexualizing of all things in Durrell's Alexandria comes partly from his overcharged self-engendered landscaping; behind it is also that tradition, which goes back to the Romans and the medievals, which portrays the luxury and sensuality of the land of Cleopatra and of the 'Soldan of Babylon'.[8] Certainly, also, there is a distortion of veracity brought about by changing the proportions of components, suggesting for example a blown-up Levantine population, a sparse native one. Durrell's sensitive, witty, sensual and uprooted characters walk the pavements of a town remarkably depleted of average man. I am reminded of Arthurian knights-errant who rove fields and forests with scarcely ever a cottager in them. And yet, unlike many of the Sojourners' fictions, the *Quartet* is not only the study of a lonely central consciousness cut loose from its original environment: its episodes contain some very fine description of place, and the whole subjective structure has indeed been inspired by the objective existence of one aspect of a city, one component of a society, which acted upon a sojourning poet at the appropriate time in that city's history and in that poet's growth.

The author is partly to blame, I think, for a vagueness about the objective veracity of his portrayal. The really depressing act, however, is that legitimate works of imaginative literature should be seized upon by the educated western public, and thought to have a documentary value which they do not claim. There is a disparity between the educated public's notion of Egypt as derived from the Sojourners' works, and the detailed accurate information available today. An unthinking notion of a Double Truth seems to grip readers who turn from an article on social change in Egypt in the *Economist* to a wholly contradictory picture of Egypt in a review of a novel in one of the desperately-named 'quality Sundays'. Do people who ask one how accurate Durrell's portrayal is, genuinely think it likely that a middle-aged upper-class Coptic woman like Durrell's Laila would, in the middle years of this century, keep a pet cobra in her summer house and feed it on milk? It would seem that the distance between, say, the Middle East Centre at St Antony's College, and Fleet Street, is a long and winding one, with no direct line of communication between the two places. In the same way, the nineteenth century visual arts kept two traditions going side by side, the luridly sensual pseudo-oriental paintings of odalisques and snake-charmers, such as those by Jean-Léon Gérome, and the delicate, exact documentary sketches of mosques and street scenes by artists like David Roberts.

Before leaving the fiction of the Sojourners, one might speculate upon the one outstanding novel that was never written. E. M. Forster's homosexual attachment to a young tram conductor produced no fictional reflex. There are perhaps two reasons for this. First, and obviously, the artistic and social reticence of Forster, which would prevent him from constructing a literary display around a private experience. Secondly, the curious way in which

Forster seems to live out in actuality the art he has previously produced, his life reflecting anticipatory writings. His return from Alexandria to home-counties respectability—and, as he would have it, Respectability—lives out the frustrated return of the elderly hero of his 'Road from Colonus', away from his vision of exaltation; Forster's affair with Muhammad el-Adl seems to be the living-out of the already-written *Maurice* in an exotic environment. Whatever the reasons, we were not to be given *A Passage to Egypt*.

The sharpest contrast with the Sojourners' work is that of the Indigenes, written in a foreign language by persons fully part of the life of Egypt. Clearly, the greatest such work is the poetry of Cavafy, but there is a certain amount of fiction written in French, including two nostalgic novels about pre-Revolutionary Alexandria, Albert Bidaros's *La caverne* and Ayoub Sinano's *Artagal*. Sinano wrote his novel long before he had any notion that he would become a Canadian immigrant. Recently English has been used with great success for short stories by Ahdaf Soueif (*Aisha*, 1983). The reviewer in the *London Review of Books* claims to find in them a new feminine sensibility and a new boldness—in fact she is continuing a realist tradition which goes back to the twenties in the Arabic literature of Egypt, and a feminist affirmation which goes back in the Arabic literature of Lebanon to at least the fifties. What is valuable is that Egyptian women's sensibilities are being presented directly by an Egyptian woman, in work written in English and addressed to the non-local public. Soueif's stories are sufficiently in the mode of modern Arabic fiction for one to regard them as instantaneous self-translation. While an English-speaking reader can study the Egyptian imagination by reading in translation a short story intended by Naguib Mahfouz to be read by an Egyptian, in Soueif's stories the same sensibility is present in works directed straight at the English reading public.

The most remarkable studies of Cairo life, however, remain the French short stories and novel of Albert Cosseiry (b. 1913). A humane Marxist with no doctrinaire blinkers, he movingly presented the life of the utterly destitute and underprivileged in the short story collection, *Les hommes oubliés de Dieu* and in the novel *La maison de la mort certaine*, before emigrating for good.[9] Cosseiry's empathy with the people who form his subject is so great that his work can scarcely be distinguished from the translations of authenic Arabic works which are the indigenous literature of Egypt—instantaneous translation again, and of work with a deep resonance.

A wrily amusing novel, Waguih Ghali's *Beer in the Snooker Club* (1964) is the work of an Indigene which, nevertheless, belongs to the English Angry Young Man phase of writing, and, indeed, is partly set in London. Ghali's sensibilities are formed by an English education, and this is an English novel which deals with a problem familiar to some of us: the only 'reality' which the hero knows is the waterskater's unreality of the thin film of cosmopolitanism in which an 'English' life can be lived by Cairenes (the time is soon after the July Revolution). It is as though one of the Egyptian characters who frequent the English people in a Visitant's novel has snatched his pen away and written that novel himself. It is, to use Toynbee's term, the self-portrait of the 'internal émigré'.

The work of the English Habitants is never so empathetic, nor is it intended to be. They do, however, understand what it is like to belong to a culture different from their own. Often, they show an involvement, personal, professional, political, or religious. Arthur Weigall was an antiquary working in Egyptian government service. Sir Gilbert Parker was an Establishment figure with a personal knowledge of Egypt; by contrast, John Knittel, Desmond Stewart and James Aldridge shared the Egyptian distrust of British political activity. Marmaduke Pickthall soaked himself in Arabic and Turkish culture, excelled in the Arabic language, and became a Moslem. Many of the stories by these knowledgeable writers cluster around cataclysmic dates in Anglo-Egyptian relations: 1882, 1906, 1919, 1956. Pickthall's Syrian protagonist, Saïd the Fisherman,[10] arrives in Alexandria in time to be killed in Gladstone's attack; Mabrûk, the Egyptian peasant hero of *The Children of the Nile* takes part in Orabi's revolt, and his English convert heroine Barakah (née Mary Smith) sees her son Muhammad killed in the same movement by his own exasperated troops; Norma Lorimer's *The Shadow of Egypt* bases its events on anti-British violence in Assiut in 1919; the climax of Aldridge's *The Last Exile* is the blow which Scott receives on the face from Fahid when a child is killed by a British bomb in 1956.

It should be noted that a large proportion of these Habitants wrote their works in the first third or so of this century, so that in taking a look at them, after the Sojourners, the centre of gravity shifts back from the years during and after the Second World War to the years around the First War.

The buoyancy of the Egyptian mind is cheeringly illustrated again and again by Weigall, Knittel, and, outstandingly, Pickthall. But the difficult life of the Egyptian, living in unjust conditions, under oppressive authorities, is a more general theme. The high Tory Sir Gilbert Parker evokes the people's fear of foreign exploiters, and of the Khedive, his entourage, and his concentration camp of Fazoughli. Sir Hall Caine, a radical and a sympathiser with nationalism, condemns the limited and autocratic outlook of the British Consul-General, Lord Nuneham. Knittel portrays some foreign medical men as quackish exploiters. Pickthall, for all his sympathy with the Egyptian people, does not only castigate Gladstonian Liberals, but the leaders of the Orabi Revolt, and the sectarian fanaticism of the ordinary man. His documentary details of nineteenth-century upper-class harem life spare us none of the horrors and absurdities.

Just as some of the English educators in Egypt have been perambulating professors, who have taught in several different countries, so some of the writers have been ambulating regional novelists, who have covered many lands in the way a historical novelist covers a variety of periods. The backgrounds are not always exotic to the writer. Parker, a Canadian, set novels in Canada, as well as the Channel Isles. Caine's settings include his own Manx background, as well as Iceland, Morocco, and Rome; most of Pickthall's novels, when not set in England, concern parts of the Arab world outside of Egypt, principally Palestine. Knittel wrote about his own Switzerland as well as about Algeria. Carrying on Scott's tradition of the documentary picturesque, some of their best passages are genre scenes of everyday life in Egypt in its variety, and the tensions created by the differences between two world views, two clashing sets of assumptions and loyalties. A dominant theme is that of East-meets-West, worked out in the encounter of two individuals who learn to understand each other. This is an update of the theme of Walter Scott's *The Talisman* with its central dialogue between Richard the Lionheart and Saladin. These bridgings are sometimes portrayed, somewhat patronizingly, as taking place between a British official and his Egyptian subordinate, as beween Parker's Donovan Pasha and his servant; they may be between two men of equal status involved in a common task, as between Aldridge's Scott and his friends in the Egyptian air force; or, as in the same author's *I Wish He Would Not Die*, the English narrator may see a common pattern in his own conflict with his authorities and the revolutionry activities of a young Egyptian; or, again, the hero may develop an emotional bond with the destitute, as Desmond Stewart's hero does, in *The Men of Friday* with the young men who make their homes in the rooftop village above Cairo's blocks of flats. For more than one writer homosexual attachments seem to have been a genuine bonding element, but this is not made explicit in their works. The principal human bonding that embodies the theme of East-meets-West is, naturally, the mixed marriage. Norma Lorimer's *A Wife out of Egypt*, written in 1913, stands as an admirable example of the Near Eastern Higher Novelette, a genre of which she is mistress.[11] In the same year, Pickthall published *Veiled Women*, set in the 1860s to '80s, and so portraying a more violent contrast. In spite of the restrictiveness of harem life Mary Smith likes its warmth and vitality, preferring it to the British consular drawing-room, of which she says, '...all was tidy and precise, a hostile element to one in love with the untrimmed profusion of the Pasha's palace. She hated it as servants hate a nagging mistress'. Because of the defective structure of Pickthall's novel, its underlying philosophy is not clearly exposed, but has to be disengaged by the reader. Barakah, while aware of the defects of Egyptian Moslem life under the Khedives, realizes that Islamic spirituality is to be discovered not *in* this but *through* and *beyond* it; as Pickthall puts it, 'through her striving after Christianity she reached at last the living heart of El Islam'. Since Pickthall became a Moslem in the year following publication, one surmises that there is much of the author in Barakah-Mary. Perhaps as a final fling of speculative boldness before his final acceptance of his new faith he makes Barakah, in the closing words, petition God that women may one day be allowed four husbands each. If this is so, the novel becomes, uniquely, an imaginative vehicle in English for heterodox speculations by a partially islamised mind.[12]

Eleven years later (1924), Weigall published his account of a mixed courtship in *The Way of the East*. The heroes and heroines of his earlier 'high life' novels had been lovers of the beauty and genuineness of desert living; there is a distinct development away from the manner of his popular *Dweller in the Desert* (1921) in *The Way of the East*. Not only is the racial exclusiveness of the stereotypical English in Egypt satirized, but the unattractive womenfolk of Miriam Marcos's Coptic family are also made the butts of Weigall's humour. Like Jane Austen's *Mansfield Park*, the novel is a sympathetic study of social embarrassment; like Fanny Price, Miriam is caught between the snobbery of her adoptive milieu and the slovenliness of her original family. Like Elizabeth Bennett and Darcy, the heroine and (when he has overcome his snobbery) the hero are sensible and sensitive persons fighting against the comic deficiencies of their ambiences. The evenhanded double satire is an unexpectedly enjoyable result of Weigall's knowing both environments and submitting them both to a healthy irony.

It is never the English mind which is satirized in the work which is, I believe, the earliest of all in the modern Anglo-Egyptian tradition, Gilbert Parker's collection of short stories, *Donovan Pasha*.[13] Nevertheless, his empire-building outlook includes a sympathy for the underdog, though, unlike Kipling, not an understanding of him, and as in his novels about Quebec, he includes verse translations of colloquial folk poems with evident appreciation. The confrontation in Parker's short stories is a triangular one, between the simpler members of the Egyptian nation, a class of exploiters based mainly on the khedivial court, and the upright English proconsul. Perhaps for reasons of tact, he sets his stories a generation earlier than his time of writing. This is so, too, in his novel *The Weavers* (1907), in which Parker abandons his public school heroes for the village Quaker David Claridge, who, in an involved and unconvincing plot, becomes an adviser to the Khedive Ismail—here named Prince Kaid—and defeats the machinations of a character who is recognizably Nubar Pasha. David's character, and some of the events, derive from the figure and actions of General Gordon. This novel by a Tory Imperialist is as critical of palace and pashas as any good modern Egyptian republican could wish.

The portraying of characters based on recent historical ones is carried to surprising lengths by Hall Caine (1853–1931) in *The White Prophet* (1909). The book contains a delightful vignette of Princess Nazli Halim, the Khedive's nationalistic cousin, with some mimicry of her English conversational style. More important is the portrayal of Cromer under the name

Lord Nuneham. Nuneham, however, has a son named Gordon, who joins an Islamic revivalist leader, a quasi-Mahdi given the name Ishmael, who has come out of the Western desert, but who sets up headquarters in the Sudan. Gordon, in disguise as the Sheikh Omar Benani, helps to overthrow his father's anti-nationalist policies. Allied to him is his foster-brother, who is one of Egypt's young and discontented officers. The astonishing plot combines fervid melodrama with documentary accuracy and continual fictional parallels to actual political events. Ishmael's Messianic faith is in part a reflex of the universalist spirituality which the author reveals in other works; the title he had planned to give the book was *The White Christ*,[14] and the British proconsul is specifically compared at one point to that Roman governor of Palestine who is most infamous in Christian annals.

Caine's radicalism sharply contrasts with the views which Pickthall held before his conversion, in the years when he wrote his Egyptian fiction. For Pickthall at that time not only thought little of Orabi's movement, but even supported the Denshwai[15] sentences. When he grew disillusioned with British policy, it was because of his sympathies for the Turk and for the Palestinian, rather than over Egyptian affairs. His sense of humour, it must be said, is of that slightly callous, Stalkyesque kind characteristic of his class and period. And yet, he more than any other can understand an Egyptian, especially a working class Egyptian, from the inside. Barakah-Mary finds at one point that she is beginning to think in Arabic. There, again, she probably reflects Pickthall, who can reproduce the turns of phrase of Arabic in his English, and who can alter his style so radically when he shifts his narration from the consciousness of an English character to that of an Egyptian. He reproduces, too, the moral outlooks which his characters would have, sometimes simple and confused, often prejudiced and cunning. His picaresque protagonists, Saïd the Syrian and Mabrûk the Egyptian, might strike a present-day reader at first as drawn by a patronizingly superior outsider. Yet the same sympathetic but ironic view is taken by him when he deals with Sussex rustics in his English stories, while in Youssef Idris and other Egyptian writers, the same attitude is taken towards those simpler protagonists who do not reflect the author's own more sophisticated personality. The flawed morality of his picaroons, so close to that of the heroes of Arabic *maqamat* is the ethical equivalent of the rustic grammar of his Sussex characters, equally understandable, and not requiring forgiveness. The adventures of Mabrûk in *The Children of the Nile* form his fullest study of an Egyptian mind. Many of his short stories[16] portray the flawed understanding which leads to failure of communication between Englishman and Arab. At Kefr (*sic*) Ammeh,[17] the villagers hurry to protect themselves when they hear the coarse and menacing sounds that some visiting Englishmen are making in the night, but the Nubian servants explain, 'Englishmen were most benevolent when thus elated. The dreadful roaring was the mode of singing in their country. They would roar till there was no more voice left in them, and then betake themselves like lambs to bed'.

The wrong-headed efforts by one or other to adopt foreign moulds become the subjects of amusing and finely crafted stories. Ahmed Abdel Cader[18] becomes a nationalist when his English office-head snubs him for being too familiar; this is after many years of efforts at self-anglicization such as this one: 'He bought a little dog and tried to like it, but every time the creature licked his hand he shuddered, conscious of extreme uncleanness.' To return to Toynbee's terms, Ahmed goes from being a compliant member of the 'internal proletariat' of English culture, to becoming a fighting member of its 'external proletariat'. What would Pickthall have made of Ghali's hero Ram? (The pet name is, it would seem, short for Ramses.) Half a century younger than Ahmed, his story is still one with comic tensions, but he is a character whose dilemma of cultured uprootedness gives his life the bruised pathos of the Absurd—in the contemporary 'metaphysical' sense of the word—and that is the same predicament in which Ghali lived his own short life.

One type of portrait of which Pickthall was incapable was successfully produced by a lesser writer. John Knittel developed rapidly away from the melodrama of his first Egyptian story. For *Nile Gold* (1929) is a mummy fantasy of love for the resuscitated Princess Nitocris, in the same line of pretentious works of which a recent and dispiriting example is Norman Mailer's *Ancient Evenings* (1983). But Knittel's major contribution is *Dr. Ibrahim*. In spite of some unlikely twists of plot, this is a true novel in a recognizably twentieth-century manner, and follows the fortunes and the developing views of a poor young Upper Egyptian who becomes a distinguished medical man. The problems, the response, the variety of attitudes encountered, make this a very authentic study of modern Egypt: the depiction of the hero's conscience is wholly interior. It is the only one of these works to have been serialized in Arabic—and that not long after its first appearance.[19]

Two writers who belong after the Second World War must be called Habitants. James Aldridge takes a phrase from Abdel Nasser's biography, the words *I Wish He Would Not Die*, as title for his interwoven account of an English officer's conflict with military authority, and the early careers of a thinly disguised Nasser and Abdel Hakim Amer.[20] Nasser's renunciation of terrorism is described, and a tentative comradeship across national and cultural lines is well drawn, though in a stiff masculine way. In the lengthy sequel, *The Last Exile* (1961), the British attack almost ruins an Englishman's hopes of acceptance in his new home. Again, the focus is upon the comradeship of men brought together through their work. It is perhaps Aldridge's Marxism which explains the resemblance to Soviet novels about communion among those who share in a public enterprise. The combination of Kipling as model and Zhdanov as preceptor makes for rather dessicated fiction. It is certainly a very authentic account of life under Nasser: perhaps it is this veraciousness which makes it dull. The slap which the hero receives on his face does not occur until page 591, and remarkably little has developed until then.[21]

The involvement of Desmond Stewart's heroes has less stiffness. In *The Men of Friday* the visitor whose viewpoint we follow is, significantly, not a European, but the son of an Egyptian exile, visiting Egypt for the first time. It is an Egypt poised for revolution, and Layth's main friendships are with the Egyptian Jew Tollo, and with Hameed, the intellectual with village roots. Stewart's trilogy, *The Sequence of Roles*,[22] covers three generations of Egyptian, Levantine, and British people interconnected through marriages, and deals with the tug between the attraction of Egypt and family roots in Britain. The lives of the successive protagonists cover precisely the period in which the fiction I have dealt with was written, and the different points of view presented in the story reflect the various attitudes found in this literature.

Throughout this period, Kipling was available as a master for imitation, while in the second half of it, Forster's *Passage to India* provided a model: English literature about India sometimes rose to notable heights—yet the Anglo-Egyptian writers only attain very occasionally to such levels, even though, among Habitants, the writing of Pickthall stands out, and, among Visitants, that of Durrell. In contrast with this negative assessment, it is salutary to turn to a western writer whose work seems to have all one might wish in a novelist in this field. An Italian living in Egypt is almost *ipso facto* a Habitant; the Italians had a larger, more varied, more rooted community there, as well as sharing with Egyptians a common Mediterranean outlook. This is demonstrated in three novels by Fausta Cialente, *Ballata levantina* (1961),[23] *Cortile a Cleopatra* (1962), and *Il vento sulla sabbia* (1972), though their success is surely due rather to her own individual fine artistry. She portrays the life of the Alexandria Levantine—beautifully, with directness, a feel for place and for human relationships, and a nostalgic poignancy. The life and place she understands from the inside, and the meretricious elements of showmanship are absent. Fausta Cialente is a pellucid and Cartesian Durrell—and some of her writing has a lyric beauty unmatched in the English writers. As an Alexandrian, I find no point at which the events and descriptions clash with my recollections, and yet they have an imaginative resonance well beyond the merely documentary. What makes them so surprising to me is that these literary artefacts have the same effect upon me as my own memories of true experiences filtered through time. It is pleasant, even if one has go to outside the field of English writings, to be able to end with this taste of what is perhaps the clearest, the least brackish of the many mouths of the Nile.

Postscript

It is hardly necessary to add that there is no attempt at complete coverage in this survey, though the footnotes should provide sign-posts for any who wish to follow this topic up further. I particularly regret having said nothing about the American Edward R. F. Sheehan's *Kingdom of Illusion* (1965); the account of Aldridge's novels does not allow for mention of his illustrated documentary book, *Cairo*, which is an outstanding work. Silence certainly implies no disparagement of the little adventure story by Keith Scott-Watson, *Achmet* (sic) *and the Colonel* (194?). I can now also report that the political melodrama of cross-cultural love is still alive and bursting at the seams in two enjoyably unprofound novels, Laurie Devine's *Nile* (679 pp.) (1983) and Noel Barbour's *A Woman of Cairo* (672 pp.) (1984).

I must thank all the members of the audience of the original presentation who gave me sound advice after it was read, in particular Mr. J. King of the BBC, who reminded me of the importance of Waguih Ghali, one of the authors who made no appearance in the original version.

This paper was prepared before the publication of Diana Athill's book about Waguih Ghali, *After a Funeral* (1986), and Peter Clark's *Marmaduke Pickthall: British Muslim* of the same year. Nor had I come to know Leslie Croxford's *Solomon's Folly* (1974), a work which comes close to those of Fausta Cialente not only in its theme but in the fineness of its vision.

Notes

A version of this paper was delivered as the IXth Antonius Lecture at St. Antony's College, Oxford, in July 1984.

[1] Similarly, there are good descriptive passages and genre scenes in Hichens's other Egyptian fiction, e.g. the short account of the little houses and sandy gardens on the outskirts of Ismailia, in *An Imaginative Man* (1913), and the orgiastic night out in Cairo in the same novel. The cosmopolitan social life of the tourist and the foreign resident in Egypt is the setting for part of the action in each of the novels *The First Lady Brandon* (1931), *"Susie's" Career* (1935), and *The Million* (1940). Hichens also sets in Egypt some of his short stories, e.g. 'The Under-Man', in *My Desert Friend* (1931). His memoirs, *Yesterday* (1947), show him to have known Egyptians prominent in the political and literary worlds, and reveal that he knew and understood the country and its people—and, indeed, human life in general—better than his fiction would suggest.

[2] See M. A. Manzalaoui, 'Curate's Egg: An Alexandrian Opinion of Durrell's Quartet', *Etudes anglaises* XV (1962), 248–60.

[3] A very recent story, *The Crocodile's Head*, now reveals Debney as rather more of a Habitant. This story has not yet been published in full: a very truncated version appears in the *New Edinburgh Review* XIII (1981).

[4] William Walsh, *D. J. Enright: Poet of Humanism* (1974).

[5] Newby deals with Egyptians and with Egypt in other novels, but the country

becomes an increasingly notional one. The main characters of *The Picnic at Sakkara* reappear in *A Guest and his Going* (1959), and there are two Egyptian visitors in the boys' story *The Loot Runners* (1949). Egypt itself is the setting for all or part of the action in each of the novels *A Season in England* (1951), *Revolution and Roses* (1957), *Something to Answer For* (1968), and *Kith* (1977).

⁶ *The Danger Tree* (1977), *The Battle Lost and Won* (1978), *The Sum of Things* (1980).

⁷ I now have to acknowledge that this notion of mine turns out to be quite wrong. Noone tells me that Tarek, one of his principal characters, is partly modelled upon myself.

⁸ The name Babylon was sometimes used in the European languages of the Middle Ages for Cairo.

⁹ There are English translations, *Men God Forgot* (1963) and *House of Certain Death* (1947). The later *Mendiants et orgueilleux* has appeared in English under several titles, first (1959) as *If All Men Were Beggars*, then as *Proud Beggars*, and later again as *A Room in Cairo*. Cossery's third novel, dealing with rural Egypt, *Les fainéants dans la vallée fertile* is translated as *The Lazy Ones* (1952). (A further work (1964) is *La violence et la dérision*.)

¹⁰ *Saïd the Fisherman* went through some dozen impressions between 1903 and the outbreak of the First World War.

¹¹ In addition to *The Shadow of Egypt*, referred to already, one can mention *The Pagan Woman* (1908), *On Desert Altars* (1916), *There was a King in Egypt* (1918), *With Other Eyes* (1920), and *Moslem Jack* (1929).

¹² As a more committed Moslem, Pickthall later translated *The Meaning of the Glorious Koran* (1930), and delivered sermons at the Woking mosque (*Friday Sermons*, 1930).

¹³ *Donovan Pasha and some people of Egypt* went through four impressions from 1902 to 1921.

¹⁴ Samuel Norris, *Two Men of Manxland: Hall Caine, Novelist; T. E. Brown, Poet* (Douglas 1947); p. 66. From this same passage, we learn that *The White Prophet* fell flat; Caine bought in the unsold copies to prevent their being remaindered.

¹⁵ One of the tensest moments in Anglo-Egyptian relations. In 1906, some English officers went pigeon-shooting near the village of Denshwai, unmindful of the fact that the pigeons were not game birds but domestic fowl owned by poor peasants. When the villagers attacked the Englishmen, they ran away, and one of them died, apparently of sunstroke. The British retaliation was to insist upon the flogging of a number of the villagers, and the hanging of four of them. The best English account of the incident is in Bernard Shaw's Preface to his *John Bull's Other Island*.

¹⁶ *Pot au Feu* (1911), *Tales from Five Chimneys* (1914), and *As Others See Us* (1922).

¹⁷ 'The Kefr Ammeh Incident', *As Others See Us*.

¹⁸ 'Karakter; A Symptom of Young Egypt', *Pot au Feu*.

¹⁹ There is much about Knittel in Hichens's autobiography *Yesterday*. John Knittel was a Swiss born in India and raised in London. After working at the Crédit Lyonnais bank in London, and in film production there during the First World War, he devoted the rest of his active life to writing. He and his family set up a joint household with Hichens, first in England, and then abroad; from 1932 to 1938 they lived in Egypt, in Dar Ain Shams, a house on the edge of the desert near Heliopolis, close to the spot where Wilfred Scawen Blunt had lived. Adrian Vereker's house, in Hichens's *"Susie's" Career*, is the fictional counterpart of this house. Knittel wrote most of his plays in German, but all of his fiction in English, from *Aaron West* in 1921 to *Jean-Michel* in 1954. Hichens already knew Egypt in the 1890s, and, in the thirties, he and Knittel lived an identical life in the same environment. The deeper understanding of Egypt which Knittel shows is a prime illustration of the importance of individual potential, as oppsed to adult environmental factors. And while Hichens belongs to the Visitant

group, in spite of their shared experience, Knittel belongs with the Habitants.

[20] Nasser's chief lieutenant and early friend, who clashed with him in 1967, was arrested and allegedly committed suicide in prison.

[21] Egypt is the background of short stories in Aldridge's collection *Gold and Sand* (1960), e.g. 'The Last Inch', 'Endurance for Honour', 'The Shark Cage'. In them, the central consciousness is that of an English airman, during and after the Second World War. The personal relationship between Englishman and Egyptian is the theme of 'Some of my Best Friends are Englishmen'.

[22] *The Round Mosaic* (1965), *The Pyramid Inch* (1966), *The Mamelukes* (1968).

[23] English translation *The Levantines* (1963).

The Meaning of the Dome of the Rock

TOGETHER with the Alhambra and the Taj Mahal, the Dome of the Rock in Jerusalem is without doubt the best known monument of Islamic architecture. It is visited every year by thousands of tourists, it appears on posters and stamps and its strikingly simple profile of a gilt cupola on a high drum rising from an octagon covered with glittering tiles has been copied in recent years on nearly all possible materials—from textiles to prints—as the Dome of the Rock has also become a symbol of Palestinian *nostalgies* and aspirations as well as of fundamentalist—and not so fundamentalist—Islamic ambitions and piety. This mixture of national, ethnic, and religious associations around a monument or a place on earth is, of course, not unusual and, in our days of ideological conflicts, it is intensified whenever sacred places or national monuments are *in partibus infedelium*. This is curiously the case with the Alhambra and with the Taj Mahal as well as with the Dome of the Rock, so that three of the most famous monuments of Islamic architecture are not in territories under the immediate control of Muslims. Accidents of history perhaps, but, as I shall try to show in the case of the Dome of the Rock, the complexity of contemporary meanings associated with it is, whatever modern reasons led to the complexity, more than matched by those of the past.

This is not, of course, true in a simple and literal sense, the sense of the tourist guides who provide for it a traditional explanation fully established by early Mamluk times, let us say by about 1300. The Dome of the Rock, according to this tradition, was built over the rock whence the Prophet ascended into heaven on his night journey, the *isra*, from Medina to Jerusalem alluded to in the first verse of the 17th surah of the Koran. The event itself, barely intimated in the Koran and the subject of some exegetical debate in early Islamic times, was embellished over the centuries by folk as well as mystical piety. Eventually it became fully accredited by the orthodox sunnah or tradition and incorporated with a great wealth of details in the account of the Prophet's Ascension or *Mi'raj*. Various components of the event found their place in a number of specific spots around the Dome of the Rock, where Buraq, the prophet's steed, knelt and waited, where it was tied, where the Prophet prayed, and so on. In addition, although less frequently mentioned, at least by tourist guides, a series of eschatalogical themes were woven around the Dome of the Rock, the most dramatically powerful one being that the Ka'bah in Mekkah will join the Rock in Jerusalem at the end of time. Finally, in ways which still seek their full investigation, the sacred history of Jerusalem from Adam to Jesus, and obviously with particular emphasis on Abraham, also finds its way to the Dome of the Rock and its surrounding areas in the *fada'il* which, since the twelfth (and perhaps already eleventh) century, served as guide-books and as spiritual helpers to the Faithful.[1]

A specific Muslim meaning (the Ascension of the Prophet), an old and peculiarly Jerusalemite association with the Resurrection, the Judgement, and the end of time, and an intimate relationship to the monotheistic prophetic succession as seen through the Muslim faith, these three themes created around the Dome of the Rock, on the platform of the Haram, to its North and to its West, that extraordinary Mamluk Jerusalem which Suleyman the Magnificent, the new Solomon, enclosed in a stunningly powerful curtain wall and which has very recently been made available to the learned and general public thanks to the tremendous work carried out by the British School of Archaeology in Jerusalem.[2]

Mamluk Jerusalem is well provided with monuments, inscriptions, texts, descriptions, *waqfiyahs*, and even now the fascinating archive discovered in the Aqsa Museum and slowly being published by Prof. Donald Little and his colleagues.[3] Matters are much more complicated when we go back to the three and a half centuries of Islamic Jerusalem before the Crusades. How many of the associations demonstrable for the later Middle Ages can be carried back to the early centuries? Is it justified to do so? Although less systematic than in Mamluk times, information is plentiful. There are inscriptions,[4] an important group of geographical texts, one of which, Nasir-i Khusro's, is an account which can almost be followed on the terrain,[5] archaeological studies like Robert Hamilton's masterful unraveling of the Aqsa mosque's complicated history or the largely unpublished and, at first glance, less carefully controlled Israeli excavations to the South and Southwest of the Haram,[6] and then there is the Dome of the Rock itself.[7]

It is a remarkably well-documented building, with an inscription dated in 691–2 during the reign of ʿAbd al-Malik. Except for minor details, the basic shape of the building has not been altered: a high cylindrical dome, gilt initially, over the mysterious Rock, two octagonal ambulatories, and four identical entrances preceded by a porch on slender columns. The building was lavishly decorated with marble plaques and with mosaics which sheathed it almost entirely, both inside and outside. The interior mosaics have been reasonably well preserved, but only minute fragments remain of the original external decoration. The history of repairs and modifications, such as they were, in the building are unusually well recorded, for the most part through inscriptions, and, leaving aside a number of technical problems which are bound to remain unsolved for lack of adequate documentation, it is only around the mosaics of the drum that feasible additional investigations are needed in order to determine the extent and date of restorations. Once again it is Sulayman the Magnificent who sponsored the last major overhaul of the building and who provided it with its beautiful exterior tile decoration, which, in a 16th century technique, recreated the colorful brilliance of earlier mosaics. Some twenty years ago a major reconstruction of the Dome of the Rock was completed which was superbly documented during the work itself. To my knowledge, however, this documentation has not been made available.

I have summarized the history of the building, which is probably well known to most scholars and visitors to Jerusalem, in order to make two points. One is that, whatever changes occurred, it is relatively easy to imagine and visualize the building apparently completed in 691-2. The other one is that the building contains an unusual number of inscriptions from its early period. There is the 240 metres long inscription with Koranic fragments from 691-2. In an unusual but, as we shall see, highly significant gesture, the 'Abbasid caliph al-Ma'mun replaced 'Abd al-Malik's name with his own, without, however, changing the date. Several 'Abbasid caliphs and members of their families, especially women, recorded their repairs in nearly inaccessible parts of the building and major Fatimid work was recorded in more formal and more visible inscriptions. What this means is that the Dome of the Rock was from the very beginning what may be called a 'talking' building, or perhaps better a 'recording' building which incorporated its history within its own fabric, but not necessarily in a form or in places visible to all. Its history was, so to speak, given to the building.

I shall return shortly to some further lessons to be drawn from this practice of providing inaccessible information, but it is important to note that it appears from the very beginning, as the long Umayyad inscription is only decipherable from below when properly lit by sunlight, which means that it can never be easily read in its entirety.

Over a quarter century ago I proposed an interpretation of the Dome of the Rock which has been accepted, at least in its broad implications, by most non-Muslim scholars, ignored by some, rejected by one or two, but, to my knowledge, refuted by none.[8] Since I will propose some major modification to it, I am taking the liberty of summarizing it briefly. On the basis of the inscription which contains the whole Christology of the Koran, of the presence of Byzantine and Sasanian royal insignia in the mosaics facing the rock, of its location on the abandoned and desecrated Herodian space of the Second Jewish Temple, by then replete with popular associations with nearly every major personage of Biblical history, and a number of other arguments which need not be repeated here, I interpreted the Dome of the Rock as a monument celebrating the victorious presence of Islam in the Christian city of Jerusalem by resacralizing with the new and final revelation a space made holy by Judaism. Like everybody else I attributed the building of the Dome of the Rock to 'Abd al-Malik and saw it, together with the reform in coinage, the change of the administrative language from Greek to Arabic, the forceful if not at times brutal activities of al-Hajjaj in the

Arabian peninsula, the truce with Byzantium, and the successful stemming of disorders in Iraq, as another sign, a specifically visual one, of the middle Umayyad conscious assumption of discrete imperial rule, that is the full awareness on the part of the Marwanids that theirs was a new empire continuing old Mediterranean and even Iranian ones but under the aegis of a new and final Revelation.[9] I agreed with the prevailing formal explanation of the Dome of the Rock as a minor modification of a type of centrally planned martyria or churches illustrated by the Holy Sepulchre and the Church of the Ascension in Jerusalem, the cathedral of Bosra in southern Syria, San Vitale in Ravenna, eventually Charlemagne's palace church in Aachen.[10] The style and vocabulary of its mosaics seemed to me as correctly derived from the prevailing high styles of Late Antique and early Christian art, all probably executed by Christian mosaicists. Finally, I argued that this immanent and immediate message to the Christian world soon lost its point, but the monument which was the message became the visual and eventually semantic center of a religious and pietistic transformation of the Haram, first into a mosque, as al-Walid constructed the Aqsa, then as a unique mixture of mosque and shrine, with all sorts of associations leading up, after the Crusades, to the reasonably coherent, both visually and functionally, entity sketched out at the beginning of this paper.

Much in this explanation is still, in my view at least, entirely valid. But in two areas, curiously enough the areas where I fully agreed with everybody else's views of the Dome of the Rock, I do believe it to be based on erroneous or at least incomplete analyses of available data. These areas are: the involvement of ʿAbd al-Malik in the building of the Dome of the Rock and the relationship of the Dome's forms to Mediterranean Christian or Late Antique art.

The date of the inscription, 72 (691–2), is clear and it has been demonstrated that the date was preceded by the phrase 'built (*bana*) this cupola (*qubbat*) the servant of God ʿAbd al-Malik (changed later into the *imam al-Ma'mun*), Commander of the Faithful' and followed with with a eulogy: 'may God accept (this work) from him and be satisfied with him; *amin*' and then a few damaged words. By a curious habit derived from the practice of painters and of manufacturers of objects, historians of art and by extension other historians have, therefore, tended to associate the building with events around 691–2 and to formulate through these events the psychological and ideological setting in which the Dome of the Rock was built, or rather created, for its completion may well have taken many years. In reality, however, as anyone involved with building anything, even in our times of computer controled technology, knows, it takes years to build and decorate a building of any magnitude. In the case of the Dome of the Rock, the following has to have taken place before ʿAbd al-Malik's inscription could be put up: mosaics and marble had to have been set on the walls;

1. Dome of the Rock, Jerusalem

2. Dome of the Rock ground plan

3. Dome of the Rock section on east and west axis

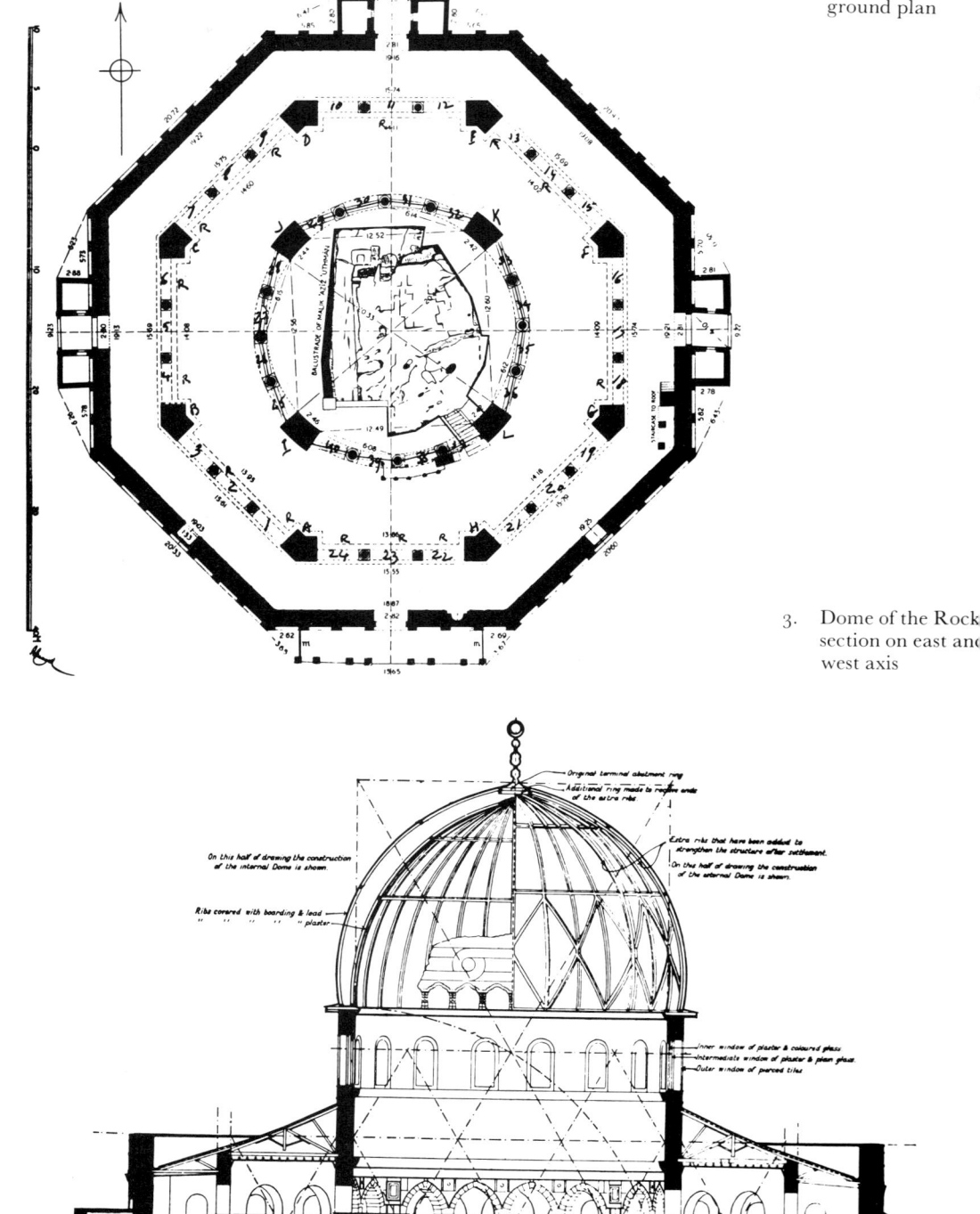

4. Jerusalem; the Haram in the foreground

Mekkah: the Ka'bah

tesserae and plaques of marble had to have been gathered from wherever they were manufactured and some designing of patterns should have taken place, a technical job for which actually a lot of information exists in the technique and composition of the mosaics themselves; building materials had to be assembled and put together, some of them taken from destroyed or abandoned ancient or Christian buildings, others cut or otherwise prepared.

So far I have only mentioned obvious building needs. In Jerusalem, there was, at this time, yet another essential requirement: the clearing of the space for the building. This clearing required the existence of the high platform on which the Dome stands, of a number of accesses (without the arcades which crown the stairs known today, most of which are dated to a later time), of the large esplanade in some sort of usable form, meaning in turn that the Double Gate, perhaps the Golden Gate, and possibly some access to the North all had to have been at least roughly cleared and flattened. I say 'roughly' on purpose, for several later inscriptions indicate that work on the outer walls continued for several centuries and, as recent Israeli excavations have confirmed the presence of a major (I suspect *the* major) early Islamic settlement South of the Haram, the southern and southwestern sections of the walls, precisely the ones which required most work, had to have been if not entirely rebuilt, at least made accessible and usable for movement. Recently it has even been suggested that the whole northern third of the Haram may well have been cut out of the natural rock under the Umayyads, and almost certainly before the Dome of the Rock was built.[11] I am not entirely convinced by the argument because, even though it solves a number of very important hitherto unresolved issues, it also creates new problems. How much really had to be done is difficult to say and the only visible documentation we possess, short of technically difficult and politically impossible excavations, consists in masonry analyses, a tediously difficult task with so many uncertainties that only very general approximations can be expected from it. But, if we recall that Jerusalem was not a major center for what would nowadays be called a construction industry and that it was not a capital city bound to attract artisans seeking employment, the effort of creating a logical space for building the Dome of the Rock was enormous and required not only huge financial investments and sizeable logistic support, but an organization in charge of the project. Even before much work had been done, someone had to have decided that it needed to be done. Even if one grants that our own progression from concept to brief, financing, design, blueprints, and execution is hardly a valid procedure for the seventh century, it is only invalid in the concreteness and specificity of the forms it takes, for the process itself is unavoidable, especially, as I shall show shortly, in a building with the peculiar visual characteristics of the Dome of the Rock. How long such a process would have taken is impossible to guess, but we are certainly talking about several years. And this is where the problem begins, for the ten years which preceded the alleged completion of the Dome of the Rock, in fact the twelve years which followed Muʿawiyah's death in 680 were years of almost unceasing internecine strife between various Arab factions and it is not until the defeat of Ibn al-Zubayr by al-Hajjaj late in 692 that peace was restored within the half-urbanized factions of Iraqi cities. By then the Dome of the Rock had already been completed.

What this rather simplified sketch suggests is that the conceptual matrix in which the idea of the Dome of the Rock, its purpose, its location, and its shape were conceived is not from ʿAbd al-Malik's time, but from Muʿawiyah's, an idea already proposed in a passing remark without substantiating evidence of the late Professor Goitein.[12] There is a world of difference between ʿAbd al-Malik, fully conscious through his reforms of the 'Islamic' character of the Umayyad empire and Muʿawiyah, the brilliant and wily opportunist ready to acquire and consolidate power through any means. The further point, however, is that there is a demonstrable connection between Muʿawiyah and Jerusalem. According to a Syriac source 'in 971 (i.e. AD 661) many Arabs gathered in Jerusalem and made Muʿawiyah king; he went up to Golgotha, sat down there and prayed, then proceeded to Gethsemane, and then went down to the grave of St. Mary, where he prayed again'.[13] An Arab Muslim source quoted by Tabari confirms a Syrian homage to Muʿawiyah in Jerusalem.[14] This is where he was offered the crown of king of the Arabs, says a third, this time Greek, source.[15] To my knowledge, no event or association of comparable importance connects ʿAbd al-Malik to Jerusalem and such references as do exist are strictly within his caliphal prerogatives as ruler of an empire, for instance the militaries recording the distances of various places to Jerusalem and a couple of other references to which I shall return. Muʿawiyah's relationship to Jerusalem is clearly that of a prince in the tradition of the pre-Islamic kings of the Arabian world and a verse from the *Mufaddaliyat* identified and discussed by Professor Caskel helps in providing a more specific explanation to the Syriac text. It goes as follows: 'I swear by Him, to whose holy places the Quraysh go on pilgrimage, and by that which is surrounded by the Hira mountains for sacrifice;

> By the month of the Banu Umayya and by the consecrated sacrificial animals, whose blood covers them.'[16]

A parallelism is here indicated between a sanctuary of the Umayyads and one of Ibn al-Zubayr, the Qurayshite upholder of an old Mekkan tradition, who had recently destroyed the Kaʿbah built with the Prophet's help and restored it to its earlier *jahiliyah* stage, the one, according to traditional lore and belief, which had been created by Abraham. In both cases the implication is downright pagan and tribal, not Islamic and imperial, reflecting a traditional Arabian perception of power struggles and power symbols, not a new one. It is in fact only within this Arabian context, still infected by paganism, that one can explain why a sanctuary would have been built around a natural rock whose only demonstrable (or at least preserved today) connotations *at that time* were with the Jewish Temple, if it is indeed *lapsis pertusus* of a western pilgrim's text, or with Abraham's sacrifice through the ancient confusion between Mount Moriah and the land of Moriah.

Within this context, I propose to see the planning, foundation, and design of the Dome of the Rock as the expression of Muʿawiyah's rule, independent of a Hijaz to which, all texts say, he did not want to return. It was set around a rock with whatever Jewish associations this rock had because there also he was establishing an Abrahamic relationship and certainly with the memory of pagan lithocracy in pre-Islamic Arabia. It was also meant to be a message of power to the Christians, whose defeated rulers had their crowns hanging in the sanctuary, as similar trophies had been hanging in the Kaʿbah, and it proclaimed the acquisition or appropriation by Muʿawiyah of *mulk*, that imperial power which had ruled the Christian world since Constantine or possibly the kingship of the pre-Islamic rulers of the northern Arabian steppes and deserts. To Muʿawiyah, in short, what was meant to be created in Jerusalem was a dynastic or tribal shrine and Jerusalem alone made sense in the world conquered by the Arabs as the location of shrine, because Jerusalem alone was endowed with the kinds of associations both with God and with kings that made an event there or a building reverberate throughout the world of Christians and of Jews as well as among the new Muslims. To try in a single monument to juggle messages to Arabs, Muslim or not, to the new leadership of a fledgling empire, to Christians and to Jews seems, to me at least, to fit beautifully with the striking and imaginative personality of the first Umayyad caliph.

One alternative to this scheme or scenario could be proposed. It is possible that the mosaic decoration and, more specifically, the inscription were chosen by ʿAbd al-Malik and his pious entourage and, thus, that, as the building was being built, parts of its program were being modified because of altered circumstances or additional meanings were given to it. The practice is not unknown in the history of mostly contemporary architecture and I know of one possible parallel in the Muslim world of the Middle Ages. This hypothesis would explain Muqaddasi's celebrated text about the Dome of the Rock which mentions exclusively the caliph's intent to compete with Christian monuments. It may also explain another more obscure statement in a late medieval text that ʿAbd al-Malik incorporated the Dome of the Rock in the Aqsa mosque, which would mean then that it is ʿAbd al-Malik who first sought to give it an Islamic meaning.[17] And al-Ma'mun's substitution of his name in the inscription can easily be explained as a last recognition of secular and imperial values in a building which by then had been transformed into a purely religious one. Solomonic lore, which has been proposed to explain certain motifs in the mosaic decoration,[18] would have affected either Umayyad patron.

Before returning in conclusion to some additional remarks about the religious meaning of the Dome of the Rock, let me turn to the second part of my argument, the visual one. For, so far, the main justifications for my explanation of the building have been, first, that the process of designing and building of this magnitude in the peculiar conditions of the city of Jerusalem compel us to propose for the conception of the building an earlier date than the usually accepted one, and, second, the contents of an inscription which is in Arabic, hardly yet the common language of the Christians and Jews to whom it was destined, but especially an inscription which was invisible to them and to nearly everyone else.

The art historical argument about the Dome of the Rock has centered almost exclusively on the question of the origins of its plan and there is a scholarly agreement about the set of Mediterranean Christian monuments with which it is to be connected. It is difficult to disagree with series of plans which are indeed strikingly alike except on one point. Only the Dome of the Rock is perfectly symmetrical on any one of its axes and does not provide a particular preeminence of one side over the others; even the doorways are exactly alike. All the comparable Christian monuments are provided with a facade, if for no other purpose than to put a single entry into the building. Where the Dome of the Rock is even more different from any one of its alleged models is in its elevation. Admittedly, most of the latter are only known as ruins, but in the Holy Sepulchre, Ravenna, or Aachen, the point of the building is always to compel entrance into it and, once in, to be overwhelmed by the central cupola. Things work out quite differently in the Dome of the Rock. Entry is difficult because of the narrowness of the doors and because not one of them has beckoning or inviting signs; the dome, twice as high as the ambulatory around it, has as its diameter the smallest circle which would encompass the rock and is therefore nearly invisible from the inside; in fact, slight alterations in the dimensions of intercolumniations always lead the eye across the whole building and over the rock rather than upward. These alterations are, however, minimal, and, on the whole, as many observers have noted, the Dome of the Rock is characterized by the precision of its geometric composition, both in plan and in elevation. As Ecochard and others have shown, the geometric principles involved are neither unique nor original. What is unique is that almost nothing breaks their harmony and proportions. The building is not only conceived in geometry, it *is* a geometric object.

In short, while the technical, phonetic, and, to a large extent, compositional structure of the building does indeed belong to the language of forms prevailing in the Early Christian Mediterranean, the effect it produces is quite different from what is found in parallel buildings: separation between exterior and interior impacts; emphasis on the dome for the outside viewer, on a unified space with multiple supports from the inside; absolute equality of all sides. To these architectonic attributes must be added the mosaic decoration. Once again, the technique and most of the motifs belong to the Mediterranean tradition. The suggestion of an iconographic meaning for the crowns and possibly also for the trees in the spandrels and on the upper part of piers is legitimate to the extent that mosaics and paintings were used for visual messages in Christian and Classical art. The absence of living beings, certainly a willed decision, makes the means for the transmission unusual and raises some questions as to whether the messages were understood, but a number of formal components like relationship of motives to each other, highlighting of some motives over others, and so on, make an iconographic reading of the mosaics not only legitimate but likely. So far, however, only the crowns and jewels on the one hand and the large trees on the other have been given some attention.[19]

In two areas, however, the Dome of the Rock is entirely original. One is the nearly total sheathing of the building with colorful decoration, in this instance of marble and mosaics. In ways which have never yet been fully analyzed and of which I shall provide only one example, this sheathing does much more than strengthen key architectonic parts; it actually modifies them, as in the intrados of arches, where the continuity of the surface design alters and softens the sharp edge of a stone arch and provides continuity to what is normally seen as contrast. The second originality of the decoration is that it also occurred on the outside. Exterior decoration is very rare in the prevailing Mediterranean *koiné* and, when it occurs there or in Iran, it tends to be limited to a specific message on the facade.

How can one explain these characteristics: differences between exterior and interior messages, perfect geometry, mosaics both inside and outside? Let me also add that there is no evidence before the Dome of the Rock for a Muslim patronage of esthetically significant buildings. The earlier mosque in Jerusalem was described as 'rude' by a western traveller and whatever can be reconstructed in Kufa and Basra does not compare in sophistication with the Dome of the Rock.

The explanation I am putting forward is that the Umayyad patrons were in fact affected or inspired by the one 'monument' in their tradition, the Kaʿbah in Mekkah. It was a simple building with the function of a shrine-treasury inside and of a magnet for ritual then in the process of formulation on the outside. Few were allowed inside, but all knew its contents. And it was covered with regularly renewed textiles, whose colors varied considerably and which, according to al-Azraqi, were more frequently changed in pre-Islamic and early Islamic times than became the practice later on.[20] All of this means that the visual impression of the Kaʿbah was that of a colorful textile fluttering under the impact of winds and covering a clearly delineated geometric shape.

It is perhaps reasonable to explain the outside mosaic decoration of the Dome of the Rock as seeking to give the colorful impression of textiles, but the building in Jerusalem hardly looks like its Mekkan counterpart. And yet, if we are mindful of the procedures of medieval architects outlined by Krautheimer many decades ago[21] and in line with my earlier suggestions about a historical context for the Dome of the Rock, a scenario for its construction can be proposed. Muʿawiyah in my hypothesis—but the process could apply to any comparable patron—decides to build in Jerusalem a shrine (understood here in a generic architectural and not religious sense as a unique monument for a singular purpose) to associate himself and perhaps his lineage with one of the holiest places in the Judeo-Christian and now newly Islamic world. He sees it primarily as a place competing in semantic value with Mekkah controlled by Ibn al-Zubayr, at least he does so with the eyes of a traditional Arab ruler. But with his eyes as the ruler of a fledgling world empire, he sees it also as a message to the People of the Book who form the majority of the population and, at least in the case of Christians, who had developed an elaborate and expensive art for their faith. Muʿawiyah turns to the building establishment of Syria and Palestine, perhaps even calls for artisans from more important centers like Constantinople, because he has extensive funds at his disposal and because, for at least one of his purposes, he has to use the language of the conquered world. Yet he also wanted to preserve something of the Mekkan world. Since no artisan was going to travel to Mekkah to look at the Kaʿbah and since there were no appropriate architectural manuals or drawings, it is orally that a brief was produced. The Kaʿbah, someone would have said, is a geometrically clear building, it creates a colorful impression, it dominates it surroundings, it possesses treasures inside and serves as a visual magnet in the city and the surrounding valley. The Dome of the Rock would then have been the translation by Mediterranean artisans into *their* language of an orally transmitted description of the Mekkan sanctuary.

The possibility of this scenario is strengthened by two additional documents. One is that several later writers did accuse the Umayyads of having tried to move the Pilgrimage to Jerusalem. They understood the connection between the two buildings, but, because the Kaʿbah had by then become exclusively the center of the hajj, they had to explain the connection in terms of the pilgrimage; the complex psychological and emotional components of generations with a foot still in *jahiliyah* times no longer made much sense to ninth century Muslim writers. The other argument is that a reliance on geometric precision and geometric imagination is often the natural instinct of architects faced with a purpose with which they are not familiar. On a different level, neither the Dome of the Rock nor the Kaʿbah were copied in later Islamic architecture, nor did they significantly affect the development of that architecture, some exceptions notwithstanding. By providing the Dome of the Rock with a unique and singular meaning at the time of its creation, its lack of impact may be explained as well, something which the traditional explanation was unable to do.

My argument tries to weave together two kinds of arguments: the analysis of a building as a perceived object and not, as is so frequently done in art historical research, as a bundle of influences; and, secondly, the elements of a process of building in which purpose, ambition, assets, surrounding events, people, ideas, and technological potential all intermingle. I have left out (or barely alluded to) a third component, which is the specificity of Jerusalem as a place and as a set of memories in the second half of the seventh century; the study of Jerusalem at that time could form a whole lecture in its own right.[22] What has emerged from this piecing together of a standing building and of processes issued from visual and written sources as well as from more general assumptions about the nature of the building?

First of all, the uniqueness of the Dome of the Rock as a work of architecture can be explained by the unique circumstances of its creation. And the uniqueness of the circumstances explains in turn why, as traditional Islam was developing and codifying its piety and its sacred places, the Dome of the Rock, with a largely different agenda behind it, was difficult to fit into anything. It was a work of state, but of a type of state that was going to be radically changed by ʿAbd al-Malik's reforms. It was also a work of art, but it was not a work of faith, while the whole history of the Haram from the moment of the building of the Aqsa mosque by al-Walid becomes the history of Muslim religious and pious beliefs and practices overtaking an ancient sacred space and eventually the Dome of the Rock itself. This was, I believe, finally achieved in a visually coherent form only under the Fatimids in the early eleventh century and the whole process is a fascinating one to which I hope to devote myself one of these years.

Secondly, even though the Umayyad period has been better studied than any other one in medieval Islamic history, insufficient attention has been given to what may be called its esthetic culture as different from its archaeology. Much too easily we have all assumed that Arabia was forgotten once the visual riches of the conquered lands became available. What these riches provided was one or more new languages of forms, but they did not, at least not immediately, eradicate memories, visual impressions, and esthetic needs from the world of Arabian oases and probably tribes. Within these memories the Kaʿbah played a far greater role than has been imagined and a continuous one because of the Pilgrimage. On a more specific level, a very fascinating Mekkah–Jerusalem dialogue and competition seems to have existed both in *hadith* literature and in eschatology.[23] Yet on another level, a pattern emerges of relationships between memory of things seen, ambitions for things to be seen, satisfying one's own sense of identity and fascinating or seducing others. It is a pattern which allows us to delve far more deeply than is usually the case into the web of motivations which surround any work of art and more specifically this pattern has fascinating parallels with the architecture being developed to-day in the Arab world.

Finally, any interpretation of the Dome of the Rock raises issues which range from psyching out the minds of patrons long gone to understanding how form and belief act with and react to each other. All these approaches help in explaining the Dome of the Rock, none is the final truth about it, for, like any work of art, the Dome of the Rock will always remain something of a mystery. It is a fascinating and yet to me by now no longer a surprising fact that, at the other end of the grand tradition of Islamic architecture, the Taj Mahal, like the Dome of the Rock, is remarkably documented and yet equally as elusive. Or perhaps the more one studies something the less one understands it. A depressing thought for an academic to expound, but a convenient way to end a paper or a lecture.

Notes

This paper was first given as the Antonius Lecture at St. Antony's College, Oxford University, in 1985. A few modifications were made for delivery at Georgetown University and later at the Universities of Toronto and of Minnesota. For publication a basic complement of notes was added.

[1] The earliest of these is Muhammad b. Ahmad al-Wasiti, *F. al-Bayt al-Muqaddas*, ed. Isaac Hasson (Jerusalem, 1979).
The most celebrated is Muji al-Din, *al-Uns al-Jalil bitarikh al-Quds wa al-Khalil* (Cairo, 1283 fl.), partial tr. by Henri Sauvaire, *Histoire de Jérusalem* (Paris, 1876).

[2] M. H. Burgoyne, *Mamluk Jerusalem* (London, 1986).

[3] Among other places D. H. Little, 'The Significance of the Haram Documents', *Der Islam*, 52 (1980).

[4] Max van Berchem, *Matériaux pour un Corpus Inscriptionum Arabicarum: Jérusalem Haram* (Cairo, 1925–27). Christel Kessler, 'Abd al-Malik's Inscription', *Journal of the Royal Asiatic Society*, no. 3 (1970).

[5] All these texts are conveniently summarized in G. Le Strange, *Palestine under the Moslems* (Boston, 1890), one of several such books.

[6] Robert Hamilton, *The Structural History of the Aqsa Mosque* (Jerusalem, 1942); his results can be interpreted in other ways than he has proposed but the book is a model of its kind. Considerable information can also be obtained from the records kept at the so-called Rockefeller Museum in Jerusalem. For the Israeli excavations, see M. Ben-Dov, *In the Shadow of the Temple* (New York, 1985), a popular account.

[7] Nothing has superceded the chapters in K. A. C. Creswell, *Early Muslim Architecture*, rev. ed. (Oxford, 1969).

[8] O. Grabar, 'The Umayyad Dome of the Rock', *Ars Orientalis* 3 (1959).
[9] Much novel cultural history has been written recently on this period. As examples, see H. Kennedy, *The Prophet and the Age of the Caliphates* (London, 1986) and various work by Patricia Crone, like (with M. Cook) *Hagarism* (Cambridge, 1977).
[10] All these examples are in Creswell. For a more imaginative but also more debatable view of the same monuments, see M. Ecochard, *Filiations de Monuments* (Paris, 1977).
[11] F. E. Peters, 'Who Built the Dome of the Rock', *Graeco-Arabica* 2 (1983).
[12] In the article 'Ḳuds' for the new edition of the *Encyclopedia of Islam*.
[13] T. Nöldeke, 'Zur Geschichte der Araber', *Zeit D. Morgenlandgesellschaft* 29 (1875).
[14] Tabari, *Tarikh*, ed. M. de Goeje et al. (Leiden, 1890 and ff.), II, 4 and ff.
[15] J. Wellhausen, *The Arab Kingdom* (rep. Beirut, 1963), pp. 100–107.
[16] W. Caskel, *Der Felsendom und die Wallfahrt nach Jerusalem* (Cologne, 1963).
[17] Le Strange, pp. 144 and ff., among several places.
[18] Priscilla Soucek, 'The Temple of Solomon in Islamic Legend and Art', in Joseph Gutmann, ed., *The Temple of Solomon* (Missoula, 1976); Heribert Busse, 'The Sanctity of Jerusalem in Islam', *Judaism* 17 (1968).
[19] See articles by Grabar and Soucek.
[20] Al-Azraqi, *Akhbar Makkah*, repr. ed. Beirut (n.d.), pp. 175 and ff.
[21] R. Krautheimer, 'The iconography of Medieval Architecture', *Journal of the Warburg and Courtauld Institutes* 5 (1942).
[22] See the suggestive recent books by F. E. Peters, *Jerusalem* (Princeton, 1985) and *Jerusalem and Mecca* (New York, 1986).
[23] J. M. Kister, 'A Study of an Early Tradition', *Le Muséon* 32 (1969).

Space, Holiness and Time: Palestine in the Classical Arab Centuries

It is under three main headings that I would like to evoke some eight hundred and eighty years of the history of Palestine, from c. AD 638 to 1516. These three headings I call (1) the texture of space, (2) the texture of holiness and (3) the texture of time. For the Judaeo-Christian–Islamic tradition, Palestine is a state of mind, a nostalgia, a homesickness, as much as it is a land with a history. All three monotheisms have attempted to lift the land above history, to endow it with a timeless radiance, to the point where the historian is drawn, almost insensibly, to abandon the normal tools of the historical craft and to follow these religions on their long pilgrimages to Palestine. Put more simply, the history of Palestine may best be apprehended, perhaps, within the patterns of centuries, where geography is as much visionary as it is real, where holiness is as often renewed as it is revealed and where history is a metronome as much as it is a time-piece.

I do not mean to alarm anyone by this dark and mystifying introduction. It is simply that, when approaching Palestine, the historian himself feels alarmed, jostled by a vast crowd of prophets, poets and pilgrims, all of whom are pushing and shoving their way into the blessed land. Palestine is a peculiar blend of experience and hope. The historian must be prepared to register both what is really there and what people imagine there to be, and to grant to both equal historical importance. This is, of course, what a historian undertakes to do in the normal course of his or her work but Palestine is not a 'normal' historical subject, since it bears an unusually heavy burden of memories, both tragic and exultant.

Let me begin with the space that Palestine occupied during these 880 years. The western boundary of the land is the least problematic. It lay along the Mediterranean, from Rafaḥ in the south, to Marj ibn ʿĀmir, the valley of Jezreel, i.e. a few miles south of Acre, in the north. The northern boundary is also not very complex. It runs down the Marj ibn ʿĀmir until it meets the Jordan river somewhere near Baisān. The southern boundary is somewhat more blurred but one must imagine a line running roughly south east from Rafaḥ to meet the town of Ayla on the Red Sea. Ayla lay somewhere beween modern Jordanian Aqaba and modern Israeli Eilat. It is in the eastern boundary where the problem really lies. The Jordan River was of course an obvious physical boundary. However, the towns of Karak, ʿAmmān, al-Salt and Jarash in modern Jordan constituted a natural human and economic hinterland, sharing the same latitude as Palestine, both commercially and in terms of population.

This, in brief, is the classical Filasṭīn of the Arab geographers. But which Palestine do we really want? or, perhaps, which Palestine do we have in mind? If the Palestine we mean is twentieth century Palestine which is generally going to be my meaning here then another slice of territory has to be added to the north, a slice that the Arab geographers of our period called al-Urdunn. Al-Urdunn ran roughly from the Marj ibn ʿĀmir to the Litani River, a little north of Tyre, and eastwards to Bānyās. In other words, modern day Palestine was made up of Filasṭīn and al-Urdunn, two provinces where the axis is east-west and lying on top of each other latitudinally.

But worse is yet to follow. For if by Palestine we mean the Holy Land, if we move, in other words from geography to geo-theology, then the boundaries begin to stretch, and be stretched by, the imagination. For then Iraq and the Euphrates are the frontiers and the whole of Syria is included in a wide arc of sanctity, the centre of which is Palestine. I shall return to the theme of geo-theology in a moment.

The classical Arab geographers looked at Palestine in several other ways as well. The tenth century geographer al-Muqaddasī distinguished four roughly parallel longitudinal zones: the coast, the mountains, the Ghawr or depression of the Jordan and what he called, rather vividly, the 'Shoreline of the desert', *sīf al-bādiya*, i.e. the towns north and south of ʿAmmān. Within Palestine itself, major geographical regions were carefully delineated. These were roughly seven in number: Gaza, Hebron or al-Khalīl, Jerusalem, Ramla, Nābulus, Nazareth and Safad. These were the seven major centres of population and commercial activity.

The immediate geographical neighbours of Palestine were the two great cities of Cairo and Damascus. The Via Maris, the Roman Sea road connecting them, was a famous road which passed straight through central Palestine. A third neighbour, in addition to Cairo and Damascus was the Hijaz, i.e. north west Arabia, with its own ancient caravan routes to southern Palestine. These three immediate neighbours were the ones most intimately concerned with the history we are reviewing.

The most widely known description of the land before the classical Arab period comes from the Bible. From the Gospels in particular, the picture we get of Palestine is one of a countryside, not of cities. Jerusalem of course towers in menace at the end of each gospel but Jesus is predominantly a countryside figure, and what we get are the pungent smells and vivid sights of the land: the fig, the olive, the carob, the earth of the parables 'yielding thirty, sixty, even a hundred fold', the fishes and loaves, the vineyard and winepress, the alabaster jar of precious ointment.

This same Palestinian countryside crops up again in the accounts of the classical Arab geographers. These accounts of Palestine are conveniently assembled in the works of Le Strange, Marmarji and others. In two respects, however, the Arab geographers were different from contemporary Jewish and Christian accounts of Palestine. First, whereas the Jewish and Christian travellers and pilgrims of our period concentrated their attention upon those sites that had sacred associations for them, the Arab accounts incorporated both the Jewish and the Christian lore within one central Muslim descriptive framework. (But more of this subject later when we come to holiness.) Secondly, the Arab geographers often came armed with the tools of the Greek geographical and natural sciences. They included under geography much information of a social, economic, demographic and ethnographic nature. This information is of course essential for the history of classical Palestine.

However, underlying this physical and human geographical literature is what one might call a *géographie fantastique*, or geo-theology, which is not so much what people saw but rather what they wanted to see in the Holy Land. This pious geography had ancient roots of course but it flourished in works on Arab Palestine, such as the large body of literature on the merits (*Faḍā'il*) of Jerusalem and Palestine. Pious Islamic geography begins with the Prophet Muhammad's well known night journey from Mecca to Jerusalem and his ascent from Jerusalem to Heaven, from the rock over which the great Dome of the Rock was soon to be built. Thereafter, Palestine was quickly peopled and then made sacrosanct by the memories and the shrines of some of Muhammad's most famous companions and by a host of ascetics, scholars and holy men, each of whom adds his or her own ray of holiness to the geo-theology of the land. Coming on top of all the Jewish and Christian associations, this body of Islamic pious associations turned the land into a veritable field of light. Prophetic, pseudo-prophetic and other ancestral sayings proliferated. Holy sites innumerable are said to be surrounded by a halo of majesty and light (*ʿalayhā al-ubbaha wa'l waqār wa'l nūrāniyya*). We are told that the only earthly speech that the people of paradise can hear is the call to prayer of the muezzin of Jerusalem. On the eve of Islam's most holy holiday, the Feast of Sacrifice or ʿĪd al-Aḍḥā, the pool of Zamzam in Mecca pays a visit to the holy pool of Silwān below Jerusalem, a geo-theological parallel to Muhammad's night journey.

But it was not all haloes of splendour, calls to prayer and heavenly pools. For the land also bore the physical scars of human faithlessness and ingratitude. The Dead Sea, the 'Stinking Lake' of the Arab geographers, was one such scar, a testimony to man's sin and disobedience. Another scar was the Wādī Jahannam, the Valley of Jehoshaphat, below Jerusalem. If one listened carefully enough in some dark corner of the valley, one could hear the cries of the people of Hell. The land to the south of the Dead Sea is called the Damned land (*al-Arḍ al-Malʿūna*), a black earth where nothing grows, peopled, says a geographer, only by ugly cylindrical boulders which look like blocks of cheese. In sum, then, we have a large and detailed body of classical Arab geography, interpenetrated by a *géographie fantastique*, which makes the land the nearest point on earth to both Heaven and Hell.

From the texture of space, therefore, I pass, smoothly I hope, to the texture of holiness. Now the Arab Muslim conquerors, bands of whom first began to infiltrate into Byzantine Palestine shortly after AD 632—these conquerors were well prepared for Palestine. Some ten years before the conquests began, and while they were still in Medina, many of these same conquerors had spent approximately seventeen months praying in the direction of Jerusalem. Looked at from a larger perspective, what happened was this. The new/old religion of Islam met Judaism and Christianity on their own sacred territory. It was in Palestine that Islam had the most urgent motive to define its relationship to its two great predecessors, and in the course of defining that relationship, Islam came to embrace them. Of course there was always the danger of religious arrogance derived from what one might call the fallacy of *post hoc ergo melior hoc*, later therefore better, the fallacy in other words of assuming that just because one religious tradition or movement comes after another, there must be some inherent fault in the first which the second has come to redress. And there was certainly some of this sense of superiority present in the Islamic conception of Palestine. Thus the eleventh century Persian traveller, Nasir Khusraw, on the so-called Jasmine Mosque of Tiberias: 'On the eastern side and in a colonnade, is the tomb of Joshua son of Nun. Below the central court of the Mosque are the graves of seventy prophets, all of them slaughtered by the Israelites', or this comment by the ninth century Jāḥiẓ on the Christian miracle called the Descent of the Holy Fire in the Church of Resurrection in Jerusalem (Church of the Holy Sepulchre), on a day called the 'Saturday of the Light', the eve of Easter Sunday: 'Priests', says Jāḥiẓ, 'have always practised all sorts of tricks with fire before their congregations. Look at the way that the monks of the Church of the Anastasis in Jerusalem juggle the lamps, claiming that the oil of these lamps is set alight without any fire touching it, on some night or another of their holy feasts'. Islam was the rightful heir of Palestine.

At the same time, and because Islam emphasized its eternity, it had also, in the Koran certainly and in much of Prophetic Ḥadīth, appropriated to itself the role of religious reformer. In the Islamic view, Judaism and Christianity were errant, not false, religions. They had to be shown the true way to go home. And it was in Palestine that Islam's process of appropriation first became manifest, assumed palpable shape as it gazed upon the holiest shrines of its rivals. Islam soon responded with two magnificent shrines of its own in Jerusalem and a host of mosques and other religious and educational institutions all over the land.

At the spiritual level, the Islamic response was the growth of a Sufi and ascetic tradition, which was a natural continuation of an already strong current of Jewish and Christian mysticism. Palestine provided the ideal setting for all three religions to meet, and the discourse of that meeting was mystical. All mystical traditions need heroes of the spirit as models of conduct and a company of such heroes was soon enshrined in Palestine. This company included some of Islam's most attractive and most universal mystical thinkers: Abū Yazīd al-Bisṭāmī, al-Ghazālī, Ibn al-ʿArabī.

But the mystics of Palestine incorporated into this brotherhood Moses and Jesus. Jesus especially became a patron saint of Islamic mysticism. A very large body of sayings attributed to Jesus and Moses was soon circulating, much of it of Palestinian or Syrian origin, i.e. from the Holy Land. These have yet to be assembled and analysed. Many of these Jesus sayings are not only of great literary and religious merit but they also throw light on the so-called 'Apocryphal' tradition in Judaism and Christianity and on the connection between this tradition and Islam. Let me quote to you some of these sayings by way of illustration. First, a general description of Jesus dating at least from the ninth century and said to have come from converts to Islam.

'Jesus was a wayfarer, always travelling in the land, never abiding in a house or village. He always wore a cloak of wool or camel hair... In his hand he carried a thick staff. When night fell, moonlight was his lamp... the earth his bed and a stone his pillow... He ate the plants of the earth and went hungry for days on end. In times of hardship he rejoiced and in times of ease he became sad.'

Secondly, a few of his sayings:

1 'The world is a bridge; cross this bridge but do not build upon it.'

2 '*Be* in the middle, but *walk* to the side.'

3 'Blessed is he who sees with his heart but whose heart is not in what he sees.'

4 'How many reminders of God who themselves forget Him! How many who frighten people with God but themselves are insolent towards Him! How many call to God but themselves run away from Him! How many recite the Book of God but themselves cast away its verses!'

5 Jesus was asked 'Why are you not married?' He replied 'Only in the abode of eternity is it laudable to multiply.'

6 'Every man slain shall be avenged at the Day of Resurrection except the man slain by the world which shall avenge itself upon him.'

7 'Let him who thinks that God is slow with His bounty beware! For God might be angry and open wide to him the bounties of the world.'

8 'Be at ease with people but ill at ease with yourself.'

9 'God said to the world "Serve him who serves me; enslave him who serves you".'

I shall not comment on these sayings except to remind you of the ascetic environment in which this Arab Islamic Jesus was born. It is this same Holy

Land environment which also created an Arab Islamic Moses. The following story comes from the fourteenth century. It is related by a man called Ibrāhīm who heard it from his father, ʿAbdullāh ibn Yūnus al-Armawī. The father says: 'I visited the tomb of Moses near Jericho. At that time, there was no dome or shrine above it. I said to myself, "O God, show me some sign whereby I can be sure that this tomb is truly the tomb of Moses". As I slept, I saw the tomb split and a tall man emerged from it. I went up to him, saluted him and said, "who are you?" "I am Moses", he said, "and this is my tomb". A man nearby was cooking in his cauldron. He served us when the food was ready. It was a rice porridge. Moses ate three spoonfuls, I ate three and the man ate three. Thereafter we sat and chatted. I had intended to return to Anatolia to my Sufi master but Moses said to me, "You shall not return to your Sufi master. Rather you shall go up to Jerusalem, marry a woman from the family of the Prophet and you shall have four children."'

The son, Ibrāhīm, now adds: 'It was as Moses foretold. My father did not return to his country, he married a woman from the House of Muhammad, that is, my mother, and they had four children, of whom I am one. When my father was on his death bed I said to him "My Lord, are you well pleased with me?" He answered, "How can I not be when Moses himself gave me tidings of your birth?"'

Nevertheless, just as the *Terra Sancta* lies close to the *Terra Damnata*, so also the very holiness of the land imposed an awesome moral responsibility upon the believers who inhabited it. This is well captured in the remark made by ʿAbdullāh ibn ʿUmar to Nāfiʿ, these two being among the most pious transmitters of Prophetic Ḥadīth in the first century of Islam. They are walking in Jerusalem and ʿAbdullāh turns to his companion and says, 'O Nāfiʿ, let us leave this holy place for bad deeds here are multiplied exactly like good deeds'. This is of course a reversal of the normal Islamic view which holds that a bad deed is recorded only once while a good deed is recorded many times over. In contrast there is the story of the inhabitant of the *Terra Damnata*, of a town called Zughar (the Biblical Zoar) just south of the Dead Sea. The story is found in a famous Arabic geographical dictionary of the thirteenth century. This is a land, we are told, often visited by devastating plagues, and the geographer continues: 'One year, a plague broke out and most of the inhabitants died. In the house of a notable there lived more than ten people and death struck them down, one by one, until only one man was left. Returning one day from the cemetery, he entered the empty house, felt very lonely, sat on a bench, thought deeply for an hour and then raised his eyes to heaven and said "My Little God (Yā rubaybī), I swear by your Majesty, if you go on like this, you will soon wipe out all your creation and you will sit alone on your throne, all by your little self (Wuḥaydik)."'

I turn to a few remarks about the texture of time. My starting point comes right at the end of these 880 years that I have been concerned with. It is a large, two volume work by a Qāḍī of Jerusalem, Mujīr al-Dīn al-Ḥanbalī, entitled *The Book of the August Companion Regarding the History of Jerusalem and Hebron*, written approximately in 1496. It is the finest work on the history of classical Palestine, a great product of the Mamluk Renaissance. With most Arab historians of today, the Mamluk Empire (c. 1260–1516) fares badly. Turmoil, incessant wars and depredations are all they see in this period. I do not share this opinion of the Mamluks, for if one examines the cultural products of those centuries, one is struck by the architectural and encyclopaedic nature of its physical and cultural remains. The History of Mujīr al-Dīn, written at the very end of Mamluk rule, embodies most of the characteristics of Mamluk encyclopaedic historical writing. It opens with a long and detailed section of Jewish and Christian antiquities in Palestine, moves to the Arab Muslim conquest, then to the history of pre- and post-Crusader Palestine and then becomes topographical and biographical, giving detailed descriptions of Jerusalem, Hebron and other Palestinian cities and ending with a biographical dictionary of famous Palestinians. From Mujīr al-Dīn and from others the following sketch could be constructed.

Under the Umayyads, Palestine was ruled by tribal patriarchs, at first loosely and later closely watched by Umayyad royal governors. Two concerns predominated: defence of the coastline against the Byzantines and the religious significance for Islam of its two holy cities: Jerusalem and Hebron. Palestine was a pivotal region of the Umayyad province of al-Shām. It shared in the general Umayyad benevolence towards that province and was probably among the very earliest regions to reassume a stable pattern of life after the Muslim conquests. An ambitious building programme and a network of roads impressed European travellers and Arab poets alike.

This benevolence slowly receded under the early Abbasids. The 'blessed dynasty' did not need domes of sanctity as much as the Umayyads. The Mediterranean was ignored in favour of the northern and eastern frontiers. In the ninth century, the Eastern Mediterranean was generally quiet and under Muslim domination. Closing in upon themselves, the heartlands of the Abbasid empire were rocked by a series of rural rebellions in protest against the rigorous fiscalism of the new breed of businessmen-Wazirs, and often assuming millenarian religious dimensions. Palestine felt these waves of rural unrest. The dissolution of the Near East into two power blocs, Syria/Iraq and Egypt, which began in the ninth century, meant that Palestine became a permanent object of interest to these power blocs, thus reverting to a pattern that had last been evident in the Hellenistic period. In the wars between the Egyptian Fatimids and the Iraqi Abbasids in the tenth century,

Palestine fell under the domination of powerful tribal groups with vacillating loyalties, entrenched in the southern and eastern regions of the country and later under the domination of bands of Turkish warlords intent upon carving private principalities in Syria. The Crusaders found them a relatively easy foe. However, from the rise of Saladin and right until the end of the Mamluk period, Palestine not only recovered its religious significance for Arab history but added greatly to it through rousing and epic associations with the great conquering Sultans, Saladin and Baibars.

Under the Mamluks, Palestine was often described as the most prosperous (arkhā) region of Syria. Apart from anything else, a peaceful and stable Palestine was essential if the two halves of the Mamluk Empire, Syria and Egypt, were to remain united. Vast sums of money were spent in Palestine by Mamluk Sultans and emirs and religious endowments proliferated, creating a livelihood for generations of Sufis, scholars and lawyers. The income for these endowments came from areas both inside and outside Palestine, linking it ever more closely to its neighbours. In 1974, an extremely valuable collection of documents was found in the Islamic Museum attached to the Aqsa Mosque in Jerusalem, all of them dating from the Mamluk period. One scholar working on them estimates that this collection equals in number all other Mamluk documents known to exist at present. The centrality of Palestine in the Mamluk Empire seems to be corroborated by the centrality of this body of documents for the study of Mamluk history in general. And Mujīr al-Dīn's work is a monumental tribute to that centrality of space and of holiness occupied by classical Arab Palestine.

It remains for me to sketch, in brief and broad outline, some of the stabilities and instabilities of peoples and places.

Although in the medieval Christian West and in classical Islam a person's primary identity was religious and topographical (one was a Christian, a Muslim or a Jew and one belonged to a town, a village or a small locality), broader conceptions of ethnic origin, e.g. Greek, Frank, Arab (Saracen), Syrian and so forth re-emerged from time to time, especially in periods of intense international wars. The term Arab as a reference to a people occurs as early as the ninth century BC. The terms Arabia and Arabian occur often in the Old Testament and in the New. The connections of this people and of its various subdivisions to Palestine are continuous and as old as recorded history. More to the point, perhaps, is the gradual infiltration of the Arabic language into the Near East from the third and fourth centuries AD, carried by successive waves of settlers, conquerors and nomadic infiltrators. It is quite evident that the Islamic conquest of Palestine, at least of the Palestine countryside, was much smoother than the conquests of other regions of the Near East. The conquerors seem to have settled down very quickly in the land, found the environment hospitable and intermarried. The local Christians and Jews seem to have been converted to Arabic almost at once, suggesting a pre-existent compatibility of culture.

The Arabic language was a much faster conqueror than the Islamic religion. Thus, while Arabic conquered by the end of the seventh century, it was not until the tenth, probably, that Islam became the majority religion in Palestine. For our 880 years, my estimate for the population figure is approximately 200,000 to 250,000: 70% Muslim, 20% Christian and 10% Jews and Samaritans, would probably represent average distribution by religion across these nine centuries, if one is allowed to do this by demography. I might add that the relative stability of these percentages suggests long periods of inter-sectarian harmony.

At approximately two-hundred year intervals, the late ninth, the late eleventh, the late thirteenth and the late fifteenth centuries, Palestine was rocked by deep social, economic and military disturbances, both civil and international. During these disturbances, the mountains of Palestine fared better, generally speaking, than the coast. Of all the coastal towns Gaza alone maintained its importance throughout our period, but the other coastal cities suffered greatly from the ravages of war. The mountain towns, that is, Hebron, Jerusalem, Nabulus, Nazareth and Safad enjoyed much longer periods of stability and thus became active centres of commerce and scholarship.

* * * * *

This, in briefest outline, is the scaffolding from which a history of classical Arab Palestine might be built. This essay is evocative, a prelude to research. If this evocation has at times bordered on hagiography, this is because Palestine, as I have argued, possesses both a history and a meta-history. The historian must strive to do justice to both.

Note

This is a slightly expanded version of the Eleventh George Antonius Lecture, delivered at St. Antony's College, Oxford, on June 16, 1986. It is dedicated to the memory of Marwan Buheiry.

Orientalism Again

THE current special meaning of the word 'orientalism' derives from Edward Said's book of that name, but in the main I do not mean to talk about Said's book, or to do more than glance at his arguments in passing. The original conflict of attitudes Arab and Western which he took up tends to get forgotten sometimes, and this is to some extent his fault. I will take as my starting point an interesting review of Arab critics of Edward Said by Emmanuel Sivan, in the *Jerusalem Quarterly*, which Dr Owen and Professor Scanlon made available to me. The crucial point of this article is that Said is himself a secularist, and seems to other Arab secularists to have betrayed his own professional loyalties and convictions, in taking up a cause, the Islamic rejection of secularism, which he and they regard as retrograde. Here and now it is not our business to harp on the dangers to Arab society that are inherent in religious extremism; we can take for granted that they threaten, in the first place, Islamic society itself, particularly the ordinary moderate Muslim; that they threaten Christians who live within the Muslim world, that they threaten foreigners there, and conceivably that they constitute an indirect threat beyond Islam itself. Having said that, in case anyone may think that I underrate, or even sympathise with Islamic extremism, I will try not to say it again. I really want to identify and distinguish an attitude, and to ask how far we should take it to heart. To fear it is not to disarm it; to understand it—if we can—is at any rate to take it as it is.

What the Jerusalem article does most successfully is to emphasize the two distinct poles, the secularist and the Islamic extremist, but the sympathies of the author are clearly with the secularists. This is natural; interculturally, it is much easier to find common ground in secularism, but to do so seems to me to beg the question altogether. It is not difficult to show that Said is very uncomfortably balanced in any conflict between his own Western standards and methods of work, and the long-standing Arab and Muslim resentment of just those standards which in part he represents. He has been much more successful in demonstrating the bias in the Western, and especially American, press against Palestinians and their case; here he has only to argue injustice; he is not quite sure what he is doing in the case of orientalism. He is certainly on the side of the misunderstood Arabs and Muslims, but equally certainly he is on the side of Chomsky and Levi-Strauss and the Annales. This brings him to commit the absurdity of confining orientalism to academic orientalists, members of one particular faculty. Then he throws his net wider, and outside the academic world, somewhat at random among the Romantics. Some of his particular judgements do not go necessarily with his main thesis. Many people will agree that his criticism of Lane is a fault in his presentation, and there is much to be said for including Massignon more firmly than he does among the colonialists. Here I leave Said and his critics and turn to the rejection of orientalism which has been fairly constant in the Arab world since Western ideas of the Arabs and of Islam first began to be known in the Arab world itself. This is the original Arab opposition to secularism.

It is impossible to quantify the two hostile camps, or the forces arrayed in intermediate positions, with anything like accuracy, and it is out of the question to try to foresee future developments and the extension or contraction of existing schools of thought. A generally anti-secularist point of view is often heard, in one form or another, and both faintly and strongly, but there is no basis other than personal experience for estimating numbers. Academic attitudes certainly relate to the widespread political and social resentment of Western (or Northern) privilege and advantage; but again I do not know how calculably. Apart from the unrepentantly secularist point of view, there are only two possible positions for those to take up who want to take the matter of orientalism seriously. One is that scholars will always be limited by the current cultural perspectives that they share with their contemporaries. They may strain to achieve objectivity, but will inevitably take for granted much that is in fact subjective, so as to flaw their objectivity, not only in the eyes of Arab critics, but even in those of their own successors. Nevertheless, they will have achieved a good deal that survives subsequent criticism, and in so far as they do so they may be said to have advanced in the direction of the unattainable objectivity, and a little success is still worth having. We of the present age cannot tell how much of our own attitudes and propositions is 'objective', or how long our work will survive, or even perhaps just what its ultimate significance will turn out to be. But we shall probably be disinclined to make any further concession than that, and we should be very dishonest if we continued to work at what we believed to be valueless. If we are not perfect, we are not perfectly awful either. The alternative is quite simply the opposition maintained by a section of Arab opinion that has always resented Western orientalism, and springs from the virulent, underlying, often atavistic resentment of 19th-century Christian colonialism. It questions in particular the right of any Western scholar to examine Arab and Islamic subjects—presumably any other oriental subjects either, but only the Arab and Muslim are here in question.

Western orientalism lent its own weapons to criticism of itself at an early stage. When Abbas Muhammad al-Aqqād in the first half of this century tried to use the methods of orientalists and the authority of Western writers to counteract them, it was rather by political sleight of hand—he was a leading Wafdist—than by scholarly training. It was not so much the technique of scholarship that he perceived as the apparent implications of its conclusions. Slightly older, Tawfiq Sidky had tried to discredit Christianity by Western methods, as he understood them; and since the actual discoveries of orientalists were culturally neutral facts, there was no great difficulty in reversing matters of simple interpretation. The Arab and especially the Egyptian world was dominated for long by the figure of Taha Hussein, with all the prestige of a formation both sheikhly and Western and quite simply by his personal stature. Yet it is not Taha's achievement which made the greatest impression, so much as the reaction he provoked. He put the cat among the pigeons with devastating effect. From the traditionalist's point of view he was the first great oriental orientalist to betray Islam. He cannot be thought of primarily as a scholar, but as an interpreter; yet he undeniably did very much to revive the study of the Islamic heritage in East and to increase its prestige in the West. It is hardly surprising therefore that good traditional Muslims wanted to do the same thing within the boundaries of traditional faith. Whatever we believe, positive or negative belief, we can only assume that facts unearthed without bias will support it. This is true of every gradation of belief and disbelief, and it is hardly surprising that there should have been sincere outrage at an apparent perversion of facts through sheer cultural incomprehension. Such reactions parallel in the field of culture the political developments still very much alive just now, which reject moderate Islamic government on the ground that it represents the worst kind of infidelity.

I should like to consider as a particularly articulate representative of an attitude not always clearly expressed the introduction by Mahmoud Shakr to his re-edition, 1987, of the poems of al-Mutanebbi. I think that it is worth doing this at some length, because it is a singularly thorough-going condemnation of the orientalists, based on a view of history which must seem very idiosyncratic to us, but which seems quite normal in much of the Arab world; it represents a widespread tendency. Its methodological and historical presuppositions are directly opposed, not only to the orientalist, but to Western scholarship as a whole. This introduction has little to do with its ostensible subject; 150 pages long, with its own analytical index, it is a little short of a full-length book, but many books as short are published, and a book in it own right is the way to consider it. It was drawn to my attention by Dr Magdi Wahba, who is himself a close colleague of Shakr's on the Arabic Language Academy and one of my more distinguished predecessors among Antonius lecturers. Mahmoud Shakr is a strong and outgoing personality who is genuinely distressed to think that anyone he loves and respects should not be a Muslim. His life has been devoted to combating the influence of Taha Hussein, against whom he revolted in his student days. He is the hub of a kind of unofficial and unauthorised university or finishing school for students from, in particular, Saudi Arabia, Kuwait and the rest of the peninsula which the Americans and some others so oddly regard as 'moderate' in an unforgivable confusion of political convenience with religious conviction.

Shakr bases his thinking on a distinction between methodology and what he calls pre-methodology. For him the latter is the pre-requisite to any methodical treatment of a subject—any subject at least that relates to the culture of a society, in effect, to a culture—but it is not itself method, it is infrastructure. Shakr says that the language and culture into which we are born and in which we grow up is the essential prerequisite of our thinking. Whatever culture is, it is, he thinks, embodied in language; it cannot be acquired. He calls it inborn, though a little later he says that it is properly acquired in childhood. He is not really concerned with method at all, but with something which alone can validate method; and to the notion of language he adds the concept of faith: the secret of a culture, he says, is 'hidden in the language and faith of a community', and also, he adds, in fidelity to the past. He feels his own lack of precision here, but while he knows he must be specific, and says so, he still confines himself to generalities. He understands that there is a danger of being wrong, or, as he puts it, of 'illusion'; he does not want to be thought to 'chatter' meaninglessly. This is sound self-criticism, because he does repeat himself a good deal, and I am only afraid of doing the same in trying to expound his opinions. In fact, I must do so straight away. He accepts the ordinary sense of 'method' as enabling us to distinguish between the false and the true 'without illusion', but this has a very minor role. All kinds of writing, from poetry to algebra, all that the mind of man has emitted, is inherited by the community, and reaches the person concerned after centuries and generations in succession, and, he insists, its 'vessel and repository is language and nothing else'. So to talk about, or in, Arabic effectively, you must be an Arab, and to talk about Islam you must be a Muslim (and he presumably means, brought up as one). He accepts the corollary that no Arab can qualify to study the Western heritage, but I am not sure how far he really means this, or thinks it worth studying. His opinion of Christianity is so low that he will not allow it to interpret itself, and he himself interprets the Western heritage at length.

His interpretation is very informative, and I think that he once again expresses in rather extreme form a very general tendency. Of course I cannot take you through his entire perspective of the history of relations between the Western and Arab worlds, so I will dig a trial trench across his Middle Ages. This is not too easy; it must be rather like I imagine it to be for an archeologist digging a faked site, or more like an opinion poll. Shakr's chronology is vague and often inconsistent, even self-refuting. One is never quite sure from one sentence to the next which period exactly he is discussing, and his own thematic analysis obscures his vision of some sequence of events. The Europeans themselves, he says, think that Europe fell into the disaster of the dark Middle Ages at the fall of the Roman

Empire, AD 476, 146 years before the Hegira; but the fact is, he says, that it was even worse before the Middle Ages, there was only *jāhilīyah* and dark ignorance. The inhabitants of Europe were the worst of barbarians, and ungoverned by religion till the Renaissance. I am not quite sure what was in his mind when he said that; in any case, for him two episodes of early European history stand out, and the most important for him is the age of Crusading.

Crusades came at a time when Islam had appeared with its dominant religion and culture, and prevailed from the North of Andalus to the heart of Africa—I am not sure what that means here, it ought to refer only to Africa in the Roman sense, or Iffriqiya, but 'the heart' of Iffriqiya is ambiguous. Anyway, Islam contained Europe in a northern region where the barbarians lived. Christian armies were ineffective against Islam, and the churchmen and feudal leaders, seeing their dominance in the South disappear, decided on a strategic retreat to the North. So monks organised themselves into bands and roamed about northern Europe to convert the barbarians and prepare them to act as battle fodder to fight Islam. 'The South' here can only mean Italy. Shakr's picture of a mysterious force making plans for Christendom is faintly reminiscent of the Protocols of Zion. In any case it was at this point apparently that the monks misrepresented the life and character of the Prophet, and every monk, priest and hermit repeated these lies *ad infinitum*, and by repetition they became axiomatic. The barbarian armies, Normans, Slavs and Saxons, were placed under the command of priests and feudal kings. The Crusaders spread over Europe, killing Christians—that is right enough—and finally reached the cities of Islam, and for two centuries began to spill the blood of Muslims—that must be from the siege of Antioch to the fall of Acre. The early rejoicing of the Crusaders soon turned to the despair of failure, as they realised that their arms would not win the day. The returning Crusaders were now aware of the truth about Muslim civilisation, they had rubbed shoulders in war with a superior culture. Doubt entered into their souls, because this did not conform with what they had heard from their monks and kings. Their return to their homeland filled men everywhere with anxiety and the leaders feared that this would spread among the ignorant masses and weaken their will to fight. Depression entered into the hearts of the monks, kings and intelligentsia and they tried to perpetuate the distorting image of Islam and the Muslim, and to persuade the masses to fight to defend their new-found Christianity. Why 'new-found' at this stage I do not know. Shakr often proceeds by a series of dislocated images. 'The wandering monks'—well, there *were* wandering monks, mostly at the wrong dates. The vilification of Muhammad—there certainly *was* this vilification. There were barbarians and monks and priests and feudal kings, of course, but they were not all connected by a preoccupation with Islam. A recent Israeli historian has pointed out how much information was available about Islam in early centuries but admits that no one assembled it systematically; and the vilification followed the Crusades and did not precede or prepare for them. Perhaps this vagueness as to the sequence of events does not matter, but the false assumption that there was a pre-occupation with Islam is more significant, and the insistence on the neurotic anxiety induced by the encounter with Islam is particularly interesting. I do not know of any evidence that it existed. There is certainly more evidence of a manic than of a depressive condition in the West.

The second important event, says Shakr, was the fall of Constantinople. Europe was shaken to its roots and filled with shame, anger, terror and envy, and the priests and monks redoubled their efforts to prepare for a new and more cruel war. As a matter of fact we might admit that, yes, you can say all that, though you would have to add that nobody took any notice of the efforts of the priests and monks concerned. In fact Shakr now goes back to reflect on the Middle Ages, and in so doing makes some interesting points. I think he confuses what we usually mean by the Renaissance with what is also called the Renaissance of the Twelfth Century. War, he says, now became a battle of knowledge, because the Muslims had been victorious on the basis of their superior strength and knowledge. Several times he remarks that Islam spread rapidly among the peoples conquered by the Arabs without compulsion. The monks and kings were dazzled by the beauty of Islamic morality and civilisation. They were desperate, and did not know what to do, especially about the willing conversion of Christians in Islamic territory. Why was this? Was it because Christianity had failed to convince its own people? No answer, he says, has been found. But something happened to dispel the sense of despair and to raise new armies. The Christians who had lived as good neighbours to Muslims returned to Europe and would talk about what they had seen and touched. Their hearts were filled with yearning for all that had enchanted them in Islam; and it was this contact with Islam that had produced the sense of anxiety on which Shakr continues to insist. Islam in fact had a secret power: this was its knowledge of this world and the next—that was how it had convinced all the people who had then freely entered into it. It was knowledge of this world which had given Islam power to control enormous forces. So now there appeared Europeans who learned from Islam, who went East and to Andalus to study science and knowledge in the lands of Islam. He instances Roger Bacon, who was indeed interested in accounts of travels, but never travelled himself further than Paris, and Thomas Aquinas, also a traveller no further than Paris, and whom he sees, of course, as no more than an adaptor of ibn Rushd and ibn Sina. He shows no sign of having read either author. The motive, he says, was to heal the breach within Christianity between the monks and the illiterate peoples, and this is also how he explains the rise of the vernaculars and the occurrence of the Reformation. There is nothing much new about this except the linking of it all with Islam and the fear of Islam. The return of Crusaders to Europe is a theme to which he returns constantly; he even calls them *kataᶜib*, militias; and he harps on their fear and anxiety under the impact of Islamic civilisation. It may of course have been like that, but there is no evidence of it. It is an achievement of his imagination. I am perhaps being too imaginative myself if I ask whether he has not transferred to his hypothetical medievals much of the experiences of Arabs under the impact of colonialism, especially in the last century, when the power of the West was indeed based on knowledge, knowledge of the mechanics of war; and its victories did cause dismay among Muslims who have never seen their own culture as anything but vastly superior. But those Arabs, often Muslims, who did not reject Western ideas, not altogether and in some cases not at all, are these the prototypes of the neurotic and anxious monks and feudal kings of the barbaric Western Middle Ages? We know of course that there was great anxiety and what we might loosely call neurosis in the fifteenth century about death, but not associated with the splendours of Islamic civilisation. The remark several times repeated that Christians were easily and peaceably converted to Islam, as some indeed were, suggests that the author is aware of the constant Christian accusation against Islam that it spread by the sword and forcible conversion. It is interesting that he makes no mention of the forcible conversions of pockets of Islam in Europe which certainly occurred.

I have said enough of Shakr's history. The most striking point about the long account he gives of Bonaparte's invasion of Egypt is his insistence on characterising Napoleon and the armies of revolutionary France as Christian. For him Europe and America are no less Christian now than ever. Changes in opinion and religious allegiance do not signify for him. Christianity is the enemy and the enemy is by definition always Christian.

All this has been leading up to Shakr's description of orientalists. Why did they write as they did? Their hearts were still burning with the anger and conflict of besieged Northern Christianity, to which *dar al-Islam* had never surrendered (exactly what he means by that I do not know); and they reflected the desire of the kings and their subjects to plunder the treasures of Islamic civilisation. They write, he adds rather more justly, for European readers. Their work is not scientific 'in any sense of the word'—I am quoting—'they do not have our language, do not live our language, do not live our culture, do not live our mood'. This is what disqualifies them. They have neither method nor pre-method, because they are born English, French or German, and cannot share our language or culture or our innocence of prejudice. Note the deliberate use of the word 'scientific' to denote what we call unscientific, in the sense of subjective: one suspects that he is trailing his coat. If he is thinking at all of a Western readership, he is certainly coat-trailing.

He devotes time and space to the training of the orientalist, who, embedded in his own literature and culture, is already mature when he turns to a quite new and different language, and studies at the feet of someone who has learned the same way, and is equally foreign to it. After 20 or 30 years of study he may, under the best of conditions, know as much as an Arab aged 14. It is not possible, therefore, for an orientalist (and that means a Western orientalist) to satisfy the very minimum requirement for a man learned in Arabic. Even more questionable is his competence to be familiar with the culture generally. Faith, and actions, or works, and belonging, are all essential. Man cannot be a witness to his own creations or creatures, and he needs the language to attain religion. Religion is the master of the human being, and language is inseparable from it. As for international culture, there can be no such thing, because people are divided by language and culture (this last point of course begs the question). Cultures clash; the best we can look for is co-existence. Cultures may compete, but they can never mix; neither can one derive anything from another. Knowledge can be shared, cultures never. That is an important remark, but again it begs the question, how much knowledge is the product of the culture. The orientalist's motivation may be various: it may be his own advantage, or his country's, or he may simply be trying to acquire learning; or again he may be trying to discover secrets, and so to dispute about them. From his studies he can derive only as much truth as he can understand, and he will be able to dispute only in so far as he has glimpses of the true connotations of his understanding. If, says Shakr, he is neither trying to derive benefit nor to dispute, but instead claims that he comes as a scholar and student, then he is wearing the robe of the professor. Then he *is* guilty of arrogance, because his real motivation is tribal—he is an instrument in the long centuries-old struggle of Islam against the Christianity besieged in the North. Perhaps he is entitled to act like this, but elements of cunning and hypocrisy are bound to enter; he may pretend to seek only the truth, but he is really looking for a weapon to continue the battle between Islam and Christianity. Machiavelli has become gospel to most Europeans. European civlisation is drenched in prejudice which it shamelessly regards as normal; it is based on self-interest, plunder and exploitation. In exploiting others, these people make use of the greatest myth of all—a world civilisation, i.e. a world subservient to their interests.

I have been repeating what I do not doubt we all think is nonsense for a good part of my time, though I do not think that this is time wasted, because it expresses exceptionally well the state of resentment that the Western world, and especially its orientalists, have aroused among many who might not subscribe to everything that Shakr says, or to the way in which he says it. The word orientalist has habitually become a pejorative. I would like to suggest that buried in the constant repetition, circular arguments, questionable statements, emotional denunciations and improbable hypotheses are a number of assertions that are well worth thinking about.

Can we claim universal validity for the objectivity at which we aim and which we hope to achieve, at least to some extent? It is certainly possible to believe in the validity of a law or a procedure, even though its principle is not universally accepted. It is generally accepted in the case of natural or physical science, at least in our world; some Muslims think they know what they mean by 'Muslim science', but most are content to claim an historical priority in science. The principles and their application in techniques may be understood in one area and understood differently, or not at all, or not so well, in another. Can we be sure that the objectivity of the orientalist scholar comes under the universal heading? *We* would say that much of the orientalist's method does indeed do so. Mahmoud Shakr is in fact well known for his editions of old texts and he gives variant readings like any other scholarly editor, in fact like any orientalist. However, it is this process (he thinks) that the absence of the 'pre-methodology' invalidates. A collection of studies of Arab science, now being prepared in Paris for simultaneous publication in three languages, is a good example of the kind of orientalism that is resented, mistakenly, but understandably. It will have contributions by seven Arab writers and one Pakistani (one of the Arabs making three contributions) out of 35 specialist contributions. Most of the Arab contributors are largely or entirely of Western formation. I cannot say whether the standard of contributions will ultimately prove uniformly even, but I think we can assume a very high level of scholarship. It is still what Shakr means by 'arrogance'. I simply cannot be sure how we should react to a book about English culture entirely dominated, not even by Indians with their considerable British cultural background, but by Thais and provincial Chinese. We might expect to find unexpected or original aperçus, but perhaps we should also expect the book to miss a good many points familiar to us from childhood. Yet, though the orientalist's arrogance consists in making judgements about a culture which he was not born into, we can hardly agree that he fails to be objective and accurate every time that he alleges a fact that conflicts with some cultural apprehension, and he is not necessarily wrong when his interpretation, or just his selection, of facts conflicts with traditional Arab and Muslim interpretations—which might, and may yet, develop under a purely internal impetus. Obviously, he may or may not be right. We do not have to assume that the insider view is the right one, but conflict may reasonably be considered a warning light and it would really be arrogant to take it as a green light. We do have to assume that the orientalist's view is influenced by his own cultural perceptions. We may I suppose claim an absolute validity for our own culture, and in that case there is no more to be said; but I do not think we can. The value of any man's research is likely to be affected by some bias or other. Facts are facts, but can we be sure that we have all the relevant facts or have rightly interpreted them? The constant revision of so many ideas, theories and systems shows that we cannot.

I suppose that I am only stating the obvious, when I say that our method is subjective in so far as it depends on the preselection of its direction as well as on interpretations that often derive from presuppositions. So the use made of a technique depends greatly on a cultural context that makes them in one aspect or another, or one connection or another, largely relative. Conclusions have been different from generation to generation. We generally welcome a new interpretation, if it is not too wild, and, while we do so, we give it a conditional acceptance, forgetting that, even if it is accepted, it is no more likely to survive the next good idea than its predecessors were. We can judge the quality of work by its own standards; for its value, we must depend on our own, and those offer no certainty, because here we are insiders, with no external standard of comparison. We can compare past results, but we believe that we are improving on them; the future we cannot get at, and often assume without justification that it will be on our side. In our day we rather like to construct an imaginary model, on a foundation of facts which are selected in order to suggest it, but which do not compel assent, because they leave so much out of account. Yet the greater mental discipline of other ages has done very much the same thing.

If we analyse Western orientalism over the ages, wholly forgetting Shakr's contentions, and without benefit of being born Arab and Muslim, we may yet find in the end that some of his claims are right enough. No one would doubt that medieval writers about Islam were prejudiced. We may not like to think that this has anything to do with modern orientalism, but some of the things of which orientalists are accused their medieval predecessors were certainly guilty of. We do not have to go further than the writings of orientalists to identify direct continuities of thought, and, even when the contents of what is said has been modified, there is continuity in the modality of thought. Shakr sees Islam as peaceful, Christianity as dependent on the force of arms, but the opposite perception, which was plugged for all it was worth in the Middle Ages, survives in the West. It is more interesting that the orientalists' claim to objectivity also dates from the Middle Ages, from those polemicists who believed that they must research into the most authentic sources, because the truth was what would most likely and effectively refute Islam. From that time forward accuracy and even empathy of a sort increased, and gradually the original polemic purpose faded—it survived unchanged at least until Muir—it was replaced by anti-religious theses and ultimately by a cold indifference, which particularly in treatment of the Prophet's life and work itself provoked resentment. If medieval polemic gave birth to authenticity, and it in turn grew into objectivity, that is only what Shakr and others like him expect of inherited prejudice.

Among the unchanging modalities the most important is the unbroken disbelief in the revelation of the Qur'an. The medievals sought to prove that God is not its author, but almost every modern assumes the same thing. To the Muslim this is obviously crucial and limits, if it does not entirely exclude, the usefulness of what an orientalist has to say about his sacred text. There is another and finer point. When a medieval writer used authentic sources, al-Bukhārī for example, his quotations were so extremely apt as to give a very wrong impression of the total work, of which they represent only a minute fraction. The work of selection and elimination that this implies would be an enormous operation to be undertaken by at most a small group of learned clerics. These points might more easily have emerged from the interrogation of, or dispute with, a sheikh, but there is no evidence of that. In any case we are left with a vast amount of discarded Arabic text which was useless for the purposes of the Christian writer. Yet methodologically the modern orientalist works similarly to pick out what he thinks is significant, and he thinks according to the cultural bias of his time. He is not, or he rarely is, looking for what the Muslim thinks significant. I do not think that Islamic priorities or interests have much influenced the course of Western research. There are plenty of studies of the political and theological schools of early Islam, and a good many of modern schools of religious opinion, but they are observed strictly from the outside, and perhaps with less understanding than they would get even from a Muslim who did not agree, or even sympathise with, them personally. There are dangers in both external and internal standards. If we simply substitute for the uncritical admiration of the believer the unrestrained denigration of an unbeliever, we have not achieved greater objectivity. If 'external' means 'unsympathetic', we have gained little and lost much; understanding can be as much or more limited by dislike as by affection. We recognise this by sending students to spend some time in an Arab country, but this is still a somewhat amateur process and can result in either uncritical liking or intensified dislike. Another side to this is the absence in a number of cases at least of widespread and continuous contact, even where there is a strong common interest among both Arabs and orientalists. This was once extreme, and contact was only occasional; as we know, things have much improved. But even to-day, although Western scholars take care to examine original sources in discussing Islamic extremism, there is little sign that they follow, and it is clear that they do not take part in, the disputes and discussions that Arabs conduct on the subject in newspapers and journals. This may well be from delicacy and from fear of intruding in a particularly delicate matter. It might well be resented; and it is far from certain that it would be welcome. But the fact remains that Western and Arab comments on the same phenomena are a good deal cut off from each other. I am probably saying this to an audience to which it applies the least of any, but I suggest that it is always something of a problem that the Western orientalist will treat an

Arab orientalist, one who shares his attitudes, as a true colleague, in a way that he will not or cannot extend to an Arab scholar who makes it difficult for him by repelling his approach, and who thereby becomes an object of study rather than a colleague.

There is clearly a real difficulty in the lack of continuous communication and shared interests, something which can be improved but probably never eliminated, and something which conforms to an attenuated version of some of Shakr's views. It is much more questionable whether we can accept anything at all of his idea that everything Western is 'Christian', and in a sense of 'Christian' which includes perpetual animosity. Of course our Europe descends from the Europe that expressed its aggression in Crusading, but the line that connects the two is fairly long and tenuous. The society which the extreme Muslim groups demand to-day is in many ways much closer to our Western medieval society than we are ourselves. It can only seem quite grotesque to us that the armies of revolutionary France should be identified as specifically Christian: in fact it looks like an extreme either of ignorance or of obstinacy, and in either case deliberate. But I do not think that Shakr is making a statement about Bonaparte. Of course, the link between the invasion of Egypt and the orientalists is beyond question, but even the conviction that anything whatever that comes out of Europe is Christian can be explained. Just as an individual who is born in what was once a Christian world is always considered a Christian in the Arab world, even if he is a devoted Marxist, so apparently is Europe as a whole to be delineated by its remoter origins. How can this stand up to a moment's analysis? The answer seems to be that it hasn't had to. In an Arab country the police want to know an individual's background, not his beliefs, which are purely personal and no doubt ephemeral; he may be an atheist, but it is more important to know what kind of atheist he is, Muslim, Christian or Jewish, and not because that tells anyone anything about his kind of atheism. Certainly it is of some practical use to know about any man's background, though I do not think that is the motive here. It is according to the pattern of origins that Europe, postchristian and often antichristian, is still forever 'Christian'. Pehaps this is partly because Islam must be forever Muslim; and also perhaps because it is thought of as the enemy to whom the label first attached still sticks. Whatever tricks they get up to, they are still the same. Or can we see this in any other way? In *their* way, an outsider way, the orientalists have often said that in Islam society and religion are inextricably joined, and Muslims do not deny this, though they may not like the terms used to say so. If all this contrasts with the West, then the difference must be that the word 'Christian' may as well attach to the society, in any form that may take, as to the religion. 'Christian' for Muslims has nothing to do with the ʿIsa of the Qur'an; but this use of the term is alien to all shades of Western opinion.

We can dismiss altogether what Shakr says about anxiety among medieval Europeans, overwhelmed by the beauty and morality of Islamic civilisation; there is no evidence for it, although we do find admiration occasionally for the wealth of the countryside or of buildings and sometimes for Arab ways and customs; it is straightforward, a little surprised perhaps, but in no way associated with depression or disenchantment with the Christian way. I have already said that I can only see it as a transference of Arab reactions of the last century and their vestiges to-day.

In what sense do the orientalists represent that besieged Northern Christianity, except only that they are a manifestation of the supposed long heritage of animosity? In one way they fit into the political scene, and that has its cultural parallel. Colonial rule was succeeded, in the main, by nationalist rule, and in the cultural scene an Arab orientalist was perfectly acceptable. He had mastered and taken over a Western skill. But nationalism did not put things right, and so the Islamic movement built upon the slogan: 'the only thing we haven't tried is Islam'. Its parallel was clearly the rejection on the cultural side of everything Western, and orientalist skills in particular. We can also admit that there was a real connection beween colonialist practice and orientalist ideals. I am thinking not so much of the active intelligence work of academics, such as M. Reid has documented, but more of the hankerings of the real practitioners after academic distinction— in Kipling's 'Kim' the secret service chief Creighton and his agent Hurree Babu both cherish ambitions of being elected to the Royal Society for their anthropological work. DCs in the Sudan, apparently without ambition for recognition, spent time and energy on studying the peoples of their districts; McMichael, a colonialist *par excellence*, wrote a classic on the Western tribes. The work of French colonialists in Algiers is well known. I am not making a catalogue and the point is perhaps not very important, that those who ruled were also attracted by the lure of fact-finding. But should we not have to say that these were points of weakness in European aggression? Yes, if there really were an unending conspiracy of malevolence. No, if we remember that the fault, as Shakr would see it, was not the colonial rule in the first instance, but the orientalism itself, the cultural intrusion. The orientalist who never left home and treated classical Arabic as a dead language, and the colonial administrator were guilty of the identical cultural fault, if the latter's was not the lesser. The scholar who remains at home may well be the worse for it. The man who knows even a little of the Arab world may understand with more sympathy than the high and dry scholar of another age who could dig out facts but lacked the terms of human reference to interpret them.

If we accept that our judgements will always be a little twisted by our own unrecognised cultural bias, can the extreme Muslim accept that his own bias makes him uncritical? We can only accept Shakr's thesis if he will accept that his own love of his language, religion and culture obscure his judgements too. Is he, and those of the same mind, right to see in international culture a trick to impose alien ideas? Even if not a deliberate trick it might be a sort of natural trap. External danger and confrontation are essential to his position, as he states it, but would he reject an international Islamic culture? One that was led by Arabs? In fact, the weakness of the attack on the orientalists is the failure, so far, of the Arab-Islamic critics to produce a comparable body of scholarship.

When he touches somewhat obliquely on the training of the orientalist, Shakr is thinking of the traditional and classic past of the discipline, and he is not allowing for the practical bent of recent developments, and the employment of Arab teachers of Arabic which is surely modifying the old 'arrogance' in the direction of learning a modern culture—not nearly enough to satisfy his pre-requirements, of course. He would probably say that he likes it none the better—but it sends him back to his starting point, the rejection of Taha Hussayn, of 'secularism' and of the Arab, or oriental, orientalist. The modern Western undergraduate does not penetrate deeply into Arabic or into Islam, but does that, did it ever, need saying? The modern Greek is inclined to regard classical Greek studies as a tribute to his own modern culture, and an Arab in the professions who is not playing at internal politics, very often the same. This is the international culture which Shakr is right at least to identify as his principal enemy.

I do not suppose that any of us who share in this current international culture is particularly attached to all or any of its individual and separable aspects. It is more that the momentum of technological advance pre-supposes a philosophy, one that assumes that we should make more and more new kinds of thing, and mostly, of course, to our great advantage. Islam is not hostile to technology, not at all to the power it confers, not even to the comforts it brings. It cannot afford not to be; but it would not put it so high on its list of priorities. But then neither would the orientalist, if he thinks of himself as committed to knowledge for its own sake, put it at the top of his own list. Real sympathy, we have conceded, is needed for true and objective understanding, but the practice of empathy has its dangers too. Shakr is empathising when he pictures the neurotic feudal leaders and priests and monks of the European Middle Ages. He has no evidence to support his vision but he does vividly imagine their dilemma. He has projected himself into the minds of those he is writing about; he has projected himself wrong, because his projection must serve his thesis, and, living his main theme so profoundly, he can project nothing else. Hostile empathy, if I can use the phrase, is clearly dangerous, but it may represent a successful methodology—in Shakr's language, pre-methodology—I instance volume one of Caro's Life of Lyndon Johnson.

It should go without saying that what is needed is Coleridge's 'suspension of disbelief', not the projection of some alien faith; but can this suspect 'international culture' do any better? Very likely, not much better. If international culture is genuinely seeking facts, its goal is irreproachable; if it is trying to exclude or absorb and digest Islamic culture or any other particular culture, it is betraying its own goals. 'Suspension of disbelief' must exclude any presupposition whatever, even a negative one; it may be easier for a believer in one faith, who has a habit of believing, to suspend his disbelief in another faith, than for an unbeliever in any faith to do so. If international culture cannot embrace Islam as alive, it may well be 'arrogant' as alleged, and its achievement will surely be limited and is internationalism in the long run self-defeating.

A scholar would have to be very cocksure to think that a born Arab has nothing to teach him, even an Arab who does not understand or respect his methods and aims. Arab criticism, including, or especially, hostile criticism, can only help the orientalist to overcome an obstacle which Shakr believes to be insuperable but which surely we can minimise. I have nothing new to propose. There is a possible future in collaboration, even more in consultation, in any case one form or another of co-operation, if suspicions permit. The Arab orientalist, although by definition a secularist, may still be able to help because he should understand his compatriots of a different persuasion, and especially if he was brought up a Muslim; for this, he should not of course have an axe of his own to grind. I see no reason to despair of collaboration between people of conflicting beliefs, so long as they have good will, which any collaboration requires anyway. Why has the attack on orientalism caused some heart-searching? It was not on the whole just shrugged off. A number of orientalists have wondered what truth there might be in it. Feeling rejected as alien, as unsympathetic, deluded by ignorance and diverted into wrong paths, some conceded the fault and suspected that it was not in the individual or even in a conglomerate, but in the system, in the methods and aims of objectivity itself. This is a dangerous thought that can and does encourage the wildest fancies and speculations. Objectivity is wholly defensible; the question is not whether we should have something less, it is about what more we should add. Is it a sufficient aim? How reasonable it is to question this, I find myself quite unable to decide.